Now That You Mention It

Now That You Mention It

MELVIN L. KRULEWITCH

73 74 75 5 4 3 2 1

Thanks go to *The Ring* magazine for permission to reprint what here goes under
the chapter headings of "A Child of Misfortune" and "Orchids for a Change."

The articles "Belleau Wood," from the November 1971 *Marine Corps Gazette,* and
"Skirmish on the Hudson," from the September 1972 *Marine Corps Gazette,* are
reprinted courtesy of the Marine Corps Association.

Library of Congress Catalog Card Number: 72-90462

International Standard Book Number: 0-8129-0325-0

Book Design by: Ben Feder, Inc.
Jacket Design by: Diane and Leo Dillon
Production by: Planned Production

TO THE FOUR
WOMEN WHO HAVE
MADE MY LIFE
BEAUTIFUL:
ANNE, HELEN,
NAN, AND HELLEN

★

Acknowledgments

I thank my friends Guy Richards, author, editor, newsman, and inspiring fellow marine over the years; Dan Daniel, writer, columnist and editor, both of whom encouraged me to write; and Punch Sulzberger, who gave my script a left hook in the right direction to Herb Nagourney, President of Quadrangle. I am in their debt. I also express my appreciation to Donald Goddard, who, over my cries of anguish, cut out a third of the script to comply with publication requirements, and was most helpful to me at a time when he was heavily engaged in the writing of two of his own books.

★

Contents

Foreword

I AM A VERY LUCKY GUY, far more so than I have any reason to expect. At 77 years of age I'm in good health, considering a few battle wounds and what begins to show up in the seventies. During my terms as boxing commissioner, my blood pressure took a long high jump and continues to gallop after each anonymous telephone call. On balance I can pass a physical, but the credit goes to the two women who have made my life beautiful—my beloved first Helen, mother of my children, wife of my war years, and then my second Hellen, a great lady, born to the purple, who never lost the common touch, and was not averse to scrubbing the kitchen floors of our country place on hands and knees when her "Old Dutch Cleanser" thought transference goaded her into frenzied activity against an infinitesimal speck of dust. Our Dutchess County home is known as The House the Helens Built. Both girls have given me devotion, companionship, and love, and it is they who have extended my life to this happy season.

The appeal of the different led me from the even tenor of my way, groping for the answer, from a happy home life and Columbia to war, to law, to politics, to the Semper Fi of the Marine Corps, even to the challenge of the boxing world, brand new to me, with its shadowy line between right and wrong, and then again back to the law, my first love, and the beauty of the legal tradition, with its centuries of painstaking dedication to the written word and its unyielding determination to decree what is right and what is wrong.

These stories were mainly written not at the moment of action, but during the restful years in the islands of the Pacific and the Mediterranean—although my correspondence with Max Schuster of

Krulewitch kissing the Blarney Stone in Blarney Castle—Cork, Ireland. Now that you mention it, that's how this story began.

Simon & Schuster was written at the moment and the letters were despatched from the front by Marines' Mail.

My dividends began. Of the children, Dick was the intellectual, outstanding in his choice of career, the diplomatic service. Nan, our sugarplum, tied in with world affairs. Through Sandy, her husband, a keystone in worldwide news media, they flew in the President's plane during the recent Moscow trip. Peter, hurt so much as a young boy by his mother's death, is now building up the old New York family tradition in the land. The six grandchildren are my windfall.

This is not my autobiography or a diary. The bulk of it is pure, unadulterated fact but there are occasions where "fact and fiction are so intermingled in my work that now, looking back on it, I can hardly distinguish one from the other."* There are contrasts and opposites in this catalog of doubtful virtues. What started in the Gemot at Kent Hall, or even earlier, kept going through the years and decades—war and peace, law and violence, life and death. Despite the marked contrasts they were very much the same. I must agree with those that say "war rests one." While our times of peace are disturbing, so are growing pains, and this has been the score in over a century of recollections, including the pre-Civil War family wives' tales, with their crinolines and courtesies. The transformation of the sweet repose and the love of home with its close family loyalties into the decaying moralities and unrestrained language of today differs from the tearing violence, blind obedience, and unyielding discipline of the battlefront only in degree. The battle between the law, with its just and prescribed authority, and trial by fire and water still continues, but there are compensations in the excitement of great music, the beauty of nature, and the fine arts, which are always new.

A final word as to the greatest of all institutions over the millenia—religion. My fundamental belief is that God is, among other things, Justice, Love, and Mercy. This has carried me through all my lives, from my confirmation in the faith, to (although not a Zionist) my pilgrimage to the battles in the then Palestine and now State of Israel, in its War of Independence. My steadfast con-

---

* W. Somerset Maugham, "The Summing Up," Penguin Books, 1963.

viction continues loud and clear that religions are good, and that
if all men lived up to the tenets of their respective religions, something new could be added to the world in which we live.

Ranging from early New York before the turn of the century
to the return to Belleau in 1972, these are what General David D.
Porter would have described as "mental meanderings." It's all
yours.

M.L.K.

Now That You Mention It

1. East Side

MY GRANDFATHER LEWIS was a kindly old gent. He belonged to the blue-eyed Krulewitch clan, and all of them were either good or bad—there was no middle ground, no in-between. Coming over to the New World during the Civil War, he landed at Castle Garden, made famous by Jenny Lind, the Swedish Nightingale, who sang there in 1860, and joined the "rags-to-riches" group during a half century of battling in the community he loved—New York.

His life was warmed by an affectionate, running battle with Betsy, his wife, my farmer grandmother, who was both a cut above him in size and a cut below him in social status. They came from the small Baltic state of Lithuania, where Lewis, the city dweller, and his wife, the country girl, had known each other as young people. Betsy was tall, strong, and dark skinned, like her three giant brothers. Their size, and the family name of Lieber, indicated a North-German infiltration, perhaps on both sides of the blanket.

Betsy Lieber had married at 16, but the following year, in the presence of the entire community, she denounced her husband as obnoxious in her eyes. This was an unprecedented step—divorce initiated on the distaff side was unknown. In a state of shock, the elders of the congregation granted her an ecclesiastic divorce without the consent of her husband. At 18, she married her childhood chum Lewis, whom she always called Eli, after the prophet Elijah. She outlived him by 10 years, although she was the older of the two. Of sturdy farmer stock, she was fascinated by the tally-ho fours driven up Fifth Avenue, where she lived in later years, and was heard to remark that as a girl she had driven heavy-timbered freighting vans with six horses. She was someone to remember. At the age of 80 she stubbornly refused the almost tearful pleas of the family to take on a housekeeper, and kept house for herself. Stern, spartan, puritanical, and frugal, she ruled the roost for half a century.

Grandpa Krulewitch was quite a boy. Under his bed, concealed by the quilt which hung to the floor, was the ever-present demijohn of hard liquor. He never was the toper that several of his grandchildren proved to be, but there was always a shot glass of whiskey at his second breakfast each morning to take the curse off the day. (Earlier, at dawn, he would have his morning eye-opener, black coffee, after ablutions and prayer.) His friend, Pete Kelly, worked in the Custom House and would pass the word when a shipment of liquor was up for confiscation sale. Eli, usually the only bidder, would appear at the auction, and would acquire a sufficient stock for home, for business, and the for Irish Tammany Hall echelon, whose goodwill was so necessary in his growing real estate business. That little dram of whiskey at breakfast was as typical of Lewis Krulewitch as his silk top-hat and the heavy gold chain across his modest paunch, from which depended a gold cigar cutter presented by an admiring petty-political chieftain. Eli had gotten this man the job of swamper aboard the ferry plying across the East River to Greenpoint—and with it, the title of captain.

My mother's side of the family had everything except money. The Levins and several of their widely scattered connections came over long before the War Between the States, and flourished in little settlements of the South. Grandpa Harris Levin, a gentleman by instinct and cultivation, came from New Orleans. His ease of manner and southern-style goatee earned him a place of distinction in any gathering, but his antecedents were shrouded in mystery. We knew he had been English, because he spoke like an Englishman, always a source of inward joy to us children, who made conversation so that we could hear him say "clark" for clerk, "darby" for derby, and "shedule" for schedule. When mother sang us the song "In Days of Old When Knights Were Bold and Barons Held Their Sway," we pictured him jousting in the tourneys of the plumed knights of the songs brought to the South from the old country.

But the best thing was when Grandma Deborah told an open-mouthed circle of listeners at her feet the tales of the Battle of Drewry's Bluff and the Siege of Richmond, how she visited and tended the wounded in the tobacco warehouse that served as a hospital during the siege. And then there was the tale of the occupation of Charleston by "Mr. Linkum's men," as the slaves called the Feds, and the family's ill-judged flight to Columbia just before Sherman, suiting the action to the word that War was Hell, burned Columbia down. The old family wedding cup used when Grandma married Grandpa Levin in Richmond was brought forth and the date of the wedding, 1859, carefully inspected. Then Grandma would repair to the kitchen, where Nancy, a freed slave who had stayed with the family throughout all their wanderings through the South during the miseries of Reconstruction, was preparing bowls of cornmeal for a regular winter ritual. And soon the squawking would begin, for Grandma, in anticipation of a harvest of goose liver, goose fat, and goose *grieben,* forcibly stuffed her geese *à la Strasbourg!*

I was born in New York City on November 11, 1895. My sister Ethel beat me to it by a couple of years, and Frances came in third a year and a half later. My earliest recollections, apart from memories of periodic visits to the South, were of New York City, where we lived just off Fifth Avenue on 106th Street, facing Central Park. I remember enthralling visits to secret and strange places, such as the Italian iceman's cellar, where he kept his ice covered with sawdust, next to supplies of stovewood and coal for cooking; and visits to the candy and cigar store, with its frightening wooden Indian, where we agonized over the display of candies—licorice in bundles for chewing and sucking, shelves loaded with brown and white sugarloaves in cans tilted so you could see inside, and hard candies with scoops for those who would buy in quantities beyond the reach of the 1-, 2-, and 5-cent customers. One cent was a respectable purchase, providing a choice between the 20-for-a-cent sugar peppercorns, two-for-a-cent peppermints and horehounds, and the one-for-a-cent chocolates. A tiny committee of four would ponder long on the choice but would always decide on the sugarcorns since the expenditure of a penny would otherwise present problems of distribution. A 5-cent all-day sucker was something else. It could be passed around.

Although we lived uptown, the Lower East Side always drew us. Grandpa Krulewitch owned an entire street, a narrow passageway between Madison and Monroe, and he was once caricatured in the press, with his General Grant beard and high silk hat, holding the street under his arm with a tag of ownership floating in the wind—"L. Krulewitch, Prop."

I. A. & H. Krulewitch, Merchants—my father's and Uncle Ike's firm—conducted their flour business at 2 and 4 Birmingham Street, where they had a warehouse and offices. On an occasional Saturday night Pop would take me down to his office, and after he had finished his business affairs, we would walk through the hustling, bustling streets lined with pushcarts, to make a few purchases for the house. Then we would go to the winding streets of Chinatown, where my portion was a bag of lychee nuts and a piece of sugar cane to chew. With us went Pete Kelly, my father's henchman, who would carry the packages and later take the trolley car up to the house. After Chinatown, Pete Kelly, my father, and I would generally repair to Essex Street, where Isaac Gellis had begun to pack frankfurters, salami, corned beef, smoked tongue, and all the mouth-watering accessories, and we would fall on a plate of what later came to be known as hot dogs. (This nickname came about when a dog accidentally fell into the sausage-grinding machine in a pork-packing plant.)

One holiday we really looked forward to was the Fourth of July. School was out and summer had come. The blue denim had been nailed down by Pop, with much grunting and wheezing, over the carpeting in the front and back parlors, which were separated by velvet portières hanging from large wooden rings to provide an extra room in the back where our parents slept in their large double bed. Both parlors had wooden shutters inside, which, folding into three hinged portions, fitted back into the sash on each side of the window sill. These would be closed and the blinds drawn against the heat for most of the morning and afternoon, and sometimes in the evening as well. The only air conditioning in our railroad apartment was the breeze—when it blew.

The crowds of children playing in the streets and in the vacant lots were sure signs that school was over. The hokey-pokey man would be out in his white suit, selling bricks of ice cream wrapped in paper, but if you were thirsty you went to the ice-ball man. Standing behind his oil-cloth counter with its massive cake of rapidly melting ice and row of bottles of red, green, yellow, and brown flavors, he scraped in his metal ice mold a ball of shaved ice, slapped it onto a piece of paper, and then sprinkled it with the chosen flavor. It cost 2 cents. For a nickel you got a larger ball with two flavors.

There were other harbingers of vacation time, like the muffin man with his stove and cart and his row of black muffin and waffle irons. We had been ordered never to eat his delectable crunchy-brown wares, liberally sprinkled with powdered sugar, because of the lard in the shortening and in the grease he spread on the irons, but we bootlegged them with many a wary, over-the-shoulder glance.

Then there was the hurdy-gurdy man, who introduced us to grand opera with the "Anvil Chorus" and the "Toreador Song," interspersed with Neapolitan and Sicilian folk songs.

All was in preparation for the Fourth of July. The money we managed to save was spent the day before on fireworks from the candy and stationery stores, or from the Chinese laundryman. Spread out on a plank table, they were dangerously attractive— Roman candles, sky rockets, Mount Pelias, pinwheels, snakes, large firecrackers that were known as salutes, and smaller ones in bundles. Our parents were always annoyingly nearby when we lit the slow-burning punk for a lighter and set off the displays, but this could be the reason why we managed to grow up with the normal complement of eyes and fingers.

We were too young to be taken to the beer gardens and saloons, but we would stand near the so-called family entrance and watch the ladies of the afternoon and evening go in. The singing and merriment increased the later it got, and occasionally before bedtime, as the doors opened for the coming and going, we might see some blowzy, frowsy blonde at one of the small round iron tables brazenly crossing her legs to display, for those who cared, her brilliant, red-ribbon garters. Our Independence Day celebration usually ended when Pop fired his revolver, loaded with blanks, through the kitchen window.

But Election Day was the day to conjure with. The run-up would begin months before when Tammany Hall and the Democratic leaders started to pile up points for that part of the legitimate vote that could not be stolen. The May parties would be followed by June walks, all free of charge to the families of the voting public, and no expense was spared with the taxpayers' money. Ice cream, lemonade, bolivars, pretzels, and souvenirs—mostly caps and flags—were dispensed everywhere, and each precinct captain had to produce a good showing.

The Republican Party, however, was given more to dance socials and balls. Our Uncle Sam being the assemblyman and later the leader of our district, the family was always in the swim.

I remember when the 1904 campaign was drawing to a close and President Teddy Roosevelt was to make his last New York City campaign speech at the Star Casino on Lexington Avenue and 107th Street, in the heart of the growing, bustling, white Harlem that was in those days. Roosevelt, a former governor of the state and police commissioner of the city, had come home. That dynamic personality was leading a young America along the road to *Weltpolitik* with a versatility previously unknown in the White House. Our interests had extended to China, the Philippines, the West Indies, and Panama during Roosevelt's terms as Vice President and President. Teddy was always where the action was.

The Star Casino was a commodious ballroom with boxes around the floor and a second horseshoe of loges one flight up. It was used for political gatherings, boxing matches, athletic meets, weddings, even an annual "Fairy Gala and Extravaganza" —and it had been repainted, decorated, shined, and polished especially for the President's visit. My parents had been invited to sit in Uncle Sam's box. Pop was dolled up in white tie and collapsible opera hat, and Mother was wearing a white lace dress with long sleeves and a whalebone collar up to her chin, topped off with a wide-brimmed, white felt hat, swept back by three ostrich plumes fastened to the front of the crown by a rhinestone buckle. They were a handsome couple, and Mandelkern took their picture in the lounge at the entrance to the Casino.

Uncle Sam's associates included Robert F. Wagner, father of New York's mayor, Ezra Parmelee Prentice, later my first boss, and Alfred E. Smith, four times governor of New York. Sam was constantly referred to in the press as "Czar," largely because during a Republican primary fight for the leadership, the inspectors of election in his home district had counted and reported more votes for Sam than were registered in the district. When a criminal proceeding was filed against all the officials involved, including the leader's henchmen, it was discovered by a disappointed district attorney that the ballot boxes had been used as weapons during a fracas between the opposing captains and their respective gangs of guerillas and had been smashed to smithereens. Their contents, the ballots, had been swept out into the gutter and lost. But I didn't care about any of that. The important part of this affair for me was that I was to see the President that night and would go with my father and mother to the ball.

From all over the city a long stream of coaches, hansoms, and here and there one of the new horseless carriages, moved to the Casino. Pending the arrival of the President, there were speeches and, in between, music. Though only 8 years old, I was allowed to wander around in this wonderland and was at the side entrance when the President arrived. He was escorted to the stage by Uncle Sam, with me trailing along to watch from the wings.

Roosevelt breezed into the room—I know of no better way to describe the tremendous personal magnetism of the man. He wore a brown tweed houndstooth suit with wide lapels, a vest buttoned up almost to his collar, and a large, four-in-hand necktie as fat as the present mode. With his shining spectacles, heavy white teeth, and scraggly mustache, he made a powerful impression on me, although I can no longer recall what his speech was about. As he left the stage, escorted by his guards and Uncle Sam, he stopped short at the sight of me. My uncle made the introductions, and the President seized my little paw in his bear's grip, smiling his great toothy smile. I nearly fainted with pride.

On Election Day itself the fires burned in the streets and every boy had to get out and prove himself as a forager. Nothing combustible was safe—boxes, barrels, crates, discarded house furniture and even broken wagons from the nearby stables went into the flames. The winners of the elections were our guarantors against prosecution. The bonfires of Election Day were, so we thought, the beacons of liberty.

Relations with the Irish and Italians in our neighborhood were also fairly inflammable, although we had close friends among both. The spaghetti-benders as they were called—without malice —were the poorer of the two, accounting for most of the rag and coal pickers, who gleaned fragments of cloth and partly consumed cinders from the ash and trash cans, and the flock of beggars who pleaded with their heads on one side for a penny. The Irish did not beg for a living, but in desperation and despair would often bum a nickel for a drink near the saloons. Skid row claimed a lot of Irishmen. We never saw a Jewish or German beggar, although there must have been some.

The Italians often had a fondness for the knife when it came to the brawl, while the "harp," with a fighting temper brought from the old country after generations of battling with the English, would fight with his fists at the drop of the hat—particularly with a "Christ-killing Sheeny," who had to defend himself with his wits. But by and large the melting-pot worked. Mr. Bandini, who gave me music lessons, and Pete Kelly, who later worked for my father, and all of their clans, helped form a strong alloy in the American crucible.

But what of the "native" Americans, the early families of the Revolutionary War and the Civil War? Where were they in New York? Certainly not in the bustling, hustling, boiling and moiling neighborhoods of the new Americans. For us, they were the people who drove every Saturday morning in their tally-hos up Fifth Avenue for lunch at Claremont or further up to Westchester for a horse show or a hunt or weekend party in the country. When we wandered south on Fifth Avenue and got down below 59th Street, a good two-mile walk—and you had to walk back as well—we'd come to the great Fifth Avenue homes of what my Uncle Sam, mimicking his Irish associates in politics, would call "the big boys."

Even so we were a cut above our friends and neighbors, because our family had come through the Civil War. Grandpa Harris Levin had signed up with Company L, 2nd Virginia Reserves, had run the blockade and lived to tell the tale. Cousin Mamie Winstock, a sweet maiden lady, told us all about our southern connections when she visited us in New York. She also gave me the names of relations who had moved to France after the War. A generation later I called on them when I was a sergeant of Marines and had been given leave to visit Paris. By then they were French. Fifty years in another country had broken the family ties. They were polite to me, but they were big people in France and I, of their blood, was just a sergeant of Marines.

But the Krulewitches were getting to be big, too. Grandpa Lewis had been doing well in the real estate business for 20 years. The New York *World* had published articles about him and his holdings, and he had calmly admitted he was no Hetty Green (the fabulous female millionaire of the turn of the century). Nothing was written about Grandmother Betsy, however, who still ruled the roost and was much against schooling for the children. In her day a boy of 14 became a farm hand and held his own with his elders. Of her eight children, few had any formal education, although my father bootlegged high-school courses at night. The Levin-Winstock family on Mother's side was just the opposite. Aunt Bertha graduated from Bryn Mawr and most of her family went to college.

Lewis Krulewitch had four brothers, and together they were known as the five grandfathers. When he came to the United States during the Civil War, there were already branches of the family in Illinois, Massachusetts, Texas, and Maryland—not always of the same name but certainly of the same blood. The Keenes of Fort Worth were Krulewitches who had tired of the difficulties of spelling and pronunciation, and so were the Thomas Leavitts of Massachusetts. Eighty years later, when I rented the rifle range at Wakefield, Mass. for the use of Marines stationed at Charleston Navy Yard, I was astonished to learn from the mayor, Honorable Thomas Leavitt, that his grandfather's and his father's name had been Krulewitch and that he was a blood relative.

My wife always said that to judge by their progeny, the five grandfathers never got out of bed—but this, although complimentary, was far from fact. The five brothers were Lewis, Benjamin, Philip, Judah, and Joseph. Judah was the handsomest—blond and blue-eyed—and his descendants include the Krulewitches of New York and the great lawyer and chess master Lester Samuels, now deceased. Benjamin, who settled in Maryland, had two large families, which include the Grants of Baltimore and the Millers (Adam Hats) of New York. Joseph's family dropped out of sight for a couple of generations and then reappeared when I received a bill for a pair of ladies' Bermuda shorts, which I hadn't bought for anyone, dead or alive. It was an error in billing, and the purchaser turned out to be a fine young mother of a Westchester Krulewitch family we had not previously known about. Philip, the last of the grandfathers and I believe the oldest, was the progenitor of the New England branch.

Our own local group, starting with 27 grandchildren, achieved a certain prominence when Grandpa Lewis authorized his son Emanuel, now living in Beverly Hills, to build a mausoleum on Long Island with 40 catacombs. This became a source of much irritation and discord within the family. Most of us hardly cared who qualified for admission, and it was finally and unhappily decided that the principle of "first come, first served" should apply—but only after one candidate had remained for an embarrassingly long period in a receiving vault.

The living were not forgotten either. Around 1906, Lewis built a clump of apartment houses on West 122nd Street near Columbia, cannily renting a few floors to the college as dorms. Sensing an opportunity, the family swarmed down upon the buildings like a cloud of locusts. My father led the gold rush, taking two adjoining apartments, and was quickly followed by two of his sisters and their respective broods. Sam, however, being a politician, had to live in his district on the East Side, where the oldest brother, Isaac, called the big fellow, still lived. Manny, the youngest child, had married Sadye Vivian Weinstein (a family name soon to succumb to "Winston"), a beautiful, charming, and altogether lovable blonde, for whom he presently built and named The Sadivian Arms.

With very little education—primary and grammar school plus a little more—Manny achieved lasting fame in the building trade; his profits and his losses were both gargantuan. In his hunger for social position, Uncle Manny drove both a Rolls Royce and a Blitzen Benz, employed a Japanese chauffeur, bought the Stokes Estate on Schooley Mountain near Hackettstown, and raced his own horses at Saratoga. His jockeys wore the Krulewitch colors, a nauseous purple and green.

In contrast, my father, Harry, was modest and self-effacing. He was a member of the New York Produce Exchange for so many years that he was almost regarded as its dean. Even so he was at a tremendous disadvantage against such great flour merchants as George Zabriskie, who represented Pillsbury, Ed Broenniman, the friend of Herbert Hoover in the Belgian Relief, and Van Boskerk and Van Alstyne, merchants of long tradition. They were old line and he was the new arrival. Though his credit was of the highest and his bills of exchange and acceptance were eagerly sought after, he was barred from a membership he never sought in the tight business and social clubs on Hanover Square and Madison Avenue.

And so in 1906 we moved to the West Side, taking with us memories of Central Park that are still alive after nearly seven decades—the skating pond when the red ball was up, showing it was safe to use; M'Gowans Pass Tavern, part of Washington's defenses covering the retreat of the Continental Army across Manhattan into New Jersey after the disastrous defeat at Long Island; and above all, the hothouses where the banana palms towered over us with their huge purple blossoms and fingerlings soon to grow into fat golden hands of bananas and red plantains.

2. *West Side*

THE WEST SIDE was another world—different people, different geography, and a reserve and dignity unknown in the screaming, boiling currents of the East Side. Much of the area was undeveloped. Adjoining our apartment house was a squatter's shanty built, we were told, in the early 1800s—it looked it, with its weather-beaten sidings and two stone chimneys cemented with field clay. A pair of goats roamed around inside the enclosure and were staked down and belled when grazing outside. There was nothing else on our side of 122nd Street as far as Broadway.

When I walked to P.S. 165 on 109th Street between Broadway and Amsterdam, joining up with friends along the way, the daily competition in winter was to see who could kick the same piece of ice all the way to school. The problem was twofold: to keep the ice from shattering into bits, and to scoop it up niblickwise at the street crossings, where the curb separated the pavement from the sidewalks by a good six inches or more.

Our neighbors were no longer in the upper-lower classes but were straining into the upper-middle class. As is typical of New York apartment house society, none of the tenants socialized with anybody else in the building, and except for the three Krulewitch families, most of them were strangers to us. We knew Spitler, the janitor, who lived in the cellar with his growing family and did more than his share of running two apartment houses for owners who were not good managers. The Krulewitch Realty Company did well in building, as did Manny (Mr. Emanuel M. Kay, today), many of whose great apartment houses are still standing, but in management and the safety factors in conservative financing, the great family fortunes—and they *were* great—lost out.

Spitler, the janitor, left after his wife was delivered of a stillborn baby in the following year, and was succeeded by an elderly black man, Farmer, who had been born a slave. The fact that he owned a rusty frock coat qualified him for family service—in addition to cleaning the halls and sidewalks, hauling ashes, loading and banking the fires, and pulling garbage—and so Farmer was drafted to help at family parties, serving at the punch bowl and waiting on table. He was kind, courteous, and a gentleman by instinct. Farmer reminded me slightly of my grandmother, the Confederate lady of the siege of Richmond: both of them had acquired a gentleness and humility through suffering.

P.S. 165 was as different from P.S. 171, which we had attended on the East Side, as a private school is from a public one. The principal was Mr. Gaddis, whom we called Doctor, a veteran of the Civil War who set much store by the school's drum-and-fife corps. We also had a German class, presided over by Herr Olmsted, who lived in a perpetual shiny sweat due to the indignities perpetrated upon him by the class. A boy called Farrell, an expert spitball thrower, sat at a desk adjoining and slightly in front of the teacher's desk where he had been placed for close supervision. He used to convulse the class by his careful mispronunciations in the song, *"Ich hat ein Kamerader, ein bessern findst du nit,"* when the eagerly awaited line, *"in gleichen Schritt (Shit) und Tritt (Tit)",* was reached. Worse still, with Machiavellian cunning he would chew up a massive, sloppy spitball while all were studying and Herr Olmsted was marking papers, then, eyes fixed all the while on his book, innocently reach around his neck, as though interested in a flea bite, and throw the spitball at Herr Olmsted's red, perspiring face, with its two spare tires beneath the chin and one at the back of his neck. The hit would register, and Farrell would innocently continue his reading. With a roar, Olmsted would heave himself up from his chair and out would fly his starched dickie, to stand out stiffly under his chin for all the world like a slightly soiled cardboard bib—(he wore no shirt). To laugh was of course a sign of guilt, or at least of conspiracy—we knew this from experience. But on one occasion, the combination of Herr Olmsted's dirty undershirt, his protruding dickie, his rage, and the saintly Farrell, looking innocently around at the direction from

which the projectile was supposed to have come, was too much—
I laughed out loud. And when the class followed my lead, I was
grabbed by the scruff of the neck and unceremoniously hauled out
of the classroom to the assistant principal's office as the guilty
one. Protesting my innocence to no avail, I was sent home with
a letter, and the following day my mother had to come to school
to patch things up.

My big year was 1908–1909—graduation from public school,
my Bar Mitzvah and the transfer into "longies." This move into
long pants was an important event in the life of a growing boy. We
had all been wearing knee pants, and if a young kid had gone to
class in long trousers, he would have been set upon at once as a
show-off or mother's darling, and marked as fair game for the
pack to annoy, humiliate, and drive to desperation. But I was now
13, and like a young Indian ready for initiation into full membership in the tribal councils, I had been preparing for full admission
into membership in the temple.

The difference between Hebrew and tribal ritual, however, is
that the Jewish postulant must complete a comprehensive course
of study, address the congregation, and pass an examination covering the Bible, Jewish history and religion, and the Hebrew language itself—no mean task for a 13-year-old boy who worked after
hours and on weekends and coped with all the other demands of
school, family, and community.

In my case, all this extra work had to be done at the Jewish
Theological Seminary on West 123rd Street. We were members
of its small congregation, which my father had helped to organize.
As a boy, and at times in later life, I had a tendency to stammer
—the result, I believe, of my parents forcing me to use my right
hand instead of my left—and the pressures and anxieties of preparing for my Bar Mitzvah began to have their effect on me. I even
wet the bed for a few months. I was very conscious that the faculty
of the Seminary, headed by the famed Dr. Solomon Schechter,
whom Jacob Schiff of Kuhn, Loeb & Co., had brought to America
from Cambridge University, comprised the greatest minds in Judaic
religious study in the world. The prospect of running the gauntlet
before these great figures was no help to my morale.

In the first week of November the day finally dawned. My father had bought me a new suit, with an extra pair of trousers, and a new hat, and I was washed and shined as never before. The family had come from the South and the West and dinner had been preparing all week. I was the first grandson on the Krulewitch-Levin side to reach 13.

All during the service my mind was closed to everything except my part. I knew it by heart. Then came the summons in classical Hebrew, "Stand up, the young man Bar Mitzvah," and my legs somehow took me up to the platform. Looking neither right nor left at the awesome, world-famous figures of the faculty, I made my way to the broad reading desk and the scroll of the Torah, unrolled to the portion of the week in Genesis. It was the life of Sarah, the matriarch. I recited the blessings and then read the concluding portion of the chapter in Hebrew from the scroll itself. After the second blessing, the Torah was most reverently lifted for congregational view and dressed for return to the ark. Having recited the further blessings upon the prophetic portion, I began to chant in Hebrew the Haftorah, upon which I had labored so long:

> Now King David was old and stricken in years and they covered him with clothes and he gat no heat.
> Wherefore his servants said unto him, let there be sought for my Lord the King a young virgin and let her stand before the King and let her cherish him and let her lie in thy bosom that my Lord the King may get heat.
> So they sought for a fair damsel throughout all the coasts of Israel and found Abishag, a Shunamite, and brought her to the King.
> And the damsel was very fair and cherished the King and ministered to him; but the King knew her not.
> Then Adonijah the son of Haggith exalted himself saying I will be King and he prepared him chariots and horsemen and fifty men to run before him.

I knew nothing about the ministrations of Abishag, the fair one, nor had anything upon this subject been included in my curriculum, but it didn't matter—the ordeal was over. My beautiful mother was smiling through tears as I closed my Bible, shook hands ceremoniously with the great scholars on the platform, and walked to the family seats for handshaking and kissing.

In the excitement I had forgotten all about my stammer. This was a happy world. I was wearing longies and would enter Townsend Harris Hall in the spring.

Townsend Harris Hall, with its conservative Gothic decor, gray fieldstone, and shining white terra cotta trim, crowned the top of the hill at Amsterdam Avenue, where the trolley cars of the Third and Amsterdam Avenue Railway Company plugged up to the crest. It was the best high school in the city—a three-year prep school with a college faculty, part of City College. Getting there was a challenge to those of us on the hill at 122nd Street, because the car barns were at 129th Street and we had to pass through the Irish neighborhood as we came and went each way. We became West Harlem mountain men, vigilant at every block and crossing, although issue was only seriously joined on Saint Patrick's Day and Halloween. The Irish were gallant but never smart. We outflanked them by taking Riverside Drive, or if the weather was bad, by using the trolley car.

The teachers at Harris were superb, since the faculty of C.C.N.Y. worked both the prep school and the college classes. We were even given college subjects in our curriculum. We took courses, unknown in high school at that time in the regular yearly schedules, such as solid geometry, spherical trigonometry, descriptive geometry (drafting), and Latin prose composition. My favorite subject was mathematics, and I believe I was one of the few students at Harris and even at Columbia, who took math on the outside and in extension courses, for the pure love of it.

I also took to sports at Harris as my thin, wiry frame began to fill out—in particular, to wrestling, a sport that brought me again in contact with an old P.S. 165 schoolmate of mine, Nat Pendleton, who went on to become a champ and a Hollywood star. Harris wrestled Polytechnic Preparatory in a dual meet and who should show up but Nat, wrestling about two weights above me. We did not meet again until we were both at Columbia in 1916 and Nat was the star of the team.

Townsend Harris also had a football team of sorts. I don't recall whether we ever won a game, but I remember I played on the line, usually left tackle, although my lack of speed usually ruined my chances for playing out a full quarter. We had to provide our own equipment. All the school contributed was a pair of pants and a jersey, to which my mother carefully sewed elbow and shoulder pads. My father did the rest, supplying shin guards, an enormous beak of a nose guard, and a yellow leather headguard that singled me out from every other member of the team. Late in the season I managed to camouflage it with shoe polish, but that did nothing for the fit!

Uncle Louis Levin, of Levindale, a convalescent center named for him in Baltimore, came to New York to visit us once when we were scheduled to play De Witt Clinton High at McCombs Dam Park on a Saturday morning. It being the Sabbath, Uncle Louis, who was pious and observant, walked all the way over to the field and back again to see the game. He described it to the family at lunch that day: "Mel ran out with the squad and he looked fine. He had more equipment than any other member of the squad. He had shoulder guards, elbow guards, shin guards, a nose guard, and a helmet—and what a helmet. De Witt Clinton smeared Harris 65–0. It wasn't much of a game." Mother asked, "What about Mel in the game?" My uncle, avoiding my eye across the table answered, "Mel sat on the bench, equipment and all. He didn't play."

The sin area in those days was 125th Street around Seventh Avenue. There was the Harlem Opera House, which offered travelogues and songs with illustrated slides, special vaudeville acts, and straight plays (which we avoided). Nearby was Hurtig and Seaman's Burlesque House, where the great headliners like Billy Watson's Beef Trust topped the bill. Around the corner on Seventh Avenue was the Alhambra, a stop on the vaudeville circuit, and further West was Pabst's, a glamorous beer garden which we only visited in company with the family.

Saturday afternoon was the time when, under the pretense of family visits, we slipped away to the Alhambra with our cousins to buy 20-cent tickets to the second balcony, affectionately called the pit. We saw all the great names—Sarah Bernhardt in *"Une nuit de Noel sous la Terreur,"* Lillian Russell, beautiful to the end, in "My Evening Star," as well as Williams and Walker, Eva Tanguay,

Eddie Foy, Maggie Cline, the Irish Queen who sang "Throw Him Down, McCluskey," Norah Bayes, Pat Rooney, the fabulous Weber and Fields, Valeska Surrat, and a host of others.

Downtown was something else. The *crème de la crème* was Hammerstein's Victoria on the northwest corner of 42nd Street and Seventh Avenue, which was later succeeded by the Palace as the pinnacle of vaudeville in New York. There the spectacular and the very special performed, and we would slip away downtown to see Gentleman Jim Corbett bag punching and shadow boxing, and Red Helen Stokes, who had recently shot her husband.

The New York Times had an office on 125th Street just west of Seventh Avenue, and there we went for the latest sports news. The baseball scores were painted onto large squares of manila paper by a black youth, who likewise reported other sporting events on the bulletin boards. On July 4, 1910, we turned up there for news of the great attempt to produce a White Hope who would take the title away from Jack Johnson, the champion and the greatest fighter in the world at that time. Jim Jeffries had been dusted off and brought back from retirement to regain the title he had relinquished and as the telegraph tapped out the news from Reno, Nevada, it was rushed out to be painted up as a round-by-round description of the fight. Excitement mounted with the end of the 14th round, and then came a roar from inside the office that swelled to the crowd closing in on its doors. Skipping all the intermediate rounds, the black youth tore off the last bulletin sheet, scrawled in heavy black paint "Jeffries knocked out in the 15th round," threw down the brush and paint pot, hurled his cap high in the air with a great shout of triumph, and disappeared in the crowd. Jack Johnson was still champion of the world.

My work at school had been passable, and when I graduated from Harris my father let me finish the freshman year at City College. That fall and winter of 1912–1913 were marked by several milestones. Woodrow Wilson, the second Democratic President since the Civil War, was elected as a result of a split between Taft and Teddy Roosevelt. His honesty was patent and his tenacity of purpose obvious to all who heard him speak. During the campaign he enthralled his audience at Madison Square Garden by a brilliant, statesmanlike analysis of governmental and international problems. But to a young college student jam-packed into the balcony at the Garden, the long face, toothy smile, and rimless pince-nez were competing with the pince-nez and toothy smile of the rugged bull-mooser, Teddy Roosevelt.

The next milestone was my switch to Columbia, where in the following semester I entered my sophomore year. It was like going back home, since I'd lived most of the first 10 years of my life on the fringe of the campus. Then the Krulewitch Realty Company sold the houses in which we lived, and we moved to Manny's new Court Rebelle, at the entrance to Morningside Drive, just a block away at 416 West 122nd Street. Here we joined a slightly more select coterie of tenants in what Simeon Strunsky, the erudite editor of the then leading American conservative newspaper, the *New York Post,* called "Belshazzar's Court."

★

3. *Columbia*

COLLEGE WAS A JIGSAW PUZZLE for awhile, as I tried to fit new relationships into the pattern of growing up. The required classics had an iron grip on my life until the end of my second year, when I celebrated the Soph Triumph and could smoke my pipe with the 16 insignia on the bowl. Latin, math, history (ancient and modern), literature (English and American), Spanish, and science (feebly represented by psychology), were required subjects. Later on, when we could elect, we picked courses not by subjects but by profs: Charles A. Beard, loved by his students, in government; Carlton Hayes, later ambassador to Spain, in history; Edwin R. A. Seligman, the banker, in economics—he stopped the show one day when he said the City Sanitation Department's chief problem was the horse; Brander Mathews, who smoked in class and allowed us to, in American literature; and John Erskine, author and musical buff, in English composition and literature. In life you learn more from people than from books.

My lighter moments were spent with a group known as "The Soup." One of our number, an enterprising young gentleman, had a contact at the Metropolitan Opera and was retained to supply manpower for the crowd scenes in its massive productions. The pay was 50 cents a night gross—carfare came out of that—plus the opportunity, if you were fleet of foot, to hear and see the operas.

My first experience was in *Aida*. Seven of us met at the 116th Street subway station, bought our 5-cent tickets, dropped them in the chopper, traveled to Times Square, and were then escorted by our hiring boss to the stage door of the Metropolitan Opera House. Threading our way through a barrage of deep breaths, hawking and clearing of throats, practice arpeggios, ahs, ohs, and grunts, we arrived at a large, filthy dressing room without windows, where the supers for Aida were assembling. Little or no English was spoken—communications were in hisses and gesticulations—but we got the message even in Italian. Dressed in pink tights, with a headband and a long cloak slashed in the front to the waist, I lined up with the other boys, variously costumed, for inspection by the prop manager. A makeup man dabbed some suntan color on our cheeks, and we were ready to perform with our fellow artists, Enrico Caruso as Radames and Geraldine Ferrar as Aida. My job was to carry shoulder-high the front end of a stretcher upon which was seated an enormous papier maché cat. As soon as my part of the procession had passed into the wings, I was supposed to rush around backstage and rejoin the tail, so as to help the illusion of a cast of thousands. In this way I got to know *Carmen, La Gioconda, Tosca, Boris Godunov* and other operas very well. When I was not required on stage, my favorite hideaway was in the prompt box, where two men read the entire libretto in whisper to the artists.

All that clouded those happy days in 1914 was the death of my grandfather, Lewis Krulewitch. I had never seen men cry before. On the day he died, his five sons and their wives were present in the large living room of his apartment, to which his bed had been carried. My grandmother sat waiting in a small adjoining room with her daughters, my aunts. I stood at the bedside with the male nurse and watched. It was spring, and the afternoon sun streamed through the windows. Suddenly there came a slight rattle as the air left his lungs, and the nurse, stooping over the body with his hand on one wrist and his head against the chest, called out, "Dead." All five sons burst into tears and went to console their mother before giving away completely to their grief.

But I was young, and life went on. I made the wrestling team, fiddled around with track, and tried out for crew. I liked rowing and I liked Jim Rice, the crew coach, but it wasn't mutual. His comments about my rowing were biting. A favorite instruction of his was "knock off that Hester Street stroke"—Hester Street being in the heart of the Jewish ghetto. On the machines I got as far as the Junior Eight, but on the fateful day when they announced the names of the crews to go to the boathouse on the Hudson for training, Krulewitch's name was not listed. I continued to row single or double sculls and went to Poughkeepsie for the races, where Columbia swept the Hudson, winning the American championship. Rice met me after the regatta and ingenuously asked what had happened to me, that I hadn't shown up with the crew squad. "You happened to me," I replied. Anti-Semitism was then prevalent, although the quota system had not yet been devised at Columbia. That came later.

I was on the water when I learned of the next great milestone in my life. It was the spring of 1917. I had graduated with the class of 1916 and was now enrolled in the Law School. The ice was out of the Hudson and I could smell the fresh earth and the budding trees of Riverside Park. I rowed back from the New York Yacht Club to the float at Columbia's Gould Boat House. Fred Plaisted, aged 65, the hale and hearty boatman in charge, who did his thousand every day on the machines at University Hall, stood at the head of the ramp. I unlocked the port oarlock and held the shell in with the oar on the float. Unlocking the starboard lock, I up-oared the eight-foot sweep and laid it on the float. Then, one foot on the float and holding both sides of the shell with the seat forward, I stepped out, lifted the shell by the gunnels, swung it overhead, walked up the ramp to the house and shelved it. Fred watched me without a word, with a copy of the *New York Sun* in his hand. How well I remember that day. The western sun, piercing the overcast sky, sharply lined the choppy whitecaps and the foaming wash of a tanker moving downstream in the main channel. The strong west winds predicted that morning were blowing the murk over from the factories and yards on the west shore, dappling the air with patches of haze. It was April 7, 1917—the day America became a world power.

The paper Fred held out to me announced that the state of war which the Imperial German Government had thrust upon the United States was formally declared. Wilson had proclaimed:

> I, Woodrow Wilson, President of the United States of America, do hereby proclaim, to all whom it may concern, that a state of war exists between the United States and the

Imperial German Government, and I do especially direct all officers, civil or military, of the United States that they exercise vigilance and zeal in the discharge of the duties incident to such state of war. . . .

Downstream at 96th Street, the boat landing was busy receiving liberty parties from the two cruisers anchored in the channel. Close by, the gray *Noah's Ark,* built on the shell of the old *Granite State* and used for training reserves, stood out like an early Victorian navy brig, wallowing in the sewage from the houses and apartment buildings lining the drive.

Upstream, the 125th Street ferry was making for Fort Lee, loaded with laughing groups of boys and girls on their way to the new amusement park on the Jersey side. Soon they would be followed by their elders, heading for the Jersey night clubs, road houses, and gambling casinos. There were freighters loading, and pleasure yachts anchored at the boathouse of the New York Yacht Club. It all seemed permanent and stable. And yet only a few weeks before in the Gemot at Kent Hall, my classmates Ed Spafford, an Annapolis graduate, and Willard Straight, later of J. P. Morgan & Co., had predicted war before the grass was green, and both had suggested joining the Marines. The double-decker Fifth Avenue buses were already plastered with recruiting posters: "Join the Marines—First to Fight." Now it was upon us.

When diplomatic relations with Germany were broken off after the sinking of the *Lusitania,* a military training group had been organized at Columbia. We drilled in the 22nd Engineers Armory at 168th Street and Broadway, and learned the rudiments of drill, 1898 vintage, using Krags, campaign hats, and civvies. The National Guard drill instructors were assisted by some of our classmates who had put in time at Virginia Military Institute and West Point. This training was naturally intensified in the weeks that followed the declaration of war, and on May 17, 1917, we had a chance to show off our prowess when Joseph Jacques Cesare Joffre, Marshal of France, paid us a visit. Known affectionately as Papa Joffre, he had been acclaimed as the Hero of the Marne in 1914, when the French turned the flank of the German drive on Paris, although much of the credit belonged to General Joseph Simon Gallieni. It was he who urged Joffre to counterattack at the height of the French retreat and electrified the sagging spirits of his country by bringing 6,000 troops out of Paris in taxicabs to help in the victory.

Plump, fair, heavily mustached, and wearing the brilliant red and blue of the French Army, Joffre looked for all the world like a genial Santa Claus in uniform. With René Viviani, Premier of France in 1914, he was to receive an honorary LL.D. degree from Columbia. I was posted near the statue of Alma Mater in front of the Low Library and came to "Present" as Joffre moved by with his procession. He returned the salute in the French manner, with his hand flat and close to his gold-braided marshal's kepi.

That made me, Mel Krulewitch, American, part of the war. Behind us now were the slogans "Too Proud to Fight" and "He Kept Us Out of War," which had elected a President.

Columbia had its School of Engineering summer camp at Bantam Lake, Connecticut, near the Revolutionary town of Litchfield. The following month it combined with the Military Training Unit and there we learned elementary surveying, leveling, mining and sapping, road mapping and night scouting. We built a range, and using National Guard rifles, fired a course. Standard equipment included dummy rifles, Spanish-American war canteens and haversacks, campaign hats, and our own khaki uniforms. We trained under Captain Ralph Hodder Williams, M.C. of the Canadian Princess Pats, who taught us English bayonet fighting. A week later, on July 4th, we marched in the Litchfield parade, and I went down to the recruiting station on 23rd Street, between Fourth and Madison Avenues, climbed the rickety wooden stairs to the second floor, and enlisted in the Marines. I still had a year to do in Law School.

4. Boot Camp

THE SIDE WHEELER *Savannah,* pride of the Oceanic Navigation Fleet, plying between New York and Savannah, eased slowly into its slip and made fast to the rusted bits above the string piece. As its gangplank hit the dock, out belched a motley horde of sweating, stinking, stumbling recruits, who were assailed immediately by the hoarse commands of Marine sergeants ordered from Parris Island to escort this latest levy to the depot.

The Marines were still recruiting as they had in the past, from less privileged groups, Bowery flops, and occasional runaways. No sooner had I gone aboard in New York and checked into my tiny stateroom, with its upper and lower bunks, wash basins, and thunderbowl, then I discovered my wallet had been stolen. In the crowding and jostling on the gangway, one of the Bowery boys, signed up for a warm winter away from New York, had obviously continued with his profession. The Marine Corps hates a sneak thief, but all the sympathy I got this time was, "You're on your own now. Watch your gear."

Falling into a scraggly line on the pier, we were counted by the noncoms and then marched to the railroad terminal, where we joined groups from the southern and middle Atlantic states aboard second-class coaches of the Charleston and Western Carolina Railway for the trip through Yemassee to Port-Royal, South Carolina. From there we were ferried across to Parris Island and marched to the boot camp, which was already bursting with recruits awaiting processing, who by virtue of one or two days' seniority, considered themselves old-timers.

For the first time we heard the calls of the wild. "S.O.L., S.O.L. —Shit Outa Luck, Shit Outa Luck." Sweating in the hot Carolina sun, disappointed and disillusioned, loaded down with packs and baggage and goaded by taunts and jibes, even the hardest case among us had misgivings about this poisonous reception into our new life—and worst of all, by our own kind.

The jeers stopped magically at the approach of a trim, smartly starched khaki-clad Marine with the white stripes of a sergeant on his khaki blouse. He led the boots into a stockade at the barracks where we were confined in virtual quarantine until the incubation period for possible infections—fevers, measles, the clap, and the like—was safely over.

As the days passed, farmers, college men, clerks, coal miners, cowboys, adventurers, rich men's sons, poor men's sons, all the melting pot of America continued to pour into the stockade, each new trainload and shipload straining the depot to bursting point.

After a week, the men were assigned to drill companies. I went to the 12th Drill Company with two corporals and a sergeant, all regulars, in charge, and the murderous routine beneath the broiling South Carolina sun got under way. As usual, no adequate preparation had been made for the flood of recruits at the boot camp, and for the first 10 days we drilled in issue pajamas, heavy felt campaign hats, and field shoes.

First call for reveille went at 4:55 A.M. with reveille at 5:00 A.M. The junior drill instructor, a corporal, would put his head into the doorway of the bunkhouse and rouse the men with the time-honored call: "Rise and shine. Hit the deck. Show a leg. Up a-a-all hammocks. Fall in with rifles in five minutes." Every bunk would then explode into action, the men grabbing their hats lying on the ditty boxes at the foot of the bunks and their rifles slung from the bedrails.

"Standby for Swedish" would be the next command, and we would then begin our physical drill under arms—the Marine Corps had adopted the Swedish system as part of the training and hardening process. Exercising with the nine-pound Springfield included vertical and horizontal swings, side and forward lunges, rifle twists, and most difficult of all, the torturing front sweep— you held the rifle overhead with hands on the stock and the muzzle, and lowered your arms at full length to touch your toes without bending your knees. This was accompanied by gasps, wheezes, coughs, grunts, and occasional farts. Again and again we did this, pushing endurance to its limit. Then we were allowed to fall out and clean up for chow and drill call at 6:30. Between "Bumps," first call for chow, and drill, a 20-minute respite was allowed for "the three Sh's—shave, shower, and shit—and the makeup of bunks for inspection.

The day's work then began on the maneuver grounds. Our senior DI was Sergeant "Horsh" Skoda, a Marine by trade for 12 years and a veteran of China, Nicaragua, and Haiti. He had 90 days to make Marines out of a collection of ridgerunners, hayshakers, crackers, muleskinners, clodhoppers, punks, college boys, and clerks. Drawing his saber, he called the men to attention and set them off on a 10-hour grind toward the blessing of "Recall." Day after day, we would plod back over the long haul to our clapboard bunkhouse with the sweat running down our chests and bellies, drenching our thighs, and blackening our khaki slacks. (The sweat would dry out, leaving a white, salty rime—anathema to a DI.)

Then, over the last long mile to the barracks, Skoda would begin to holler "Cadence," which meant the chain-gang stamp of each left foot as it hit the ground, for the purpose of keeping step, and then "Cadence" again, and "Let's hear it." One day, looking back over his shoulder from the head of the column, Skoda pushed so hard with his "Cadence" and "Let's hear it" that discipline broke. A coal miner from West Virginia, followed by a farmer from Iowa, shouted back at him, "Horseshit"—and there were faltering echoes of this defiance all the way down the line. Affronted and for once at a loss, Skoda spun around and uttered the line that made him immortal. Marching backwards, facing the company, he screamed, "Who said that *last* horseshit?" He was known as Horsh ever after.

Back in the bunkhouse, the company showered, scrubbed skivvies and slacks, and waited for chow call. The evening slop usually consisted of sowbelly, boiled and greasy, speared by a dozen forks as the KP detail banged down the platter in the center of the mess table, with coarse barracks' bread to sop up. Dessert was blackstrap, a by-product of the first grind of sugar cane, and

not too bad when scraped on a crust of bread and washed down
with black coffee.

"This is the Marine Corps?" I moaned in my beer. "What
happened to that vision inspired by the glamorous posters of
Howard Chandler Christy and the cartoons in *Life* and *Harper's*
and *The Saturday Evening Post?* Where are the Floradora beau-
ties, wasp-waisted in their straight front XYZs, hand clasped on
their ample, billowing bosoms as they gaze longingly at those lithe,
khaki-clad, Arrow-collared Marines leaping from a motor sailor
onto a romantic, silver, sandy beach, led by a young god, pistol in
hand, gold hat cord precisely fitted around his neatly blocked field
hat and his leather puttees mirror polished? What is this hell I let
myself in for? Who is the Slovak bastard, five ribbons on his
blouse, shining drill saber in his hand, sticking his venom and DI
authority up my ass every moment of the day?" There was no
moment of repose in this new life, no time even for thought, except
for the last moment before taps, with its blessed blanket of drug-
like, beaten sleep. Nor was there any privacy, even in the head.
Seated on the hard, bare rim of an open toilet, one of a long line
of porcelain stools with no partitions between, you were in full
sight and sound of all the others in the row and of the "captain"
of the head, usually a half wit leaning on his mop, alert to any
emergency amid the disquieting echoes of a dozen adjoining
assholes operating in symphony.

There seemed to be no end to the daily, grinding agony. The
days stretched from morning twilight to night marches under the
stars, and yet somehow we lived through it—from moment to
moment, hour to hour, and then, as training advanced, from day
to day. The last 30 days were spent on the range, in the butts and
on the firing line—prone, kneeling, sitting, and standing, both
slow and rapid fire, holding and squeezing until the rifle barrel
got too hot to touch and you fired from the heat of it. And somehow, as the end of that three months of boot training came closer,
the miracle of the Marines broke through. You lost your searing
hatred for the DI and began to think of wearing your tin of accomplishment—a "safety pin" or a sharpshooter's Maltese cross or
even the crossed rifles over a laurel wreath, the mark of the
expert. There quickened in the march that first hint of assurance,

that swagger in the swing into line. The heavy felt field hat was no longer at the back of the head or hanging over the bridge of the nose, but straight and square.

I found I was doing well, and one afternoon after drill on the maneuver grounds they made me an acting Jack and put me in charge of the company. I was ordered to bring it back to camp.

We returned by way of the main road, and were nearly there when we approached a prisoner chaser who was guarding two men working a mule alongside the road on the line of march. He was lounging against a split-rail fence on the other side of the road, and made no move to cross over and join his prisoners as the marching column approached. This was an infraction of discipline, since the regulations say that a guard shall permit no one to come between himself and a prisoner, the chaser being primarily responsible for any such violation.

All would have been well, however, had not one of the men in the marching column goosed the mule in passing. This was the work of Ranny Reed, a Georgia cracker, who was always up to something. His reputation in the company was based on his frank admission that he could not return home because of an incident involving the "borrowin' " of a horse. He also started the company singing a mournful dirge called the Ranny Song:

> Raaaany O Raaaany,
> Raaaany O Raaaany,
> You take Sal and I take Sue
> Cross the river to the barbecue.
> Raaaany O Raaaany,
> Raaaany O Raaaany.
>
> Raaaany O Raaaany,
> Raaaany O Raaaany,
> If it wan't fo' the bull
>   and his long rod,
> We'd have no milk or
>   butter, by God.
> Raaaany O Raaaany,
> Raaaany O Raaaany."

At the head of the company, I turned at the commotion. The outraged mule had leaped over the fence and was bucking across the field, dragging a scraper behind him, with the prisoners in pursuit. The guard was trying to fight his way across the road through the marching column of men, but couldn't make it and yelled over his shoulder, "Halt that company!" Eventually the prisoners caught up with the mule, the guard caught up with the prisoners, and all four returned to the road. The chaser took my name.

That night at about 6 o'clock, after evening chow, a detail of regulars led by a corporal, appeared at the barracks and spoke to the DI sergeant in charge of the 12th. The DI then called out in a loud voice, "Private Krulewitch," and ordered me to fall in between the guards Indian file. Without further word, we marched off to the brig, located in the old barracks some two miles away. I was under arrest.

Arriving at the brig, I was turned over to the sergeant of the guard, an extremely uninviting individual, big, swarthy, and mean-looking. He reached up to a shelf for a hidden piece of rubber hose with a wooden handle.

"You see this?" he shouted, fanning the air with the hose.

"Yes," I gulped.

"My instructions are to shake well and use freely!" he roared, and with that he grabbed me by the shoulder, threw me into a cell, and clanged the door shut.

I sat on the edge of the hanging metal bunk lashed to the bulkhead and took stock. Sharply before me was a vision of the sergeant with the hose. I decided to ask no questions.

An hour or so later, the turnkey opened the door and took me to the brig warden, who sent me back to my company with orders to report at 7 o'clock next morning to the sergeant major at Post Headquarters for office hours.

Back in the bunkhouse, I found I had become the first hero of the 12th. There was some disappointment when I showed up in one piece, but they brightened up when I came to the part about the rubber hose. The sole topic of conversation was what was going to happen to me. Then, Ranny Reed began his ditty to the tune of "Oh Susannah," about the sad case of the "Hill-Billy Marine."

Ah cum fum wha' the blue grass grows
    In the hills of Old Kaintuck
Ah got tarred o' eatin' corn an' beans
    And ah thought ah'd change mah luck.
Ah met a snappy sergeant and he looked me up and down.
He made me sign a paper and the world turned upside down.

All joined in the chorus:

Oh Susannah,
Wha did ah leave home?
Fo' when this war is o-o-o-vuh,
Ah nevah mo' will roam.

The drill sergeant called me into his office and discussed the case with the two corporal DIs. There was a touch of condescension, even of friendliness in their attitude. Their suggestion was to plead guilty and get it over in a hurry. I was to hear this advice, more or less, for 30 years, yet despite the one-sided nature of military discipline, I rarely came across a miscarriage of justice. But this time I was not guilty and was not going to plead guilty. My plan was to bring out all the facts and show the CO the whole picture. I was not, repeat not, going to remain silent in seven languages, as the saying went.

After reveille and chow, I scrubbed and polished my leather, cleaned and blocked my campaign hat and put on freshly washed khaki. Loyal friends in the company helped me get into uniform and look my best. No neckties had been issued, since these were only for officers and gunners. Carefully lacing my leggings, folding in the slacks, regulation style, and guarding against Irish pennants, I checked out with the sergeant.

The Headquarters building a mile away was one of the two brick buildings in camp. The sergeant major, the first I'd ever seen, was a burly, paunchy, shiny, moon-faced individual, sporting two spare tires under his chin and a third at the back of his neck. He checked off my name on his list, gave me that sergeant-major look, and grabbed me by the shoulder.

"Stand by until your name is called," he said. "And when I tell you to march, you march. When I tell you to halt, you halt. I'll give all the orders when I take you in."

I had finished two years at Columbia Law School and worked in a law office one summer, so I was no stranger to legal tribunals. Except for a frosh-soph fight on the campus, during which we had all been arrested and later discharged, this was my first appearance as an accused. After the new and old officers of the day had marched in, the colonel called for the sergeant major and the sad parade for company punishment began. When my name was called, the sergeant major grabbed me by the shoulder, apparently a favorite grip, and hauled me to the door of the commanding officer's room. "Forward march," he called, so that all could hear. I marched in and just as I was about to crash into the colonel's desk, the command came—"Halt!" I stopped directly in front of the CO.

Colonel Treadwell was a compact, serious-looking officer, bald-headed and black-mustached. Seated to his left and right were the officers of his staff, a formidable company with all eyes on me. The prisoner chaser appeared from somewhere, and the sergeant major began to read the charge.

I missed the beginning but caught on before long. ". . . and Melvin L. Krulewitch, private, United States Marine Corps, attached to the 12th Drill Company, while so attached and serving and then being in command of said company, did, while proceeding from the maneuver grounds along the Post Highway give the wrong word of command and as a result thereof did march his Company between one James Haunce, Private, United States Marine Corps, duly detailed as a prisoner guard, and the prisoners he was guarding, thereby placing in jeopardy the performance of the required regulations, in such cases made and provided, for the safety and security of said prisoners and other property of the United States in the possession of said prisoners, to wit, one mule, the United States then being in a state of war."

The colonel turned to me and asked, "What do you say about that?" I answered that I had been marching the company along the road, that the prisoners with the mule had been working on one side of the road, and that the prisoner chaser had been sitting on the rail fence on the other side of the road. I added that when the company had almost passed by, the mule became frightened and ran away, with the prisoners in hot pursuit. They caught up with the mule, brought him back, and went back to work.

As I talked on, the sergeant major's face turned from a happy pink to an angry red. The colonel continuing with the case turned to the chaser and asked him where he was standing when the company passed. On the horns of a dilemma, the chaser gulped and blurted. Without further ado the colonel turned to the sergeant major, now an irate purple, and said, "What do you mean by bringing in a case like this?"

The sergeant major looked at me. "About face," he bellowed. "Forward march."

I about-faced, forward-marched, and walked out to freedom. I even stopped to say good-bye to the sergeant major, which turned out to be a tactical error. He grabbed me by the shoulder, leaned into my face, and muttered, "Get the hell out of here, you sea lawyer son-of-a-bitch. And if I ever see you again. . ."

That was all I heard. I was gone with the wind.

Somehow we survived those brutal three months. One morning in November, 1917, Skoda's whistle and the call, "Fall in on your bunks," brought the 12th Company together. Outside, the sun glistened pleasantly on the palm trees, and far in the distance, the palmettos fringing the maneuver grounds fluttered good morning in the breeze. In our high-raftered room, the floor, bleached by innumerable scrubbings, had been swabbed immaculate. The round-bellied coal stove, now shiny black after its ruby dullness of last night, was silent and cold. On each side, the long rows of evenly-spaced bunks were made up "regulation"—mattresses, sheets, and blankets triple–folded at the head, equipment hanging at the foot, and the rifles slung, bolts downward, along the edges of the iron springs. In front were the ditty boxes, neatly stowed and always ready for inspection.

"You'll be shoving off out of here pronto," Skoda began. "You ain't no Marines. You got a long road to go before you know what it's all about, so keep your khaki clean, polish them shoes, shine up your brass, keep your ass and your feet dry and maybe some day someone'll take you for a gyrene."

He turned to his assistant, "Take the outfit down to the QM to draw equipment." Without a further glance at the company about to leave his jurisdiction after three long months, Skoda strode majestically through the bunkhouse to the squad room appropriated by him for his own personal use and reached for the corn liquor hidden behind *Courts and Boards,* the court martial manual.

For us there were three more months training in the mud at Quantico, the new camp on the Potomac, before we were ready to shove off in the 133rd, commanded by Captain Francis Burns. By now I had made corporal, and became a bayonet instructor, thanks to the technique taught by the Canadians at Camp Columbia in June. What had been a 60-man drill company at P. I. was now one of four platoons in a regular company.

In December we entrained for Philadelphia, where we boarded the U.S.S. *Von Steuben* and sailed for New York. After anchoring in the upper bay for three days, we shoved off for France.

5. *The Green Monkey*

IN THE FIELDS surrounding the tiny hamlet of Chatillon-sur-Cher, Department of Loire et Cher, the crimson trêfe, blood brother to the American clover, shimmered in the warm breeze and brilliant May sunshine. Beautiful and placid, France's garden, the Touraine was worlds removed from the turbulence of the western front. The villagers had made us welcome, although what the boys most desired to uncover was not much in evidence. For once, the Marines had failed to live up to their reputation that "If it's there, the Marines will find it." To paraphrase an immortal line heard a quarter of a century later, "Never in the history of the world had so many chased after so few and gotten so little."

We trained in Chatillon for three months, practicing the best of British and French combat techniques, and we became part of the life of the village. Each week, I accompanied our battalion surgeon on his rounds among the civilian population, a grassroots community long used to wars. For most of us it was a flashback into history—ancient chateaux, peasants in wooden shoes, pissoirs in public view, and universal wine drinking.

One of my duties was to march the venereal brig detail each morning to the sick bay. Upon discovery, all venereals were sent to the brig for disciplinary action, since they had deprived the Corps of the services of a fighting man. This melancholy group formed each morning at Sick Call to receive a primitive and painful field treatment for their respective disabilities. And painful it was, to hear the naval lieutenant, Medical Corps, joke bleakly about "your little brother who weeps," and about his cure—"Too bad, too bad, six months of Mercury for one moment of Venus."

35

The three noncoms—Sergeant Dutch Friedman, Sergeant Red Fitzpatrick, and myself—were billeted with an ancient dragon known only as Marie Justine. Wooden shod and in her eighties, she would talk incessantly to anyone who would listen, about the good old days of the "Empéreur."

One day Sergeant Friedman, heavy set, swarthy, and blue-shaved, looked gloomily across the street and spat. Directly opposite our billet was the shop of the village shoemaker. His daughter, known to the unit as Horseface Harriet, was busily dusting off the large glass bottles of urine, animal and human, which her father used for the polishing and finishing of fine leathers. Many a villager in his Sunday best owed the brilliant finish of his slippers to the combined personal efforts of the shoemaker and his family.

Harriet looked with interest and hope through the store window at the Marines. Long in jaw and tooth, her nickname was not inappropriate. At the first sign of attention, however casual, she would break out in a cavernous smile exposing to the startled observer a vast expanse of wet, red gums. The extent of her sex appeal may be gauged from the fact that, surrounded by hundreds of Marines suffering acutely from the absence of female society, she had never managed to hook one, drunk or sober, for a date.

Harriet saw the three of us at the entrance to our billet and smiled. As one man, we turned and went inside.

Red Fitzpatrick, a snappy line sergeant of middle height with blue eyes, snub nose, red hair, and a scrubby red mustache, took off his fore-and-aft, wiped the sweat from his brow and sat down on the tongue of a heavy cart parked in the courtyard.

"It's getting worse here," he said. "I'm about ready for a bust."

Friedman smiled smugly. "I got a thirty-six for Saturday morning after inspection. Top wants me to do some business for him in Tours and I'll look around. I hear it's a good town."

Fitz looked shrewdly at Friedman. Pals for 12 years, they had been through the campaigns of Nicaragua, Haiti, and Vera Cruz together, so there was little one could hide from the other. "Come clean, you bastard," he said.

"We got a cash warrant to buy fresh stores, and Babcock wants met to get some fresh meat," Dutch answered. "Besides, I got some friends in Tours."

"Why you mitglommer punk," Fitz exploded. "Holding out on your pals. You're after tail. Well, I'm going too."

"Sure, you can come along—and Krulewitch too," Dutch said, nodding at me. "We'll need him to talk French."

"What's this business you're talking about?" I asked. "If you want me to write out another receipt in French for a pig you didn't buy, I can do it here. How much did you make on the 300 francs you didn't pay?"

Red howled and pushed Friedman in the chest until he had to smile as well.

"I'll give you the skinny," Dutch said. "One of the frogs I do business with gave me the name of a cathouse in Tours and I figured we could have some fun. But we'll need Kruley to help us get around and talk to the frogs. It's good he knows the lingo."

"I never supposed you had to do much talking in a whore-house," I said, "but if I can help, I'll go along. Besides, Tours has the beautiful castle of Francis the First with the salamander stair-case, and I'd like to see it."

Friedman and Red exchanged looks. "Okay," said Fitzpatrick. "Let's go up to the company office and get the passes. But don't say a word about the dive," he added quickly. "Babcock can smell cunt a mile away, and that will be the end of it for us. This won't be the first joint he took over for himself."

Dutch nodded. Babcock, the first sergeant, tall, handsome, and debonair, was a bitter, knock-down fighter, and a whole party unto himself for the women. He was too much for any of the outfit and could take over any outing at will.

Saturday morning, we were waiting at the tiny railroad station of Chatillon for the shrill toot of the 10:30 train which stopped on its way from Paris to Tours. Shined and polished for inspec-tion, we were stepping out for our first liberty after two months of combat drill and intense training for the trench warfare that lay ahead on the western front. With our wrapped puttees carefully rolled, forest greens sharply pressed, new fore-and-afts jauntily cocked, and gleaming fair leather belts across our blouses, we had to look good. In came the train, and an hour later, with a whoosh and a screech, the train pulled in at Tours.

The city was impressive after the weeks at Chatillon. Our first objective was a small restaurant near the Metropole, a hotel set up by the YMCA for the services. After French-fried potatoes, called *frites,* fresh eggs, and beefsteak, washed down by drafts of beer, we got around to the main object of our mission.

"Where is this dive, Dutch?" asked Fitz.

"I don't know the location, but I got the name." Friedman pulled a crumpled bit of paper from the sweatband of his cap, and handed it to me.

"Le Singe Vert," I said. "You know what that means?"

Both shook their heads.

"The Green Monkey."

"Not a bad name," Dutch volunteered. "Although I dunno about the green part."

At that moment, a benevolent old gentleman came walking down the street. He was pink-faced, with sparse white muttonchop whiskers.

"Ask the old guy," said Fitz. "Maybe he remembers it from his college days."

The ancient had taken off his hat in honor of France's newly embattled allies and greeted us with a polite salute.

"Sir," I began in my best college French, "could you convenience us by directing us to the Green Monkey?"

The Frenchman recoiled as though bitten by a snake. "Why, messieurs," he faltered. "That is a very bad place."

"What's he say?" asked Friedman.

"He says it's a bad place."

"It ain't so bad from what I heard," he said. "Maybe he knows a better one. Ask him."

"He doesn't mean it's a bad joint," I explained. "He's just saying it's bad—like saying it's bad to go to any whorehouse."

The old gentleman, who had paled at the intensity of this argument, started to move on. I asked him politely where the chateau was, and beaming this time, he gave us directions. As he left us, lifting his hat in farewell, he said again that Rue du Singe Vert was a bad place.

We held a council of war. All we knew was that it was on Rue du Singe Vert, and we had to find the street.

"Don't ask nobody who don't look like he knows what tail is," counseled Fitz.

"All Frenchmen know about tail," Friedman sagely contributed.

"I'll ask the cop," I said, as a gendarme, smartly dressed in leather helmet and cape and with a small bayonet as a side arm, came towards us.

"Maybe they haven't kicked in and they're out of bounds," said Dutch. "But what can we lose. Cops always know the best places and sometimes they get a cut. Ask him."

I got as far as "Singe Vert" when the cop beamed and wagged a coy finger in our direction. "Why certainly, messieurs," he began, and gave us explicit directions. Dutch and Fitz, on solid ground at last, smiled and passed out a package of Camels.

"Ah, Chameau, bon cigarette," said the gendarme, and with a last friendly warning, *Attention à ta bite* ("watch out for your tool"), we were on our way. I thought of the venereal brig, and the torturous treatment for that unfortunate detail.

It turned out that the Green Monkey was a well-established house in Tours. When we knocked on the door, it was opened at once by a fierce-looking concierge with an enormous rippling bosom and a luxurious mustache. After a second look, she opened the door wide and let us inside.

Passing through the foyer into a large salon with a small bar at one end, the madame made a brief announcement to the girls sitting at the tables against the walls. *"Americains,"* she said. The girls, who had been sitting with civilians and two French soldiers in horizon blue, immediately dumped their companions and flocked to us.

Dutch and Fitz picked their company. "I'll take the ass-blonde Kewpie over there," Fitz quipped and beckoned to a doll-faced girl with long blonde hair flowing to her hips. They joined hands and fled. Dutch giggled and pointed to a dark, well-built girl. "Meat for the monkeys," he said. "Dark meat for me." He walked over to the girl, lifted the hem of her silk chemise high above her downy furrow, grabbed her arm, and ran upstairs with her. The girls in the room began to sing the popular bordello ballad,

> *Relevez, ma belle, ton beau jupon*
> *Qu'on peut voir le cul, on voit le con!*

I walked over to the bar where a slight, attractive, blue-eyed young girl in evening dress was standing, and offered her a drink. She smiled politely and we drank for a while and chatted in French. I was a little embarrassed at first, but warmed up after awhile and began to enjoy the conversation. After the third drink, the madame came up and asked me what was going on. I answered that we were just drinking. "Don't waste your time with this one," she said angrily and pulled her away.

I had another vermouth cassis and looked around. The boys had disappeared and no one in the place was paying attention to me any longer. It had begun to get dark. I was hungry again and I decided to go back to the Metropole for dinner and a room for the night.

The hotel was crowded and the meal was American canteen chow. By 9 o'clock most of the patrons had left. I paid my check, walked to the desk and asked for a room.

"Nothing doing, not a room in the house," said the clerk. "This is Saturday night and we've been sold out for a week."

"How about letting me sleep on the billiard table? I'll push it against the wall and spend the night there."

"Not a chance," answered the clerk and turned to the next in line.

I walked out of the hotel. There were no more trains for Chatillon and I had to find a bunk for the night. A young, attractive girl happened to be passing, and on an impulse I said, "Pardon me for addressing you, but I'm a stranger here and am looking for a place to spend the night."

"Think nothing of it," she answered. "I know the very place for you. It's not too far away. We can walk there in a moment."

It seemed her name was Mercedes. "What horsepower?" I wanted to wisecrack, but anxious for a place to sleep, I let her chatter on until we came to a private house. Still in my mind was the gendarme's warning and the screams of strong men when medication was applied to the venereal detail.

The door was opened by another formidable lady, this time smoking a large cigar, who ushered us into a salon opening into a small garden with a bar at one end. Still smoking her cigar, she took a few steps through the open doors into the yard, and with no more ado, lifted her skirts, squatted down, and pissed with a great hissing and splashing.

I ordered a bottle of wine for Mercedes and myself and we sat down at a small table to drink it. The lady with the cigar then came over and Mercedes explained that I wanted a room alone for the night. Without a word, Madame pushed little Mercedes toward the door. I paid for the wine and left.

It was late now; I walked to the railroad station, stretched out on one of the long, hard benches and tried to sleep. The trains rolled in and out. At 3 A.M. a large group of refugees from the northeast front arrived and changed trains for Bordeaux, to which they were being shipped by the French government.

After they had gone, I looked down the row of benches. A slim, familiar figure walked through the waiting room and down the aisle. It was Mercedes.

Every bone in my body ached. I was hungry and tired, uneasy and disquieted. She stopped as she saw me lying on the bench. Bending over, she shook a finger at me. "This is all you deserve," she said.

I returned to Chatillon on the first morning train out of Tours. It was early dawn with the gold of sunrise giving its blessing to the new day. As I walked up the hill from the river and turned into the straggling main street of the village, I saw that an astonishing change had taken place. Only the day before a peaceful billeting area far from even the echoes of war, Chatillon had burst into sudden activity. Men were rolling their packs in the billets, seabags were being piled high in the streets and loaded onto trucks. A French cart, hauled by a great, deep-chested *percheron,* had been commandeered and crammed to its limits with equipment, and the baggage detail now sat high in the air, on guard.

Down the path a Marine came running toward me full tilt. "Corporal," he gasped, catching his breath. "We're going up. Top sent me down to pass the word. We're combat-loading. We're shoving off for the front."

As I passed the galley, I saw Dutch Friedman was back. He was issuing thick slabs of meat and bread for packing in the messkits. A line had also begun to form at the listerbag, where canteens were being filled. The quartermaster was issuing 100 rounds of .30 caliber ammo for the Springfields, and the men were buckling the clips into the pockets of their cartridge belts.

We fell in and the entire population of the village lined up across from the company front to see us off as we marched down to the railroad station. There we lined up again for muster and roll call, report to the captain, final orders to the special details and a few crisp words from the CO. At a sharp word of command, the line then swung into column and marched to the empty box cars waiting on the siding. Each held *"40 hommes,"* who climbed aboard, stowed away their equipment and rations, slung their rifles carefully from the roof or sides of the car, and settled down— their high adventure had begun.

With a shrill toot of the engine's whistle, the long troop train clanked out of Chatillon on its way to the front. Sitting at the side doors, the men saw great splashes of crimson staining the green fields. In the afternoon breeze, the blood-red clover waved good-bye.

6. *Belleau Wood*

WE BOUNCED and rattled in the boxcars as far as Fontainebleau, then piled into waiting *camions* lined up along the Paris–Metz road. The front was less than 40 miles from Paris, and we could hear the guns. Heading for our regimental headquarters, 6th Marines, we were replacements for the dead and wounded of the last week's fighting. There were 20 of us in our truck, including Dutch Friedman and Red Fitzpatrick.

We rolled through the villages and towns east of Paris towards the Second Battle of the Marne. Along this road, Gallieni's taxicab army had turned the German flank, four years before, when Joffre had outwitted von Kluck. History was now repeating itself. The British and French had been pushed back and back and back, and the Paris–Metz road had become the objective for the last German drive of the war. It was on this offensive that Hindenburg and Ludendorff were pinning their hopes for final success. The advance continued. On May 30, the Germans stood at the Marne. Pershing ordered up the Second Division with its Marine Brigade, but by June 1 the Germans had moved to within 40 miles of Paris. The American defense then broke the German attack, held the line and on June 6, the Marines counterattacked and held the southern edge of Belleau Wood, the Ravine, and the town of Bouresches.

Censorship prevented the identification of particular units, but the Marines were a separate service and could be referred to as such. On June 8, 1918, *The New York Times* carried this banner headline:

OUR GALLANT MARINES DRIVE ON 2½ MILES; STORM TWO TOWNS, CAPTURE 300 PRISONERS

And the story went on:

New advance by our men

Torcy and Bouresches stormed in a drive on Six Mile Front

Enemy losses very heavy

Each man get a German, Don't let him get you, is the Victors' slogan

Nothing stops their rush

Twenty-five of them fight 200 in Torcy—German Dead Three Deep in Places

As we got nearer the front, the road became pitted with old and new shell holes, and we passed the still visible scars of the four-year-old trenches of the First Battle of the Marne. One of our group, who was a little jumpy, made us laugh like hell, when mindful of bootcamp instruction, he shouted, "Fellows, take off your front sight covers!" We were five miles from the front! At Regimental Headquarters we lay over for chow and watched Corporal Angie Cincotta, later colonel, strip down the new one-pounders, the French 37mm, a deadly accurate weapon with the precision of our Springfield rifle.

New muster-rolls were written up, and we were split into groups. That afternoon runners came up from each battalion to guide us to our company headquarters, and a few hours later I was assigned to the 78th, Captain Messersmith commanding. We left our support area to take position along the edge of the woods facing Belleau Wood.

Lieutenant Clifton B. Cates, my commanding general at Iwo Jima a generation later, described the position in a letter home:

> . . . a thick woods on the side of a hill near Belleau Wood. Luckily, we had time to dig fox holes before the Germans opened up with a heavy barrage and we had intermittent artillery fire all day. Casualties were fairly light.[1]

[1] *At Belleau Wood,* Robert B. Asprey, p. 276.

The firing had now stopped, except for an occasional long-distance shell keening high over the lines toward the ammunition dumps and the rear assembly areas.

We were the replacements of which Colonel Harry Lee spoke so highly, although most of us had had almost a year of Marine Corps training, rather than the two months he attributed to us:

> The remarkable conduct of raw replacement troops which joined this organization on the night of June 8 when thrown into the line is transmitted for the information of the Major General Commandant. The replacement detail of 213 included among it a large majority who were enlisted two months before their reporting to this organization. It was necessary to replace immediately losses sustained in the 2nd Battalion which was holding the right flank of our operations and the stronghold of the town of Bouresches, a line vitally important to the success of the present operations. The detail arrived at the Regimental Headquarters at 6:30 P.M. and were placed in the woods and organized for relief. . . . These troops were marched past the lines at 10:30 P.M. under detail from Regimental Headquarters to the point where they were met by platoon guides and conducted to their station. The Regimental Sergeant Major (John Quick) reports that the men obeyed orders without a word, moved in splendid order and across a terrain which was shelled by the enemy by high explosives and lighted up by flares. Their arrival in the lines of the 2nd Battalion relieved a pressing need for men at a vital point. The remarkable steadiness of these men . . . under conditions that would have been trying to veteran troops, is eloquent evidence of the fine material from which the Marine Corps is drawing its men in a critical hour of the nation's history.[2]

I was ordered to a listening post 100 feet in front of the line. I crawled there through the high grass, and sat on the edge of the foxhole in the darkness, sipping a mouthful of lukewarm water and chewing a bit of hardtack so tough that it had to be soaked first. In my mind as I looked up at the stars were thoughts of the past and present—not the future. A year ago I had been in the middle of a busy social and college life; that other Krulewitch had been able to go and come as he pleased. I thought about the

[2] *At Belleau Wood,* Robert B. Asprey, p. 230.

graduating class at Law School, now receiving their degrees, and about my happy family life. Standing in that shoulder-deep post at night, alone in the face of the enemy, listening to the rattle of German ambulances across the field on the hill beyond, I looked up at the stars and my throat constricted at the thought of those same stars looking down on my loved ones. But then reality asserted itself as my relief broke in with a soft sibilant call, and I crawled as silently as possible back to the line.

Then the galley came up with a mess of hot beans for chow, and the men left their foxholes to gather around. One of them went down to the food dump and came back with a giant necklace of hard brown French loaves, strung on wire. Everything looked good, but then the shelling began, making a direct hit on the galley. It rained beans and debris.

Just before midnight, the German box barrage took over. Huddling in our foxhole, we were shelled from every quarter with deadly accuracy. This was no long-distance shelling, probing our back areas. *We* were the target. First would come the crescendo screams of the shells approaching, then tearing, shattering, rupturing explosions, so different from the heavy boom of the guns themselves. In the pitch blackness of the woods, the bursts made yellow and red auroras, showering a rain of death. No Hell or Purgatory imagined by Dante Alighieri could approach that inferno of violence.

Then the sounds changed. Instead of tearing bursts, came the *plop, plop* of a different kind of shell and with it, the smell of mustard and horseradish. "Gas! Gas!" came the cry, and we put on our masks. This was the attack that cost us literally hundreds of casualties.

Lieutenant Cliff Cates told Bob Asprey the story:

> I had not gone over twenty feet from my foxhole when I heard a salvo of shells heading our way. From the whistle I thought they were gas shells, and when they hit with a thud and no detonation my fears were confirmed. Soon I smelled the gas, and I gave the alarm to the men, and they all put on their masks. By this time there was a steady stream of incoming shells—gas, air bursts, shrapnel, and high explosives. I reached for my gas mask, but it wasn't there. Natu-

rally, I was petrified. I tried to find my hole where I had left it, but I became confused and couldn't locate it.[3]

The shelling was so heavy we didn't try to move out, which I now realize was a mistake. It kept up for hours, and we suffered rather heavy casualties, both from shell fragments and gas, as many of our masks were defective. Heroes were made that night, as the wounded had to be carried to the dressing station, which was under a stone bridge down the ravine. Many of the stretcher bearers were hit while carrying the wounded. As soon as the Boche artillery fire stopped, we moved out with about half of the company remaining, and went into this hell hole Belleau Wood.[4]

I wore my gas mask for six solid hours, every once in a while removing the cover of the mask but keeping the tube in my mouth and the clips on my nose. From forehead to chin my face was covered with a slimy slobber. All around were calls for first aid for the wounded and the gassed. Men without masks lay on the ground, coughing up blood and gasping their life away.

Pierce Fredericks, writing in *The New York Times Magazine,* had the story:

> **For the next 20 days, the brigade fought in the woods, rock to rock, one German machine gun to the next, only to find that for every machine gun they captured two more were positioned to take the captors on the flank. The Germans went to mustard gas and a Columbia College boy named Mel Krulewitch remembers that they put down a neat box barrage and then sent in gas shells. When it was over, Krulewitch led out the 11 men left of a company of more than 200.**

In the early morning, with Cates the only officer in command, we gathered the remnants of his 96th Company and the 11 men of our 78th, and moved to a position in the Woods.

I made sergeant.

Later on that week, we marched back down the same Paris–Metz road to a support position about two miles behind the

[3] *At Belleau Wood,* Robert B. Asprey, p. 276.
[4] *At Belleau Wood,* Robert B. Asprey, p. 277.

front. The mules of the baggage and ration train were on picket line and I picked a dry place under one of the wagons to sleep. An artillery battery was firing nearby, but I was so dead tired, so worn out by the terrific strain, that I fell asleep literally under the firing guns. Then, suddenly, I awoke with a start. It was the silence. The guns had stopped firing.

My mother had mailed me a union suit made of linen, silk, and cotton, that was guaranteed louse-proof. When I slipped down to the Marne for a bath, I took it off—and it was so lousy it practically walked away by itself. On my chest and belly were clusters of what the newspapers delicately referred to as "cooties" —large body lice, not to be confused with the smaller "crabs" frequenting the pubic area. I scraped off all I could and took a swim but had to put on the same sweaty, filthy uniform afterwards, and so in a few days my little friends were all back again doing business at the old stand.

By now fresh troops were coming up, and among the replacements was Victor Spark, a sergeant, who had just arrived from the States. We were old friends. Five months later, during the last battle of the war, I carried him back to the first aid station. Although exhausted by dysentery and the flu, he had refused to report to the battalion surgeon. I had the melancholy honor of burying one of his Marine sons on Saipan, 26 years later. His second son, a colonel of Marines, was killed in Vietnam.

We rejoined the line. Toward the end of June, when the Wood had been completely secured, we were ordered up from brigade reserve to the front, facing an enemy who although defeated, had shown no signs of any general retreat. Our battalion was in good shape—new officers, new replacements (our third batch), good chow, and plenty of ammo and java.

As an old-timer (?), I was ordered to take out a detail to set up some double-apron wiring to the north of the Wood in German territory. On our way back along the trail amid the trees, I fell into a camouflaged German dugout. I broke the arch of my right foot, and had to limp and hop the rest of the way. That was bad enough, but worse was to come. That afternoon we were shelled again, and one of the shells had my number on it. A tremendous explosion drove the blood into my ears—my helmet rang like a bell. A sergeant near me was wounded in the knee. As the numbness wore off I felt a bite and a sting along my left leg and side. Exploring this cautiously, I was surprised to find blood running down—I had been hit in the left leg, left thigh, and left chest. I reached inside my shirt, where an itch was making itself felt, and pulled out of my left rib cage a thin strip of metal in the shape of a horseshoe.

One arm thrown around the shoulders of a medical corpsman, I limped and hobbled back to the battalion aid station. The lacerations in my left leg, thigh, and chest had stopped bleeding and it was the broken arch that was giving me the most trouble. I fell down several times and couldn't get up. At the dressing station, the battalion surgeon shot an enormous dose of anti-tet venom into my belly, and left my shoes on to keep down the swelling.

This first-aid center was in a large culvert, which afforded some protection, although most of the wounded were spread out all around—some on litters, others sitting or crouching in the scrub. Ambulances bounced in and out, taking the bad ones to the regimental collecting point, and when my turn came, I shared a ride with two others on the floor and a third suspended on a stretcher from the roof. The clearing station was a gutted church, where we were tagged and classified before moving on to a field hospital, five miles back of the line on a spur of the Paris–Metz Highway.

This field hospital was a temporary installation set up to receive the casualties of the Second Division. Its canvas walls were braced at regular intervals by wooden joists supporting temporary sashes for windows on each side. The grass in the center aisle, between the rows of beds, had been trodden down by visitors, nurses, and doctors into a soft green carpet. Here the wounded stayed until they were fit to travel to one of the great base hospitals at St. Nazaire, Neuilly, Dijon, or Bordeaux. I was brought in on a litter and an angel in nurse's uniform gave me a bath. I was grimy, lousy, and covered with mud from the battlefield. She scissored through my sodden rolled puttees, cut the laces buried in my muddy field shoes, and pried off the sticky matted socks. Except for my foot, I was in good shape, and so I was shipped out with the next batch of wounded to the base hospital at Bordeaux.

7. Behind the Lines

WE TRAVELED aboard new Pullman sleepers specially built for hospital use. Clean, shiny, and antiseptic, they had upper and lower berths and linoleum passages to enable the walking wounded to reach the lavatories and washrooms at each end of the cars. The food was excellent and the male nurses were clean and orderly. All this caused the base hospital at Tallence, a suburb of Bordeaux, to seem a sorry anticlimax. Each morning a nurse would come around with a large pitcher of Dakin solution and a small funnel, call out "tubes," and as the hands or feet went up, he would go from patient to patient pouring the disinfectant into the open ends of tubes protruding from bandages on arms, legs, and torsos, to irrigate the poisonous infections that so often proved fatal with battlefield wounds.

The French received a ration of wine every day, but we didn't. This resulted in a rash of petty larceny throughout the ward to finance a barter system with the French wounded for their wine. All in all, I didn't enjoy the hospital and was happy when I finally came before a Survey Board which recommended that I be discharged, marked B2 (no longer fit for combat duty), and sent to Ramorantin, the British orthopedic camp for treatment and reassignment.

The morning after my arrival at the B2 camp, I reported with the rest of the inmates to the exercise ground, where we were lined up sitting on the ground in two long parallel lines facing each other. We then took off our shoes and socks, and at the order began wiggling our feet and toes.

We were all B2s but for many different reasons. Some had broken shoulders ("Wiggle your toes!"), some had lost a hand

("Wiggle your toes!"), some had chest and stomach wounds ("Wiggle your toes!"). Eventually, the boy alongside me rebelled and asked, "Why do I have to do this?" We then discovered he had been marked B2 only because he had no front teeth, and therefore could not hold onto the mouthpiece of his gas mask ("Wiggle your toes!"). After the first week we were joined by a boy from the back country of Louisiana. He dutifully took his place in the row and wiggled his toes. On his chest was a tag ordering him to the B2 camp because he could not speak English ("Wiggle your toes!").

From here, I was assigned to POW 14. We picked up 300 German prisoners at St. Pierre-des-Corps near Tours, loaded them on boxcars, and after a day of backing and filling, pulled out. My CO was an Army dental officer, who was marked B2 for reasons best known to his Survey Board. Short, fat, moon-faced, and indolent, he was left alone and we ran the company without him.

The four-day trip across France from Tours to our camp at Is-sur-Tille was plain murder. We had two soldiers as guards, fully armed, locked in each freight car with 35 German prisoners. The long train would stop from time to time for sanitary purposes, and as soon as the troops from the POW companies had lined up facing the side doors, the cars would be unlocked and out would come the guards first, and then, with a rush, the prisoners. They would squat in a row in the fields and relieve themselves. Many of them had dysentery, and the scene was a shambles. Separate stops would be made for the distribution of water and canned food. The empty cans were welcomed by the prisoners, who used them for makeshift sanitation, although the floors were already covered with a layer of rotted, stinking straw, probably left over from a previous shipment of horses. The wooden walls were splashed with human soil, as were the areas near the side doors farthest away from the rows of sardine-packed men lying on their sides— the luxury of lying on their backs or stomachs was impossible in the space available.

The place was a living shithouse, and I was sorry for them. Only a few days before they had been soldiers in a proud army. I also felt sorry for the two GIs in each car, and sorry for myself —I badly wanted to get back to the clean, healthy comradeship

of my own company, fighting somewhere on the line. At each of
the stops, I was required to inspect the 10 boxcars assigned to me
for breaks in the floor, sides, or roof, and for signs of disturbances
among the prisoners. I rode with the CO in an old passenger car,
and rough as the accommodations were—no water, no lights, and
the only toilet a rusty, encrusted pipe with an open end—it was
heaven compared to the stink of corruption in which the prisoners
traveled. Our gunny, Paddy Behan, took one look inside a boxcar
and said, "They've been jalaped"—an old Marine Corps expression referring to jalap, a cathartic tropical bean.

Paddy had retired in 1912 after 30 years in the Corps and had
been recalled in 1917 and marked B2 because of his age—he was
now in his fifties. Paddy was very religious. Each Sunday morning
at Is-sur-Tille, he attended Mass and then repaired for the rest of
the day to the local whorehouse, where he could be reached in any
emergency. Blue-eyed, short, and wiry, with large hands and feet
and a deeply-marked, ruddy complexion, he was never quite drunk
and never quite sober. We admired his capacity and covered for
him when he was away.

Sunday afternoon was spent on maintenance of the prison area.
We permitted the prisoners to organize themselves into *Zugs,*
platoons, with a *Zugsführer* in command, who in turn reported to
their *Feldwebel,* or first sergeant. They gave us little or no trouble,
maintaining their own internal discipline except on one occasion
when a prisoner refused to accept it and they asked us for a court
martial. There then ensued an *opera bouffe* worthy of Bardell vs.
Pickwick.

The dental CO presided, glaring fearsomely around since he had
just been disturbed from his afternoon nap. "Quiet," he said in his
childish pipe, although no one had said a word, and Gunnery
Sergeant Paddy Behan gave me a knowing wink. Since I had two
years of law school behind me and knew a smattering of German,
he promptly turned the proceedings over to me. When the *Feldwebel,* the prisoner, and the witness were escorted into the company administration office, I stood up and ordered the German
noncom to state the complaint. He rambled on in German, some
of which I understood, but most of which was Greek to me, and
then I played my trump card. In a loud voice which impressed

even the CO—he opened his eyes—I called out, *Schuldig oder nicht schuldig?* ("Guilty or not guilty?").

The prisoner, to my disappointment, answered *"Nicht schuldig,"* which meant a trial would have to be held. Anxious to avoid this if possible, I told him it would be better if he pleaded guilty. *Das ist mir egal,* he answered ("It makes no difference to me"). I talked to the *Feldwebel* again, then to the witness, and waking up the dental officer, pronounced the prisoner guilty. I didn't listen to the defense because that might have confused me! I whispered into the CO's ear, "No tobacco and clean out the field toilets every day for a month." He looked at me as though I was imposing the sentence on him. "It's just a suggestion for the prisoner, sir," I whispered.

The CO glowered at the *Feldwebel* and shouted at him, "You've been found guilty of. . ." He broke off and turned to me, "What the hell did he do?" "It's not that one," I said, leaning over the table. "It's the one standing over there. The one you're talking to is their first sergeant." He was furious. "Why didn't you tell me?" "Let him clean out the shithouses," I said soothingly. The CO smiled. "Tell him to do it in German," he ordered, and I did. The German first sergeant winked as the sad little party left the room.

One Sunday afternoon the corporal of the relief in charge of the body count, taken three times a day, came running into the office to report, "There's something wrong with the count." A runner was sent to the bordello to summon Paddy. The call to arms was immediately sounded. The gates were manned, guards with BARs were stationed in the one-story towers at each corner. Bringing out the muster-roll, we got the *Feldwebel* to check us, and as each name was called, the prisoner stepped through the prison barracks gate into the compound.

When the last name was called, with all present, a group of four miserable prisoners in a slightly different uniform stood huddled together at the barracks' entrance. We looked them over, spoke to them in German, and as they turned around, noticed that, instead of PW, in large black letters on their backs they had the French PG—*prisonnier (de) guerre*. The mystery was soon solved. Having heard that the Americans treated their prisoners of war more humanely than the French, these four PGs had escaped, not to freedom, but to the American stockades! Reluctantly, we had to send them back.

Taking a leaf from their book, I decided to take French leave myself, to go over the hill—not to desert, but to rejoin my own company, the 78th. From a wounded Marine in the hospital, I found out that my regiment was located near Chalons-sur-Marne, and I reported there for duty. My official service record never caught up with me, which meant that I received no pay until just before our Division sailed home from Germany. But I was back home with the 78th and I managed.

After a staggering forced march to Leffincourt, to join the beleaguered 9th French Army Corps, a 50-mile hike in heavy marching order from dawn to moonlight, our battalion was ordered back to our own division near Mont Pelier.

There we prepared for the last battle of the war.

8. *Birthday Present*

Six months had gone by since that day in May, 1918, when we had said good-bye to the training camp at Chatillon. The 78th Company had fought in the desperate engagement at Belleau Wood; struggled through the confusion at Soissons to achieve the monumental victory for which Petain had given the regiment the *fourragère* of the Croix de Guerre; broke in through the salient at St. Mihiel to complete in businesslike fashion the first completely American major operation of the war; seized and held the citadel of Blanc Mont in the Champagne sector, a German fortress that had defied the Allies for four years, and finally, in the last month before the kill, had shivered and hungered in the climactic drive against the *Kremhilde Stellung* and its approach to the Meuse.

It was early morning on November 10, 1918, and all night long there had been rumors at the front of an armistice. I had been awakened by the cold of the water into which I had sunk in the boggy ground. That night Jess Hammer and I, the last of the sergeants of the 78th, had taken the precaution of building a nest of twigs and boughs to sleep on, but with the continuing rain, nothing could keep your ass from sinking into the earth and forming a collect pond for all the run-off water. Fires were out of the question. Body heat alone had to steam the damp out of your breeches and blouse. As for your feet, they just never got dry.

Jess squeezed out as much of the wet as he could, lit the bedraggled butt of a cigarette, and asked of no one in particular, "When do we eat?" In the hazy half-light, other struggling forms were rising in the scrub and trying to shake off the misery of the night. Wet, cold, hungry, exhausted, and sick, the remnants of our company rolled their packs, cleaned their weapons, huddled together, and in the time-honored tradition of their outfit, stood by for orders.

"Look what's coming down the road," Jess shouted, pointing to a muddy galley rolling along to the Company CP. "There's Kelly." "He must have some chow with him or he wouldn't dare show his mug around here." I took one look, grabbed my rifle, told Jess to watch my gear, and ran down to meet the mess sergeant by a small clump of poplars near the water cart. He did indeed have chow. I brought back a round loaf of French bread for Jess and told him, "Kelly says he's going to serve hot monkey meat and java in ten minutes. Pass the word to the outfit." It wasn't necessary. Word had already gotten around. The clatter of mess gear could be heard all down the line. By the time Kelly called "Chow," the outfit was there to a man and waiting.

The rough food was like manna from the gods—hot black coffee and French canned meat with black bread. When Kelly broke open a case of peaches it was to general acclaim, except from the old hands who began to ask themselves, "How come we get it so good this morning?" The boys hadn't seen a galley for a week. Then the rumors started up again about an armistice, adding to the sense of well-being induced by the food, and the wet night was forgotten. The sun even started to come out, its sickly rays piercing the haze.

The day passed quietly. At 4 o'clock that afternoon chow call went again. As the boys lined up, their shouts passed down the line. "Steaks and gravy." "Fresh spuds." "White bread." "Sergeant major coffee." It was almost too good to be true, but there it was.

As the men finished their meal, Second Lieutenant Robb assembled what was left of the company and the blow fell. "Every man draw four grenades, two extra bandoliers of ammunition and stand by," he ordered.

"Looks like we're going in again," said Jess. "Some armistice. Who started that shithouse rumor around here anyway?" There was no answer. For veterans of months of fighting, the routine was familiar—hot chow, then extra ammunition and hand grenades. This was another attack. No armistice for us.

The 78th had been reduced from a full complement of 200 men to 54 in the space of 10 days. We lay on arms at a crossing of the Meuse, as part of a covering force established at the bridge-head to protect the Division's advance. We moved to the attack just before dawn on November 11, 1918—my 23rd birthday.

In the previous 10 days, the Division had smashed the last remaining enemy defenses in the *Kremhilde Stellung,* seized the heights of Bayonville, and continued its advance towards the Metz–Malmedy railroad, the enemy's main artery of supply. The attack had been pressed home under almost intolerably bad weather conditions through the swamps and low wooded country south of the Meuse, and we were now forcing a crossing of the river.

During the advance, the 78th had been hard hit, not so much by enemy fire as by sickness and exhaustion. The continuous campaigning in the rain, the nightly bivouac in the swamps, and the absence of fires and hot food had knocked out all but the hardiest.

Two battalions of the brigade were forming to bridge the crossing, while a third, including the depleted 78th, had been designated as the covering force. We had taken our position along the railroad, and we were now getting ready to meet the expected counterattack. But all visible landmarks on the hills and along the roadbed had vanished under a thick yellow blanket of fog. Even the great piles of burning material and coal, set ablaze by the retreating enemy that day, could only be made out at closest range.

The covering troops lay huddled together on the rough railroad bed. The sharp staccato of machine-gun fire and the rattle of mus-ketry were sporadic, and the shelling was so intermittent as to cause very little anxiety. So far as we could tell, the crossing was well on its way to completion. The first bridge, a precarious, two-plank affair made fast to the opposite bank by the tenacious efforts of the 2nd Engineers, had been swept away by the swift current and well-directed artillery fire. The second bridge, held in place for a time by the desperate efforts of men up to their shoulders in flood water and weighed down by heavy marching gear, was thrown across in the face of withering machine-gun fire, and a desperate counterattack was successfully beaten off by the first companies across. The bridgehead was now secured.

With the crossing of the first companies, however, the enemy artillery support lifted to attack the covering troops on our side of the bridge. The shelling increased in tempo. All along the railroad the men shook off the inertia of the past two hours and prepared for action. Cries of "First Aid" were heard with increasing frequency, and the noise of ambulances bouncing across the uneven ground added to the din. Gone was the earlier quiet of the hills.

Our little company, although completely in the open, had kept up its morale and by some miracle had suffered no casualties as yet. But nerves had been drawn tight, not only by this engagement but by six months' hard campaigning, and they were now at the breaking point. The course of each incoming shell was followed with the most intense concentration by every man, from the whistling approach to the hit, the instant's pause, and then the burst set off by the percussion fuse in the shell's nose.

Suddenly there came a new note in the approach of a whizz-bang—and every Marine in the platoon froze to the spot. Each knew from experience that this particular high explosive had his name on it. Even if cover had been available, none could have reached it in time. Fascinated, immobile, they could only await the end.

The shell landed squarely in the center of the company. And in that fraction of a second between hit and explosion, there was no thought as to past or future. Each soldier braced himself only for the terrific impact of the next moment when the fuse would detonate the charge.

Nothing happened. For that little group of men came the war's greatest thrill—and my best birthday present. The shell was a dud.

At 11:00 A.M. on November 11, 1918, Lieutenant Robb, the only remaining officer of the 78th, mustered his company on the open ground behind the railroad and read them the order declaring the Armistice. Still weary from the morning's attack, cold, tired, and wet, the men looked at each other without comment. The first man to speak said, "I'm goin' to build me a fire," and started digging into the waterlogged deadfalls for some dry wood. Others followed suit and soon groups of men were standing around in the open, enjoying the warmth of an open fire for the first time in months. Far in the distance, little knots of Germans gathered at the edge of the woods.

The war was over. General John A. Lejeune issued the following order next day:

HEADQUARTERS SECOND DIVISION (REGULAR) AMERICAN EXPEDITIONARY FORCES

France, November 12, 1918

O R D E R

1. On the night of November 10th, heroic deeds were done by heroic men. In the face of a heavy artillery and withering machine gun fire, the 2nd Engineers threw two foot bridges across the MEUSE and the first and second battalions for the 5th Marines crossed resolutely and unflinchingly to the east bank and carried out their mission.

2. In the last battle of the war, as in all others in which this Division has participated, it enforced its will on the enemy.

John A. Lejeune
Major General, U. S. M. C.
Commanding

JAL:hi

While the men huddled around the fires in the cold November morning, great celebrations were taking place in New York, Washington, Paris, and London.

9. *The March to the Rhine*

As SOON AS the 78th had reorganized, we began our march to the Rhine, following the defeated armies of the Reich, in stages, as set by the terms of the Armistice. As the advance guard of the Second Battalion of the 6th, the 78th had sent out an advance party, which in turn had thrown out a point consisting of just two of us, 2nd Lieutenant Adams, a new shavetail, and myself. I had been saddled with the additional duty of billeting noncom because of my smattering of German and French.

We crossed the border into Belgium. Behind the hedgerows the bare brown wintry fields, dotted here and there with tree skeletons stretched across the lowlands into emptiness. In one grubby patch an ancient peasant was pulling a wooden plow with a woman directing it, scratching out the barest furrow in the soil for a winter planting. As the Marines strode down the road, the man straightened up in alarm, stumbled over to the road, his cap in his hand, and asked, *"Wer sind sie?"* I replied in German, *"Ameri-kaner."* His jaw dropped. Then he began to sob, *"Amerikaner, Amerikaner,"* and called to his wife, who left the plough and came through the hedge to join the point. At a word from the Belgian, she hurried ahead down the road and was soon lost to sight.

We pushed along, the stumbling, limping farmer keeping up with the strong, even strides of the Marines, and soon the squat stone houses of a hamlet appeared in the distance. At the head of the main street a knot of villagers had gathered to greet the Americans. The wife had passed the word.

As the point approached a feeble cheer arose. An old, old man in a rusty black suit and floppy black hat scraped a faltering tune on a fiddle and all joined in the Brabançonne, the Belgian national hymn. A small boy, jumping up and down, waved a hurriedly improvised American flag. It hardly mattered that the red and white stripes were painted up and down with only a splash of blue in the corner—the spirit and the warmth and the welcome were there. The waiting group broke and ran to meet the Marines, the peasant now hoarsely shouting, "Les Américains." "Welcome, welcome," they cried in French and German, with here and there a stab at the English word. I picked up the small boy with the flag and carried him high on my shoulders above my pack. The procession grew. Invitations to rest for a drink or a spot of food were politely declined, but we stopped for a moment to take a drop of the rough red wine poured from a bottle which one of the elders brought out to toast the victory.

Passing through the village, we moved on toward our first stage terminus, Arlon, the first Belgian city over the French border, which lies in the finger of Belgium thrust between France and Luxembourg. Overrun in 1914, Belgium had refused to surrender, even though it was the captive of the Hun. Defiant, though defeated and crushed, the country had maintained its unity and spirit through four years of occupation.

As we marched side by side through the flat farming country of the lowlands, more and more people joined us at each of the villages on the way to the city. At last we saw the roofs and spires of Arlon in the distance, a welcome sight after hours of marching. We were to stop there for the night before going on to Reisdorf, across the border in Luxembourg.

As we approached the town, the citizens came out to meet us. All the able-bodied young men were far away in the northwest country, in that corner of free Belgium which still flew the gold, black, and red of the national colors, and only the women and children, the disabled and the very old had remained behind. At the head of the procession were two young Belgian girls, four hands on the pike staff, carrying high their country's flag, buried in the earth for four long years but now uncovered and flown again to welcome the Americans, the vanguard of freedom.

We crossed the border into Luxembourg, and after a night in the town of Reisdorf, we received new instructions from Major

Bull Williams, commanding the Second Battalion. His high octane breath indicated that his two-quart French *bidon,* which it was his practice to replenish each morning with fine French cognac, had come in handy. He spoke to Adams: "Lieutenant, get to Ettelbruck, billet the outfit, and wait for us at the town. If you need guides the advance party will provide them." We saluted and moved off, while the major and his exec, the only two mounted in the battalion, clambered into the saddle, and rode down the long line of Marines and baggage and ration trains, to make a tour of inspection.

Far ahead, we soon lost sight of the main body. We were setting a stiff pace, and the Lieutenant remarked, "This is an eight-hour hike for the battalion. We'll do it in six."

All around were the rich farms of the Grand Duchy, well-kept gardens and busy little villages. This was no war-torn Belgium or devastated France. Though the duchy of Luxembourg had groaned horribly under the German yoke, during the four years of occupation its girth had increased. True, it had not suffered the misery and destruction of open conflict within its frontiers, but the appropriation of all its military and natural resources by its easterly neighbor had been a heavy cross to bear. Now, however, the brave city of Ettelbruck, the center of many roads and second only to the capital itself in size and importance, made ready to welcome the Allied troops.

Only that noon had the last blue-gray coated German soldier left for home. In the previous four days, trainloads of troops and equipment had moved eastward, the foot troops ahead and the artillery and motorized transports in the rear. That morning the last of the caissons, limbers, and guns had moved slowly down the highway, taking with them the remaining ordnance not surrendered to the Allies. Far in the distance could be seen the snakelike parade of retreating Germans, passing over the hills and out of the life of the peaceful little valley.

In honor of the occasion the city had declared a holiday. The schoolchildren and the city band had been rehearsing the American anthem, and as the day wore on, had been waiting impatiently, hour after hour, for the arrival of the American troops. The Burgomeister and the Town Council, as the reception committee, had arrayed themselves in musty frock coats and shiny top hats, and proceeded to the market square, word having come that the Americans were not far off. There they joined the boy scouts and schoolgirls armed with flowers. Behind them, solid ranks of the citizenry pressed forward against members of the army of Luxembourg who had been detailed as the police of the town. The Duchy's little army, with its striking blue uniforms and patent leather kepis well-known in operetta, numbered 250 before, during, and after the War.

The band played. The populace waited. The flowers wilted only slightly and the police tried to look important. Then a small boy dashed down a narrow winding street to give the word. The Americans were coming, but from a totally unexpected direction. Hastily, the entire reception party moved with as much dignity as it could muster to the top of a small hill on the outskirts of the town. There, true enough, they saw the Americans—and what a shout went up as the point consisting of the two of us approached. The boys shouted, the band played, the flowers were waved, and the committee, full of self-importance, moved forward.

I explained that we were only the point and that the main body would soon approach from the south. Hastily the procession re-formed and proceeded to the south, complete with schoolgirls, boy scouts, band, Councilmen, Burgomeister, and the police. The band played a little, first aid was applied to the flowers, and there was a general polishing of the committee's hats and boots. That cloud of dust down the road marked the progress of the troops— a little late, but on their way.

As it turned out, there were just two platoons, headed by 2nd Lieutenant Bogan; it was only an advance party, scheduled to join the main body later in the day. The Burgomeister, a bit annoyed at the small size of the liberating army, wasted no time. He moved forward to greet them, a husky shout—throats had dried in the interval—went up, and the band and children contributed their understanding of the American national anthem. The drooping flowers were presented to the astonished lieutenant, and the speech of welcome began.

Suddenly, the clear note of a trumpet was heard from the distant market square on the other side of the town, and what a sinking of hearts there was among the loyal Luxembourgers, who turned as one man to see what was happening. Presented to the gaze of the weary Councillors, the tired Burgomeister, the breathless band, the wilted schoolchildren, and the speechless policemen, was the distant sight of the entire battalion, with the major and his exec at its head, moving through a completely deserted public square.

We tramped on across the mountains toward the Rhine. Back in France before Belleau Wood, we had left our seabags and everything personal with friends or in storage. What we carried in our 50-pound packs was literally all our worldly possessions, including an overcoat, extra shoes, skivvies, socks, toilet articles, two blankets, a poncho, half of a pup tent, plus accessories, four days emergency rations, mess gear, a .45 and ammo, a 9-pound rifle and bayonet, 120 rounds of Springfield ammo, 2 canteens of water (from my first battle experience I learned that "you'll lick the bloomin' boots of 'im that's got it"), and other miscellaneous items.

Germany was enemy territory. As we passed through town after town, groups of silent, sullen, white-faced Germans lined the sidewalks. We moved into small towns at night and took over, billeting our men in private homes, school buildings—wherever there was space available without dislodging the townspeople. Leaving the mountains behind us, we marched down the Ahr Valley along the river through Altenahr and Ahrweiler to Sinzig on the Rhine, were ferried across the east bank on December 10, and billeted in Rheinbrohl between Bonn and Neuwied. The Allied Army of Occupation had four bridgeheads on the Rhine, extending from the Belgians in the north, the British at Köln, the Americans at Coblenz, north and south, down to the French at Mainz, with units through Alsace-Lorraine.

As we marched down the mainstreet of Rheinbrohl, the usual silent sidewalk crowds greeted us—but this was soon to change. The churches were much in evidence; there was the massive Catholic *Dom,* the red brick Evangelist Lutheran church, and the small one-room stone synagogue, with Hebrew words in gold above the door—*Deh Leefnay me ottaw omaid* ("Remember before whom thou standeth"). The first Saturday morning we were there, I dropped in and almost frightened to death the few at prayer. Armed to the teeth with rifle, pistol, and dirk, I pushed the door open and entered. All eyes turned my way and in them were the eternal questions of 2,000 years of suffering and wandering: Friend or foe? Life or death? I unslung my rifle, unbuckled my pistol belt, drew my dirk, and laid all at the door. The shamus handed me a prayerbook in Hebrew and I was invited to the altar to pronounce the blessings.

The battalion and the company prospered on the Rhine. Germany was a cleaner place than France; there were no long brown streaks on the walls of the toilets in the public buildings, stations, and farms as in France. The Germans used toilet paper. The *gemütlichkeit* was something nearer our own American family life, and there was plenty of "Wein, Weib, und Gesang." Strasbourg, Mainz, and Wiesbaden were great fun. We built a firing range in the hills and slept under tents in the January and February snow.

On May 1, I managed a trip to Paris. Everywhere there were flower sellers telling us *Muguet porte bonheur* ("lilies of the valley bring happiness"). We watched *cuirassiers* galloping down the boulevards to cut off crowds of *grévistes* (strikers) at the May Day parade, and then lunched at Maxim's and relaxed at the American University Club before finally heading back to the Rhine.

We had a scare in June, when the Germans refused to sign the treaty of peace. We combat-loaded and headed toward the interior, long columns of British, French, and Americans moving up. Then the Germans signed, and the war was officially over.

The march through Belgium, Luxembourg, and Germany to the Rhine passed into history, and the Army of Occupation was losing the Marines. August, 1919, had come, and with it orders returning us to our base at Quantico. Lejeune would bring home the entire Second Division, and after a parade in New York along Fifth Avenue from the Washington Monument to the Fort Lee ferry, the division would be deactivated.

On this same Fifth Avenue only a short two years before, the buses had carried the call to "Join the Marines," adding the promise that they would be the first to fight. And so it had come to pass. We were back on the Avenue with the war under our belts, seasoned veterans in heavy marching order on a blistering August day, with the bands playing and the crowds cheering. Mustering out followed at Quantico.

I was a civilian again, but not for long.

★

10. *The Compulsion of Command*

THE PERIOD AFTER the war was a toughie. The spirit of the front lines was still there—I read the same lines of Wigmore on evidence or Costigan on wills or Gray on real property over and over again without seeing them. Then came the early years with Clark, Prentice, and Roulstone, and lunches with fellow clerks at Child's on Broadway—shredded wheat, apple pie, and coffee, except on Friday, when with our $25 paychecks in our pockets, we would go to Libby's, the old American fish house on Fulton Street, to gobble Daniel Webster fish chowder.

In the old Thirteenth Assembly District, which stretched from the Columbia University neighborhood and the Hudson east to the edge of black Harlem and north to the heavily Irish Catholic section along Amsterdam Avenue and Old Broadway, we had a melting pot that did not fuse. The eight small election districts to the south were strongly Republican, but were swamped by an overwhelming Democratic preponderance in the north, and except for the rare political landslide, as in 1920, we could be counted upon to return a safe Democratic majority for Tammany Hall. It was when Andy Keating, the Democratic chieftain, turned his guns on our handful of Republican districts in the Columbia section that I got into politics.

Sarah Schuyler Butler, daughter of Nicholas Murray Butler, President of Columbia University, and Election Commissioner Valentine J. Hahn were our Republican leaders. Many students who had no home other than the dormitories, and many college professors who worked and lived in the area, voted in my election district, the 2nd, which embraced the territory west of the university and was predominently Republican. Keating's henchmen claimed that since the students had homes away from college, they were supposed to go home to vote, and they produced a section of the election law to support their view. On the first day of registration for the general election, our Republican inspector telephoned frantically for help, saying that the Democrats were turning away Republican voters from the registration booths. Sarah and I got into the car reserved for just such emergencies and drove to the polling place. A long line extended into the street from the booth, and inside was pandemonium. The room was filled with angry men and women shouting at the four inspectors of election seated around an unpainted pine table bearing the large registers in which the qualified voters of the district were listed.

Boards of inspectors of elections in New York City must act by majority vote, and since the law required that two members of the board must be appointed by the Democrats and two by the Republicans, the board is automatically deadlocked on every partisan issue, unless one of the four breaks away from his party. A young man leaning over the table and shouting at the inspectors had been refused registration because only the two Republican inspectors had voted to place his name on the register. Many of those waiting in line were in a similar category, and would likewise be denied registration. It was an obvious device on the part of the opposition to cut down the Republican vote in the district.

We took the names and addresses of all who had been refused their right to vote and I hightailed it downtown to my law office. The only legal remedy was a writ of mandamus against the board of inspectors, requiring them to show cause why an order should not be entered against them, directing them to correct the register and add to it the names of those filing suit. We brought many of these cases—won a few and lost a few—but the word got around that the party would fight for those being victimized, and we kept this small election district Republican.

After the election, Val Hahn called me one day in 1923 to say that Sam Koenig, the county leader, wanted to see me. Koenig said there was a job open at the Public Service Commission and, if I was interested, I should see William Prendergast, Chairman of the Commission. I took the job and became assistant counsel to the

Public Service Commission of the State of New York at a salary
of $4,500 per year.

My first assignment was to defend the New York & Queens
Gas Company case, quickly followed by the Consolidated Gas
Company, the Brooklyn Union Gas Company and the New York
and Richmond Gas Company cases. What had happened was that
a debonair New York state senator, Jimmie ("Will You Love Me
in December as You Did in May?") Walker, on his way to the
mayoralty of the city, had forced through the state senate the
Walker Dollar Gas Act, just weeks after the Commission had
completed the lengthy, laborious, and painstaking hearings which
fixed the rates at $1.15 for the larger companies and $1.45 for
the smaller ones. All of the companies then severally sued the
Public Service Commission for an injunction against the new
rates, an even dollar per thousand cubic feet.

I was also trial counsel for the Commission in the New York
Telephone Company case, which took nearly four years to try and
involved 35,000 pages of testimony and some 50,000 pages of
exhibits. I had to cross examine over 2,000 witnesses. In the end
we had the Telephone Company's appeal dismissed in the United
States Supreme Court, but by this time a new governor was suc-
ceeding Al Smith, a new commission was being planned, and my
private practice was building up, since counsel were permitted to
practice law while representing the Commission, as long as there
was no conflict of interest.

Around this time, Major General John Archer Lejeune, Commandant of the Corps, our old division commander, came to
New York to meet some of his old troops. Very tough and very
much of a gentleman, Lejeune has been called by the Leatherneck
Association "one of the most outstanding officers the Corps has
ever produced." Sitting around the table with him, I wanted to go
back into the Corps.

At 31, I was no spring chicken. Indeed, I was distinctly old
for a shavetail, which was all the rank I could hope for—the
Corps wasn't making field marshals of ex-sergeants. But having
dwindled to some 18,000 officers and men by 1927, it had let it
be known that applications for reserve commissions might be
forwarded to headquarters for consideration.

At the Public Service Commission, my close friend was Commissioner George R. Van Namee. George suggested that the Governor might give me one of the two letters of recommendation required with my application and he delivered. Though the Governor was on the West Coast at the time, and on the verge of a Presidential campaign, he took the time to write a letter in my behalf, carefully drafted to protect him politically, and sent it to Headquarters:

ALFRED E. SMITH
GOVERNOR

STATE OF NEW YORK
EXECUTIVE CHAMBER
ALBANY

July 22, 1927

General Dion Williams,
United States Marine Corps,
Washington, D. C.

Dear General Williams:

It has been called to my attention that Melvin L. Krulewitch, Assistant Counsel to the Public Service Commission of this State, has made application for a Commission in the Officers' Reserve of the United States Marine Corps in which he served during the War. Mr. Krulewitch is highly endorsed to me and I, of course know of him by reason of the official position which he holds in the State Service. I am therefore glad to recommend him to your favorable consideration.

Sincerely yours,
(sgd) Alfred E. Smith

To take the curse off a Democratic endorsement, I also spoke— with some trepidation—to my friend, Theodore Roosevelt. I had helped him in his unsuccessful campaign for the New York governorship (he lost to Al Smith), and we had many mutual friends. Without a moment's hesitation young Teddy wrote:

THEODORE ROOSEVELT
OYSTER BAY, LONG ISLAND

West Dover, Vermont
July 11, 1927

To the Senior Officer,
Examining Board for Reserve Commissions,
U.S. Marine Corps

Sir:

Melvin L. Krulewitch, who is applying for a commission in the Officers' Reserve of the Marine Corps, has been known to me for some time. He is a citizen of standing in New York City. He is a responsible businessman and takes a keen interest in proper public work.

Of his war record, I do not have to write, for with that you are already familiar. Suffice it to say that as ranking sergeant of the 78th Company, he fought in the engagements in Europe. He was twice wounded.

I feel confident that you should see fit to commission him, he will be a credit to the service.

Believe me,

Yours very truly,
(sgd) Theodore Roosevelt

TR/meh

On the Marines' birthday, November 10, 1927, my commission in the reserve came through—I was back in the Corps. With it came a sense of accomplishment, of security, and a pride, presumptuous no doubt in a second lieutenant, but perhaps forgivable in a young man assuming the prestige of command. But it was not until August, 1928, that I was ordered to Quantico, Virginia, on active duty.

Together with my fellow second lieutenants, most of them also newly commissioned, we were quartered in wooden barracks of 1917 vintage, neither better nor worse than those for the enlisted. The roads were also of 1917 vintage, except that instead of mud, we kicked up a haze of powdery dust as we hiked around in heavy marching order, drenched in sweat from head to toe in the searing Quantico heat. We later spent hours on the range, and still more hours cleaning our rifles afterwards.

I remember one day. I was shooting the breeze in our shack with rangy Ham Eggleston from Boston, Jack Andrews, a New York police sergeant who had served a hitch in the Corps, Jerky Perkins from Fort Wayne, Indiana, who used to earn an extra dollar here and there by cleaning the other guys' rifles, and Sandy Wellman from Tallahassee, Florida, who was going on to Pensacola for flight training. Andrews had started talking about the four fleet reserve companies which had been organized into a battalion and ordered for training to Quantico, where they were quartered in another old barracks section near us.

"You know that hermaphrodite company from New York City —half New York State Naval Militia and Half U.S. Marine Corps?" he said. "Well, they got a New York millionaire in command. DeRonde. Some CO! He takes 'em on picnics, wines and dines 'em, and puts 'em to work in his bank, like a sugar daddy. The dope is, he owns the Naval Militia. They even made him a major." He let this earth-shaking news sink in.

"Is he wearing the leaves?" I asked. I had met Captain DeRonde up at Waller Hall and found him pleasant enough, although a bit critical of the barracks.

"Hell, no," Andrews replied, putting his oil and thong case in the butt of his rifle. "That's a New York State rank, not Marine Corps. He'd get the bum's rush if he ever pulled that here."

"So what happened?" asked Ham Eggleston.

"This is one for the book," said Andrews. "DeRonde thought he was coming to Fifth Avenue, sent his Stutz Bearcat down ahead, and got ready for a bash. But he didn't like his quarters, he wouldn't eat the officers' chow, and ate in the enlisted mess with his own company. He complained loud and long to Hunt Holmes —he's in charge of reserve training—we nodded, and Hunt Holmes gave him the works. They told him he'd do like everybody else and like it, or else. And DeRonde took him literally."

We got the scoop later at the local 3.2 per cent slopshoot. DeRonde was an important citizen in the New York community, and after talking it over with Headquarters, which was always anxious to avoid a donnybrook with citizen reserve politicos, Quantico permitted him to request relief for business reasons. Having left New York with his company for its 14-day training duty on July 29, DeRonde asked to be relieved on July 31st, and on August 3 turned the company over to his segundo, 1st Lieutenant Robert Bogardus Fisher, and departed in his sports car for New York, his head bloodied but unbowed. What was of greater consequence, he was still in command of the 303rd Fleet Marine Corps Reserve Company which, in its dual status, was also the Marine Company, First Battalion, New York Naval Militia.

Though I didn't know it at the time, this was the prelude to my next war. And what a war. No tempest in a teapot this, but a knock-down, drag-out, political-military showdown between the sovereign State of New York and the United States of America. In one corner was the New York Naval Militia, (navy blue trunks, of course), and in the other, the United States Marine Corps in red and gold—the engagement being fought on the island of Manhattan, on the clean, pure Hudson. (In those days sturgeon showed up occasionally as far north as Poughkeepsie, and the shad weirs were as close as 125th Street.) The war ended, of course, with the unconditional surrender of New York State, although not, I hasten to add, until the Federal heavy artillery had been brought up in the person of the celebrated General David D. Porter—yes, the grandson of the Commodore David D. Porter whose "Damn the torpedoes, full speed ahead," won the victory at Mobile Bay.

The First Battalion, New York Naval Militia, had a long and glamorous social history, not unlike that of the celebrated Seventh Regiment of the New York National Guard. The name of the original organizers and members of the Battalion read like an excerpt from the stud book: Vanderbilt, Low, Satterlee, August Belmont, Kent, Dana Greene, Washington Irving, Townsend, Brevoort, DeForest, Rutherford, and many more of the Four

Hundred, not forgetting Louis N. Josephthal, founder of the banking and investment house of Josephthal & Company. Philip DeRonde had joined the Battalion as Captain of its Marine Company in 1926.

This was no bathtub Navy. In the first 20 years of its existence, the First Battalion numbered on its muster rolls no less than 31 Annapolis graduates. It mounted guards of honor for the visits to New York of three Presidents—Harrison, McKinley, and Theodore Roosevelt. It assisted the New York Yacht Club in its supervision of international yacht races (many of the officers of the First Battalion were members of the Yacht Club), and during the Spanish-American War, saw service in the New York harbor area aboard the Civil War monitor *Nahant* and off the coast of Cuba in the U.S.S. *Yankee*. The three months of duty on the *Yankee,* from June to September, 1898, earned for each member of the crew the coveted Sampson Medal.

There was about the First Battalion, in short, an aura of glamour and romance that still existed when, after training at Quantico, I crossed the gangplank of the U.S.S. *Illinois* on September 17, 1928, reporting for duty as a company officer of the 303rd—or, as it might more properly have been called, "DeRonde's Company."

The *Illinois* and its predecessor training ships had been permanently docked for over 30 years at the 96th Street piers on the Hudson, in the sewage disposal areas for the long lines of apartment houses on Riverside Drive. Going aboard, I saw the incredible sight of great masses of pale, ghostly, upright candle-like forms floating below the gangplank, along the sides of the ship and along the shore, nodding in unison as the swells of the mid-channel wash reached them. They were distended condoms, floating for all the world like pale sea anemones or the faded, semilucent shells of sea cucumbers, or *bêches-de-mer*. An old salt, sadly viewing the gently floating rows of thin rubber or fishskin sheaths from the deck of the *Illinois* was once heard delicately to remark, "I've been bogged down, shoaled, beachcombed, and stranded on many a rocky shore, but never before, drunk or sober, did I ever cross a condom reef."

It was good to be back with troops. The glass-encased stands of rifles midship facing the company offices, the busy clatter of the naval division rooms, the off-duty gobs lazing around the recreation compartments were all regulation. In the Marine company office, the enlisted jumped to attention. I nodded, called out, "Carry on," walked to the first sergeant's desk, and asked for the commanding officer.

Edward N. Calisch II, the top, with his deep southern accent, replied that the captain was in his quarters. Corporal Sid Kassel, the company clerk, piped up, "Sir, I'll tell him the lieutenant is aboard," and left the office. He was back in a moment. "Sir," he said, "the captain requested that the lieutenant join him. Would the lieutenant please follow me?"

We walked forward through the passageway to officers' country. Each division commander, including the Marine CO, had a room to himself. The company clerk led me to an open door. I knocked and said, "Sir, Second Lieutenant Krulewitch reporting for duty."

The captain nodded. "Come in and have a beer and a stool," he said. I thanked him, helped myself to a bottle, and sat down.

In his forties, DeRonde was of middle height, slim but not small, blue–eyed with a straight short nose. Clean-shaven, well-scrubbed, and well-groomed, he had a full head of light hair and a healthy, out-of-doors complexion. His manner was pleasant but there was a sardonic cast in the set of his mouth. I was soon to learn that he regarded the 303rd as his personal possession—like his shipping company (Oriental Navigation), his bank (Hibernia Trust), his racing cars, and his cruiser yacht. He could be as sweet as pie when he wanted to, but when he felt the occasion compelled it, as mean as cats' piss.

As a commanding officer, he went far beyond the requirements of that office. He would often entertain the entire company at a movie and dinner party. He contributed generously to company functions, and employed several of its members in his various business enterprises. First Lieutenant Fisher, who had previously been his second-in-command, was a guard at DeRonde's bank. All in all, the 303rd was very much a family affair.

But at this, our first meeting, we chatted for a moment and then he opened up about his brief tour of duty at Quantico that summer. Still smarting under the treatment he had received, he spoke of the dilapidated condition of the barracks, the poor food, and the lack of officers' comforts and conveniences. Then he hinted darkly of being relieved, which was news to me, and asked if I knew a Captain Mallen.

"No sir," I replied.

"He's been assigned to take over the company. Did you know that?" Again this was news to me, and I told him so.

DeRonde brooded for a moment. "The boys are not going to like that. They want 1st Lieutenant Fisher to take command." More news, and all this on first meeting with him. I knew little or nothing about Fisher, except that he had had some previous Marine Corps experience.

"This man Mallen is a letter–writer—watch out for him," DeRonde continued with a frown and an emphatic nod. But then eight bells sounded and we joined the company on the drill deck.

The following month DeRonde was relieved. Fisher left at the same time and Captain Frank A. Mallen took over as company commander. Attendance at drill and training at once began to drop off, but I worked steadily at my job, which included the chore of collecting an only partially sober company at 5:00 A.M. New Year's Day, 1929, loading them aboard boxcars on the New York Central tracks below Riverside Drive, and shipping them to Albany to march in the Inauguration Day parade for the new Governor, Franklin D. Roosevelt.

Through February and March, attendance at drills and training contined to dwindle. This was doubly serious because state money for the Naval Militia was computed on the basis of attendance at drills, and a slackening off meant a smaller contribution to the battalion for its operating and maintenance costs. It was also becoming crystal clear that these defections were planned. Knots of enlisted men would gather in isolated corners on the spar deck, in the head, and deep down in the hold on the range, to whisper and gossip, falling silent at the approach of an officer. Something was in the wind—you could smell it. I could sense an uprising against the CO, but not the reason for it.

The captain began an investigation, but by this time the First Naval Battalion was so concerned that, to our amazement, it suddenly appointed Lieutenant Commander A. Matheis, executive officer of the battalion, as the commanding officer of our Marine company. Thus, the 303rd now had two commanding officers, an unparalled absurdity.

As a company officer of the 303rd, a lowly shavetail in rank, my job was to serve and follow Captain Mallen loyally and helpfully, which I did. He was a newspaperman, heavy-set, somewhat below middle height, with brown eyes and receding light hair. He was a hard driver, with a sergeant-major look, but he could also relax and enjoy a good story. There was no relaxing that spring, however. We had a poor showing for the Decoration Day Parade, and worse followed. The very next drill night, at eight bells, Captain Mallen and I came up from the wardroom to the drill deck where the company fell in for its weekly drill and found exactly five Marines there in company formation. We dismissed the men and returned to the company office.

Brigadier General David D. Porter, then colonel commanding the eastern reserve area, got wind of the situation and came up for an inspection tour. He spent a long time in conference with the Naval Militia officers, including Commander Matheis, and the following noon asked me to lunch at Whyte's on Fulton Street. He was chary of the Naval Militia relationship but was coolly noncommittal throughout our talk. The only personal remark I remember him making was that the officer who had brought us drinks aboard ship, our battalion bootlegger, was wearing a stickpin with a diamond in it "as large as a horse turd."

Meanwhile, Captain Mallen had been continuing his investigation and had written to General Porter, as follows:

303rd Company, U. S. M. C. R.
USS Illinois, Ft. of W. 98 St.
New York, N.Y.

8 April 1929

FROM: The Commanding Officer
TO: The Commanding Officer, Eastern Reserve Area,
1100 South Broad St., Philadelphia, Pa.

SUBJECT: Demotion and transfer, request for; also undesirable discharge, recommendation for; Case of 1st Sgt. Edward N. Calisch, Sgt. John J. McManus, PFC George H. Wilson, Jr.

1. I hereby request the demotion to rank of Private, and transfer to inactive status, and at the same time recommend for discharge as UNDESIRABLE, the following men:

Sgt. John J. McManus
PFC George H. Wilson, Jr.

2. Request has already been made for the demotion of 1st Sgt. Edward N. Calisch, to rank of Private, and similar transfer and discharge are also requested in his case.

3. The uniform clothing and other Government property issued to these three men, are now in the process of being repossessed.

4. The above named men have caused considerable trouble in the Company and are responsible for the breaking down of the morale of the men.

5. I have proof that PFC Wilson called up a member of this Company on the telephone requesting him not to come to drill. I believe he also got in touch with other men. He refused to affirm or deny this charge and displayed a contemptuous attitude when questioned.

6. Sgt. McManus refused to obey orders and defied me to issue them to him. He said he remained away from drill because he felt like it. I also believe he had something to do with other men not showing up. He would not deny or affirm this.

7. Reasons for the demotion of 1st Sgt. Calisch were given in a previous letter. I believe he had considerable to do in conjunction with breaking down the morale of

some of the men. Since relieved as 1st Sgt., he has conducted a campaign of espionage on the Commanding Officer, even to the extent of going through confidential records in the Company office. He also questioned my authority to take action in his case, first going to the Executive Officer of the 1st Battalion, Naval Militia, N.Y., to find out whether I had said authority.

8. These three men, who have always been closely together, have tried to run the Company. When they learned that the undersigned had requested the demotion of 1st Sgt. Calisch who had previously told me that if he quit the outfit, other men would go too, they immediately took steps to disrupt the Company.

9. Since taking over the Company, I have found a spirit of unrest and defiance among the men, owing to Company politics, but the three above named members, each holding a responsible position in the Company, so disguised their activities that it was not until recently, I had found out the harm they were doing.

10. I am calling attention to the fact that Sgt. McManus is employed by Capt. Philip DeRonde, former Company Commander, who as Major in the Naval Militia, New York, has caused me considerable embarrassment and tried to create friction between myself and the Naval Militia.

11. Recently Capt. DeRonde secured a position for 1st Sgt. Calisch who told me he thought Capt. DeRonde had more interest in the Company than I. He admitted that Capt. DeRonde tried to get information about the Company from him. He encouraged the men to come to him with their complaints.

12. I firmly believe that the elimination of these three men from the company will be beneficial.

13. I am conducting a newspaper and radio campaign

for new men for the Company, which I believe will be fruitful.

Frank Mallen
CC Executive Officer, 1st Batt. NMNY, U.S.S. *Illinois.*

A few days later we heard that there had been a terrific row between Captain Mallen and Commander Matheis on the day the letter was written. It was the point of no return. The Naval Militia had won out.

Morning Telegraph
820 8th Avenue.
New York City.

9 April 1929

FROM: Captain Frank Mallen, F.M.C.R.
TO: Major General Commandant, U.S. Marine Corps.
SUBJECT: Request for Relief as Commander of 303rd Co., F.M.C.R.
VIA: Official channels

1. I respectfully request to be relieved as commanding officer of the 303rd Company, F.M.C.R.

2. This request is made because Captain Philip De-Ronde, the former company commander, using his office as a Major in the State Naval Militia, did his utmost to create friction between the New York State Naval Militia and myself. Under the conditions he has created I do not feel I can serve the 303rd Company in the best interests of the Marine Corps.

3. The opposition and attitude of Captain DeRonde toward me since I took over the company quickly spread to several men, who are either employed or have been employed, or have secured employment through him. These men had been allowed to dominate the company through a Civic Association which was operating ille-

gally. I abolished the Civic Association as organized, which called for taking money out of the pay of the members of the company which is contrary to Marine Corps regulations. I also requested the demotion of the 1st Sergeant, one of the men above referred to, who had constantly hampered me, as well as outwardly showing disloyalty and disobedience. Upon word that this action was taken the other men above referred to conspired and succeeded in keeping other men from drill. They also did all in their power to break down the morale of the men, defying me to give them orders.

4. Because of Captain DeRonde's lact of tact in satisfying his personal feud against me, which arose when I refused to permit him to run the company after relieving him, I have spent considerable time trying to straighten matters with Naval Militia officers. When I asked them to show some courtesy to the Marine Corps and for their cooperation in bringing the company on a better basis they displayed disrespect for the Marine Corps, one (Lt. Commander Matheis, executive officer of the U.S.S. *Illinois*) saying: "To Hell with the Marine Corps. I don't give a God damn about the Marine Corps and I will tell that to Colonel Porter." This was in no way provoked.

5. I have requested the demotion of three men, all of whom, holding responsible positions in the company, betrayed their trust. I have also recommended that these men be discharged from the Marine Corps Reserve as undesirable. I shall be glad to present and press charges against these men.

6. In requesting relief as commanding officer of the 303rd Company, F.M.C.R. I desire to state that I shall always be at the service of the Marine Corps in an investigation of the 303rd Company and Captain De-Ronde's connection therewith after being officially relieved.

Frank Mallen

The Marine Corps granted his request. And on April 12, 1929, while still a 2nd lieutenant, I was ordered to take command of the 303rd. Although the tension had eased, it was the calm before the storm. DeRonde had won the first round, Captain Mallen was out, but the war with the Naval Militia was still on. Having been promoted to the Fleet Reserve in the Marine Corps, a more professional cadre, all that stood in the way of my permanent command was a commission in the Naval Militia of the State of New York. No officer could keep command of this dual status company without this, and my application for it had been dutifully filed. With two United States Marine Corps commissions, I was not in the least apprehensive as to the outcome. I knew I had been running the company alone with my two senior noncoms, "Guns" Monaghen, Gunnery Sergeant, and 1st Sergeant Ed Calisch, who devoted himself loyally to the company and was a tower of strength. I had dropped all charges against Calisch, McManus, and Wilson.

But early in June, 1929, the first blow fell. One morning, in seeming friendliness, DeRonde called me at my law office and invited me to lunch at the Bankers Club in the Equitable Building at 120 Broadway. I was delighted to accept, and met him in the lobby on the 39th floor. The maitre d' escorted us to an excellent table near one of the large windows overlooking the heart of the financial district. We had a couple of martinis, chatted idly over an excellent lunch, and then over coffee, DeRonde came to the point.

"The company is doing fine, I hear," he began.

"Thank you, sir, we try," I replied.

"You're the only officer in the company?"

"That's so."

"I think you should have another officer," he said. "And this is what I want to do with the company. I'm going to put 1st Lieutenant Fisher in command, and you will, of course, continue as a company officer." I was flabbergasted, hardly believing my ears. Though DeRonde no longer had any connection with the company, and had resigned from the Marine Corps, he could not and would not disengage. He well knew I was the commanding officer, appointed by the Corps, but was nonetheless openly declaring war. "I got rid of Mallen," he went on. The Naval Militia didn't commission him, and you can't serve aboard the *Illinois* without a state commission."

This was a thinly-veiled threat—his influence could keep me from my command. I began to boil, but didn't say a word—it was all clear to me now. Behind the revolt of the enlisted, who unwittingly were serving DeRonde's purpose, Calisch, McManus, and Wilson had all been influenced by the skipper's compelling desire to keep control of the company and make life insufferable for any commanding officer not of his own choosing. And I was next in line for the axe.

Seated across the luncheon table, enjoying his calculated hospitality, I was stunned by this attack. What could he have against me? And then I realized it wasn't personal at all. In back of everything was the compulsion of command. He could not disengage himself from what had become part of himself, the 303rd. If he could not have it directly, it would be his by remote control.

"You have three choices," DeRonde said, staring me straight in the eye. "You can continue as a company officer with Fisher in command, you can resign your commission in the Corps, or you can fight me."

And as I rose from my seat to leave, he added, "If you tell anyone what I've said to you, I'll deny I said it." I bowed curtly and left, having forgotten to thank him for the lunch.

On my return to the office I reported the conversation to General Porter in Philadelphia. The General, whose family had made American history for generations, had only one comment—"This is not new!" Then he added, after a pause, "Carry on with your company." Later on I was deeply moved to receive a copy of his counterattack, addressed to the Commandant of the Marines:

> The undersigned heartily endorses the recommendation that Second Lieutenant Melvin L. Krulewitch, Fleet Marine Corps Reserve, be promoted to the rank of First Lieutenant.
>
> Lieutenant Krulewitch assumed command of the 303rd Reserve Company at a time when the morale of this unit was very low, owing to dissension between his two predecessors in command. However, despite discouraging conditions, Lieutenant Krulewitch has brought the 303rd Reserve Com-

pany back to its normal good standing and earned the high respect and confidence of the enlisted men of the company, and the various regular and reserve officers (both Marine Corps and Naval) with whom his duties have brought him into contact.

But there was still a major roadblock to overcome. The Naval Militia of the state, jealous of its jurisdiction and loyal to its staff, had arranged for me to be examined as to my qualifications for a state commission—by the same board that had promoted DeRonde to Major. I appeared before it at Naval Militia Headquarters in the Municipal Building, just east of City Hall.

The President of the Board, Captain Leo W. Hesselman, Chief of Staff of New York Naval Militia, had been a member of the old socialite group in the heyday of its fame, but General Porter had done his job. The name of Commodore Porter of Civil War fame was a name "for a blessing" among the Navy men.

I answered the Board's questions, which dealt mostly with Navy procedures, as well as I could. Then the armorer of the U.S.S. *Illinois,* who was advising the Board, played his trump card. Handing me a choked Springfield, Model 03, the standard weapon during World War I, he asked me to make it work. This was a break. I had stripped, repaired, and assembled so many 03s that it was nuts and raisins to me. Finding that the mainspring had been improperly released inside the bolt so that it blocked the firing pin and the cocking piece, I reassembled the interior mechanism, reset the safety lock, which is operative only when turned to the right, and the examination was over.

Then I waited, day after day, week after week, for my state commission.

With the company now up to strength, I had issued final orders for summer training in July at Quantico. New clothing, equipment, and quartermaster supplies had arrived from Philadelphia, but there was still no word from Albany. Deciding that he who begs in silence, starves in silence, and that the meek inherit only the meek, I called Hon. Samuel I. Rosenman, "Sammy the Rose," Secretary to the Governor, later known as the President's right arm and speech writer. Sammy was a college-mate. With some trepidation, I asked him if the Governor could send on a letter of recommendation to the board in connection with my application. Sam said he'd have to send for the papers and let me know. At the end of the week he called back and said, "The Governor won't give you a letter of recommendation." He let this sink in before blowing the trumpet of victory. "But the Governor said he'll sign your commission—and he has."

On our return from summer training in August, I received a telephone call from Major DeRonde. "I'd like to present a stand of national and Marine colors to *your* company," he said, in a pleasant and friendly tone. Nothing surprised me anymore. "I'd be happy to receive them," I replied.

I set up a review, he made the presentation, and I never saw him again.

11. *The Impossible Dream*

WITH THE END of Prohibition and the beginning of Franklin Delano Roosevelt's term, I was sent out by Val Hahn, the Republican leader, just before the election in 1932, to take a poll in my end of the district to see how the voting would go. I would very politely approach each voter, identify myself as the Republican captain, tell them about the poll I was taking, and then ask them how they would vote. I began at an apartment house on Claremont Avenue, close to the university and after a few good ones, I knocked on the door of a burly tenant who apparently disliked canvassers. Still, I went through my routine politely and told him we were for Hoover. "Hoover!" he shouted. "I wouldn't vote for him if he was God and Christ rolled into one." I withdrew, making up my mind to mark him "doubtful."

But things were going rather better for me in the law and in the Corps. As a second lieutenant, I was commanding a company, and Headquarters dug up a regulation which qualified an officer for promotion to a higher rank where his command rated it. The Tables of Organization required a commanding officer of the rank of captain for each company of the line, and one fine morning I found in the mail my promotion to captain. And wonders never ceased. My company was then transferred into the First Battalion of the Nineteenth Reserve Regiment, and I, being the senior captain, was promptly promoted to major, making it from a shavetail to a gold leaf in 3 years. The regiments and the brigade were later abolished by Washington but my rank was made permanent. Then I had to wait 6 years for my next promotion.

My legal career was also coming along nicely. After the trial of the New York Telephone Company case, I was retained by Judge

John E. Mack of Poughkeepsie—the John Mack who nominated Franklin D. Roosevelt for President at the Democratic conventions of 1932 and 1936. He once told me with hardly suppressed glee that the only reason why he didn't nominate Roosevelt for a third term was because he, Roosevelt, and Harry Hopkins decided that someone else should do it for fear it might not look spontaneous if Mack did it a third time. He had been appointed chief counsel and general factotum of the Joint Legislative Committee to Investigate Public Utilities, formed by public demand after an outcry in the press about big companies buying members of the state senate and assembly. Mack invited me up to Poughkeepsie to talk about it and I accepted at once. I had resigned from the Public Service Commission, my letter grudgingly accepted by a now Democratic agency, and was freelancing with some success.

The following morning found me in John Mack's sparsely furnished office on Main Street. There was a small, worn rug in the center of the unpainted floor and an old-fashioned, rolltop desk. The judge (he had served for a year on the Supreme Court) sat in a swivel chair facing the door, legs crossed, wearing a dark suit, black string tie, and an austere but friendly expression that I came to respect. He retained me as chief assistant at $1,000 per month, which was good money in 1935, and I was permitted to continue in private practice at the same time.

I had also been retained in the celebrated Gastonia murder case. Frank I. Schechter, lawyer, author, scholar, and life-long friend, was general counsel for the B.V.D. Company, owned by the Erlanger family, which had its cotton mills at Langerre, near Charlotte, North Carolina, close by the town of Gastonia. Labor union organizers from Paterson, New Jersey, had begun to organize the workers in the Charlotte area, and a strike had been called against the mills near the B.V.D. factories. Since the strikers lived in company houses, they were promptly dispossessed from their homes, but a neighboring farmer permitted them to set up a tent camp on his land. Social workers from the North, including Frank's sister, Amy Schechter, came down to help with the sick and care for the children.

A drunken lynch mob led by Chief of Police Overholt marched out of Gastonia to the farm to destroy the camp and disperse the strikers, and in the ensuing gun fight Chief Overholt was killed. Eight people, including Amy Schechter, were arrested and charged with murder. Frank asked me to appear at the trial at the County Court House in Charlotte in defense of Amy, who had taken no part either in the strike or the gun battle, but had helped to care for and feed the babies and small children. The strikers were mostly white adults with families earning $10 a week and children under 10 earning half.

It took two months to select a jury, since most prospective veniremen expressed the opinion when questioned, that "they should awl be hung." In a loud voice, the prosecutor would casually refer to the fact that "they brought down these Jew lawyers from the No'th," and that "down here in No'th Ca'lina, we know how to take care of these furriners." The last juryman to be selected was a 48-year-old newsboy pulled off the street. He was sworn in with his papers still under his arm, and was obviously mentally infirm. He had not the slightest notion of what was going on and answered all of the district attorney's leading questions with a vacant smile. Seated at the counsel table with Frank and me was Arthur Garfield Hays, the noted civil rights lawyer from New York, who represented all the defendants except Amy. We huddled together while the prosecutor in his opening statements to the jury again referred to "these Jew lawyers brought from New York to protect these murderers who killed our good chief of police." At this point, a ghastly, chalk-faced effigy of Chief Overholt, garbed in his blood-stained unform, was wheeled into court and placed before the jury. A startled gasp from the spectators was immediately followed by an agonizing scream from the jury box, and Juror Number 12, the elderly newsboy, slipped from his chair to cower on the floor. The bailiffs and the court clerks rushed to the box and lifted him up, trying to allay his fears, but the Court adjourned the trial until the morning.

At the clerk's call of the case the following morning, only 11 jurors were in place. A policeman called by the prosecutor testified that he had gone to the hotel where the jury had been locked up for the night, opened the door of Juror Number 12's room and found him hiding under the bed. He had refused to come out and would not return to the courtroom. A mistrial was declared and the case adjourned. This was not a total loss for us, because during the adjournment we were able to negotiate a dismissal of the charges against Amy. Later on, a long-running hit on Broadway, "The Trial of Mary Dugan," based on the Gastonia murder, used the ashen, cadaverous dummy with telling effect at the box-office.

The other big event of the thirties for me was my marriage to Helen Greene, the mother of my children. It was about time, as I was pushing 42. Helen had the courage of a lioness, and was as beautiful as she was brave. In 1938 my daughter Nan was born as the war clouds gathered over Europe, and when the storm broke in September 1939, I was then coordinator of the Marine Corps Reserve in New York and New Jersey. As a lieutenant colonel, I was ordered to train four battalions, including a Pennsylvania unit, at Quantico, Virginia, and Sea Girt, New Jersey. When Secretary of the Navy Frank Knox ordered out the Marine Corps Reserve early in 1941, I was not called in, and meanwhile politics beckoned. A nomination was available for president of the Borough of Manhattan. When called before the Executive Committee of the Republican County Committee and asked whether I would be ordered on active duty if we went to war, I had to tell them I hoped so. This ended my hopes for the job, since if having been elected, I was ordered on active duty in the Marines, A Democratic City Council would fill the vacancy. Edgar J. Nathan, Jr., a member of the Sons of the American Revolution, was nominated and elected in the 1941 campaign.

We were living at Little Orchard Farm in White Plains on that fateful day—December 7, 1941. I had been trying for active duty in the Corps for a year. On December 10, 1940, I wrote Headquarters respectfully requesting active duty and received a polite reply from Orin H. Wheeler, Colonel U.S.M.C., whom I later succeeded as commanding officer, Support Group, Iwo Jima. Writing for the Commandant, he disapproved my request:

REFERENCE: (a)   Ltr. Lt. Col. Krulewitch to MCC,
                       dated 10 Dec., 1940,
                       and end. thereon.

1. In reply to reference (a), you are informed that it is impracticable to assign you to active duty at this time, therefore your request is disapproved.

2. Your application will be placed on file and should members of your class be called to active duty in the future, you will be notified.

Orin was a conservative-type regular Marine, married to an intelligent and attractive wife, a great help in the service, but no earthy field soldier. I remember him yelling at me, years later, when I went into his dugout headquarters on Iwo with two small blocks of TNT left over after my unit, 4th Provisional Battalion, had returned from the front. Taking them out of my jacket, I put them on a shelf and sat down. Pointing at the blocks, he screamed, "Take them out!" I obeyed.

In April, 1941, I wrote an old friend, General S. M. Harrington, asking for active duty. Again, no soap.

My dear Colonel,

Receipt of your letter dated 15 April, 1941, relative to being assigned to active duty is acknowledged.

Your request has been taken under consideration and your qualifications and experience have been noted. However, your services are not required at this time. Your application has been placed on file and should an officer of your ability be needed in the future you will be notified.

Your desire to be assigned to active duty is appreciated and it is regretted that a more favorable reply cannot be made.

In Washington during the summer of 1941 I spoke to General R. S. Keyser, U.S.M.C., Director of the Reserve, and wrote him a follow-up. He replied through Jack Moe on August 29.

Dear Colonel Krulewitch,

The Director, Marine Corps Reserve, has asked me to reply to your letter of August 26, 1941, in which you requested information pertaining to a plan for the training of senior Reserve officers. I have also received your recent letter addressed to myself personally, relating to the same matter.

While some consideration has previously been given to a plan for the further training of senior Reserve officers, no plan for such training is contemplated at present. I am sorry that I am unable to give you more favorable information.

The tension was now mounting in the Pacific. In September word was passed through the grapevine that I was being ordered to the U.S. Naval base at Cavite and that the orders would also provide for the transfer of Helen and the children, together with our household effects. We began preparations for the 10,000-mile journey by finding out about local conditions in the Philippines from my cousin, Captain Josephus Maximillian Lieber, United States Navy, who had served at Cavite and knew all the answers.

Then everything came to a full stop. Because of the expense of transportation, the orders were cancelled and a retired Marine officer, living in the Philippines, was ordered back on duty. Such was the luck of the draw. Headquarters had taken from me and saddled upon another Marine Bataan, Corregidor, and the Death March.

On December 4, 1941, Don Quixote-like, I again wrote officially for duty with troops.

SUBJECT: Active Duty, request for.

1. It is requested that I be assigned to active duty. My desire is for duty with troops, if I may presume to express a preference.

2. It is not intended to qualify or limit my request for duty by expressing a preference, since it is my wish to serve in whatever capacity I can be helpful to the Corps and Government.

Again, Orin Wheeler answered from Washington on December 11, after Pearl Harbor.

REFERENCE: (a) Ltr. Lt. Col. Krulewitch, to MCC,
dated 4 Dec., 1941

1. In reply to reference (a), you are informed that at present there is no need for the services of an officer of your rank, and there is no definite information as to when you may be called to active duty. However, a notation has been made of your desire to be assigned to active duty and advance information will be given you, if practicable, prior to your assignment.

On the day after Christmas I got my first break. The wire from Headquarters read:

MARCORPS 26 DECEMBER 1941

LT COL MELVIN L KRULEWITCH USMCR
LITTLE ORCHARD FARM
WHITE PLAINS, NEW YORK

ORDERS BEING ISSUED ASSIGNING YOU ACTIVE DUTY

2 JAN 1942 FOR DUTY MARBKS NYD BOSTON MASS

HEADQUARTERS MARINE CORPS

Marine Barracks, Boston, was the time-honored Charlestown Navy Yard billet at the foot of Bunker and Breeds Hill, across the bay from the Old North Church—"one if by land and two if by sea, and I on the opposite shore will be." Not too good, but not too bad for a beginning. I was on the team, and could now operate from inside.

I drove up with Helen so she could case the joint. Reporting as directed, I met my new CO, "Biff" Pierce, Colonel of Marines, and the executive officer, Lieutenant Colonel A. B. Miller, like myself a veteran of World War I, whom I was to relieve.

When I reported in, Biff, by a casual word, alerted me to Colonel Miller's wife. She was a sturdy, attractive French girl *d'un certain age* who promptly backed me into a corner to announce that Pierce would hate me because (1) I was taller than

he, (2) I was a World War I veteran as was her husband, and
(3) he would hate any exec. This was startling to me and shocking to Helen, who wrote in her diary, "Mel and I drove to Boston.
Stopped at the Statler. At 1 P.M. Mel called from the Navy Yard.
Met him and saw our new quarters. Very pleasantly surprised.
Mrs. Miller the lieutenant colonel's wife is a very talkative vitriolic
person."

In fact I profited from my duty under the command of Harold
Clifton Pierce, U.S.M.C., and I learned more from him than from
any other officer in the Corps, except General Richard F. Williams,
affectionately known as "Terrible Terry," who had headed the
Reserve at Headquarters. Biff was an Annapolis graduate; Dick
Williams was a drop-out from West Point.

Biff and I became friends, and the poisonous prediction of the
former exec's wife never came to pass. The colonel was about
5'4"—just the minimum height for admission to the Academy—
and was sensitive about it, which perhaps made him the martinet
he was. Dick Williams was something else, a *muy duro, muy
caballero* Marine, very tough and very gentlemanly. He watched
me chewing tobacco on the firing range at Quantico one day and
told me the story of a *mohel,* the Jewish religious circumcizer, in
the small southern town in which he had lived. "He was a nice
man and we all liked him. After he died we wanted to plant a tree
over his grave but there was a difference of opinion. There were
some who wanted to plant a *Ju*-niper. But we all finally came to
agreement and over his grave we planted a eu'clyptus." He always
called me Genghis—sometimes Genghis "Kohn"—but always
with that little side smile that warmed your heart.

I strained at the leash to get away from Navy Yard duty
from the very first day I was there, although I got along well and
Biff recommended me for promotion. On July 27, 1942, I wrote
to the Commandant of the Corps:

SUBJECT: It is requested that I be considered for
expeditionary duty.

Melvin L. Krulewitch

Biff Pierce forwarded the request to Washington and I received a prompt reply. No soap.

30 July, 1942

FROM: The Commandant, U.S. Marine Corps.
TO: Lieutenant Colonel Melvin L. Krulewitch, Marine Corps Reserve, Marine Barracks, Navy Yard, Boston, Mass.
VIA: The Commanding Officer.

SUBJECT: Preference for duty.

REFERENCE: (a) Your letter dated 27 July, 1942.

1. The preference for duty expressed in reference (a) has been recorded for future consideration.

Selden B. Kennedy
By direction.

We had a command of 724 officers and men with the Marine barracks and seven outlying detachments, but no action, no war —nothing but the daily routine of humdrum military housekeeping. It was hard to take. The only excitement came about during a formal dinner in my quarters, when I was notified that a destroyer loading ammo in the Yard had caught fire. I excused myself, and in quickly donned oilskins, my OD and I rushed a detail of Marines aboard the ship, where we conferred at the bow with Captain Rosnan "(Rosie)" Grady, the captain of the Yard, who had beaten me to the fire. The ammunition barge was fended off and the fire foamed out. After cleaning up I returned to the dinner table. No questions, no answers. Service wives have plenty to occupy their minds.

My biggest responsibility was the *Queen Mary,* which came into port with 1,500 members of Rommel's Afrika Korps on board as prisoners. That was a toughie after the hue and cry which had followed the sinking of the *Normandie,* the world's fastest transatlantic liner, at its pier in New York City—a scandal for which the blame was never satisfactorily fixed. With the *Queen* in port, the finger was put on me. It was I, the sacrificial goat.

The giant liner loomed over the town and could be seen for miles. Its presence was about as secret as the presence of an elephant in a phone booth. The bitter freezing cold of the waterfront added to the misery of the Marines on guard on the pier, in small boats under the piers, and on every deck. City fire engines were stationed on the docks, and as we watched hundreds of longshoremen wheeling cases of freight up the gang into the ship's holds, we couldn't help wondering which one held the bomb. But we got through that one. Standing huddled in an ice-rimmed parka at the foot of the pier, I could have kissed the *Queen's* ice-covered stern as she sailed silently out of my life.

But the saddest break in the routine was the aftermath of one of America's greatest civil tragedies, the Cocoanut Grove disaster. Rosie Grady ordered us out to take over at the scene of the raging fire at this popular night spot and three parties moved in with trucks, stretchers, and other equipment—some 96 men in all. Fourteen loads of dead and injured were removed to the city morgue and various hospitals.

Hour after hour, with hair singed, field shoes charred, and skin scorched, the Marines gently sifted the mounds of ashes for anyone alive. Here and there a horribly burned but still living body was recovered and rushed to the Chelsea Naval Hospital. All tolled, 491 men and women lost their lives that night, many of them in the services. One Marine officer was identified only by his partially melted U.S. Naval Academy ring. He was Captain Walter C. Goodpasture, Jr., U.S.M.C., who had just returned from the Allied landing in North Africa aboard the cruiser Tuscaloosa. His wife had come to Boston to greet him on his safe return from the battle. Both perished in the Cocoanut Grove.

For me, the war seemed as far away as ever. In June, 1943, I decided I would go to Washington and ask the Commandant in person for combat duty. Major General Thomas Holcomb, my old major at Belleau Wood in 1918, was now head of the Corps, and at Headquarters, the magic words "Belleau Wood" passed me straight to the top. The General rose from his chair and advanced to meet me as I was escorted through the door by his aide. Putting his arm on my shoulder, he said, "You fought one war, Krulewitch —wasn't that enough?"

This was the moment. I had to think of a good one. "General," I blurted out, "What's one war to a Marine?" The General roared, and so did his aide. "I'll make a note of it," he said. We shook hands, I came to attention and left. I enjoyed the visit but felt again that I had been elected president of the Usual Nothing Club.

In June I rented a house on Cape Cod for the family, and I was able to get there weekends. Came the Fourth of July—real, grass-roots America, with boiled salmon and green peas, the holiday dish for 150 years—and then, in the morning mail at the office, a letter from an old friend:

Dear Mel:

You will be happy at this change in your fortunes. The Commandant is going to assign you to a new division on the West Coast.

The best of luck to you.

> Sincerely,
> /s/ Ben
> Benjamin W. Gally
> Colonel, U. S. M. C.

It was official—Ben was the detail officer at Headquarters. On July 20, I received my orders:

19 July, 1943.

FROM: The Commandant, U. S. Marine Corps
TO: Lieutenant Colonel Melvin L. Krulewitch,
Marine Corps Reserve, Marine Barracks,
Navy Yard, Boston, Mass.
VIA: The Commandant

SUBJECT: Change of Station.

1. When directed by the Commandant, Navy Yard, Boston, Mass., on or about 1 August 1943, you will stand detached from your present station and duties, will proceed overland to Camp Elliot, San Diego, Calif., and report to

the Commanding General, Fleet Marine Force, San Diego Area, for duty with the Fourth Marine Division. You are authorized to delay ten days in reporting to Camp Elliott, San Diego, Calif.

/s/
H. SCHMIDT
Acting.

I was on my way at last.

The night before we left, the officers and senior noncoms gave us a high octane party, the effects of which lasted about 500 miles. We shoved off after reveille, the trunk of our beat-up Buick chock-full of grips, valises, packs, bags, satchels, and toys for the two children—Nan aged five and Peter, three. In approved military style, Helen called out, "Count off," and began "One," Nan followed with "Two," Peter piped up "Three," and I finished with "Four." Helen then reported, "All present or accounted for," establishing what was to become our family routine for the next six days.

We made good time, the only delays occurring when we reached the deserts of New Mexico and Arizona. Peter would announce, "Haf'ta go to the bathroom," and we would pull up on the side of the road and point to a lonely cactus or yucca. Somewhat reluctantly, Peter would then go and water the plant, keeping up a running conversation with us just for company. "Daddy, there's a hoppy toad here." "He's a nice little toad," I would say. "Let him be." And so on until the next stop. Even so, we left the Mojave behind early in the morning of the sixth day—we usually started at dawn with Helen and I spelling each other—and made the remaining 400 miles to San Diego with no sweat or strain.

Reporting into District Headquarters, I was immediately referred back to the 4th Marine Division at Camp Pendleton. But I decided I would take Helen and the kids to Beverly Hills first, where a temporary apartment had been fixed up for us—I felt I had plenty of time. In my orders I had been given seven days travel time, ten days delay, and five days leave—a total of 22 days in all. The trip had taken six days, leaving 16 days in hand, but when I was ushered into the commanding officer's office, I found Major General Harry Schmidt slouched down in his chair behind the table he used for a desk, the peak of his overseas cap resting on his nose and looking thoroughly forbidding.

"Lieutenant Colonel Krulewitch reporting for duty, sir," I said.

The General sat there, Buddha-like, for a moment, then took the wind out of my sails completely. "We've been waiting for you for a week," was his first and only greeting. The endorsement on my orders assigned me to duty as the commanding officer, Headquarters Battalion, headquarters commandant and division provost marshal; Schmidt neither rose from his chair nor shook my hand. Instead he curtly referred me to the Chief of Staff for further information. I came to attention, clicked my heels faintly and moved from the CG's room to the office of Colonel William W. Rogers, division chief of staff. These two men, together with Brigadier General Jim Underhill, Assistant Division Commander, were the three officers who would lead the division on its first assault against the enemy, and three more different characters could hardly have been selected.

Harry Schmidt was a regular's regular, inspiring neither friendliness nor affection—there was no magnetism, no warmth in his manner. He was old-line, regulation Marine Corps, and there was a threat to someone in every move he made. A onetime paymaster in China, with a good record at sea, in the Orient, and in the tropics, he made his way to the throne at Washington and had even signed my original orders "by direction" of the Commandant. He must have known my name, but he was a loyal devotee of RHIP (Rank Hath Its Privileges), and demanded his in full measure. Of middle size, good-looking, with white hair and eyes of Aryan blue, he was completely devoid of humor, although he did once dance the hula at one of our division parties on the Island of Maui. Repenting this display of warmth, however, he promptly ordered his harried assistant to destroy all snapshots taken of him during his solo.

Schmidt was never friendly to me during his tour of duty as CG, which extended through Saipan, but strangely enough it was to me he complained after Iwo Jima, when his son Dick, who had the Tank Battalion, was recommended only for a Bronze Star, a worthy enough decoration. And later on, when his son was named as an accused before a court of inquiry on a technicality, the boy came to me and said his father, the Corps commander, wanted me to defend him. The charge was that his men had fired shells with Mark 4 fuses, without first pulling out the little wires in the noses. These had scratched the rifling in the bore of the guns. I accepted the brief and "sprung" him, as Dickie put it.

Harry Schmidt owed his success in part to the excellence of his chief of staff, Colonel Rogers. The keystone of the division, Rogers was a veteran of the old school tie at Belleau Wood— tough, incisive, and very knowledgeable. He looked and acted more like Churchill than anyone I'd ever met, but despite his brusqueness, there was a warm, pleasant, and scholarly side to him, rarely found in a Marine officer. Though other flag officers openly described him as the power behind the throne, he was loyal and devoted to Harry Schmidt, and we admired him for that. When I played chess with him, he could spot me a rook and still win, or at worst draw. But poker was something else. When we played at Pendleton, he would generally slander me with a paraphrase of the ancient Arab complaint, "He beat me and he cried."

Brigadier General Underhill, the assistant commander, was a gentleman to the core, by breeding, tradition, and training. Well liked by the staff, he languished in the shadow of the Buddha, and our impression was that there was no great rapport between the two generals. It was no surprise to us, therefore, when he was transferred out of the outfit after Kwajalein. I still have his photograph, autographed to me as "my good friend and comrade-at-arms." Tall and light-complected, he cared less for personal comfort than any of the brass, and his cultivated, handsome address took the curse off the martinet "penny fighters."

But perhaps the most famous member of the Fighting Fourth was Evans Carlson. He had retired some years earlier to accept a job with Navy Intelligence and had spent a considerable period of time in China with the Chinese Communist armies, including the 19th Route Army and Chang Tso-lin, a Chinese warlord. Carlson felt that the Chinese people were the real victims, not only of the Japanese invaders, but of the warmongering Chinese generals as well. He had had an outstanding reputation even before he came to the outfit, having seized Makin Island under the noses of the Japs and led a unit known as Carlson's Raiders during the earlier fighting in Guadalcanal. He joined the 3 Section, Operations and Training, and later formed a separate section with the responsibility for preparing top secret plans. I came to know Carlson more closely as our preparation for Kwajalein developed and later in the months leading up to our assault on the Marianas.

Pendleton was a massive camp with training areas 25 miles away from the main gate—a division of some 20,000 men was swallowed up there. Though a general and staff operated the camp itself, our own Headquarters section was set up some distance away, with the troops under canvas, and we all participated in innumerable landing exercises on Aliso Beach, near Highway 101, up which I drove for my weekends at home. I also took part as an observer in field problems at Las Pulgas Canyon, in command post problems near the tent camps, pillbox assaults at Windmill Canyon, and night attacks at the Santa Margarita River. As in all new outfits, a continuing problem was to get to know one another under trying circumstances, to appraise each officer's ability, personality, presence of mind, and commonsense, since when the chips were down, life or death might depend on the fellow alongside of you. The best time to acquire this knowledge is before it's too late—in the slopshoot or handling the daily problems in camp.

And there were problems enough. A Marine was charged with first-degree murder, and Rogers ordered me to get him out of civilian custody. I went to see an elderly California judge, who was happy to talk to a Marine lawyer. When he turned over the prisoner, he remarked that his father, who had lived through the Fifties before the Civil War, had told him of the old days of the California Gold Rush. "Father didn't go in much for legal proceedings," he said softly. "He always said that ca'tridges were cheaper than lawsuits." We also had one opera bouffe court martial, toward the end of December, not long before the division shoved off. An elderly lieutenant colonel, on the eve of retirement after 20 years of regular service, came to me with a sad story. A complaint had been filed against him by a girl in the administration offices, and he had been ordered to appear before a general court martial for trial. The charge was attempted rape, that he had pushed her against the wall, kissed her, and gone through some feeble motions. Affronted more by the fact that the old guy had played Conrad in Quest of his Youth, than by the act itself, the girl had reported him to the Commanding General. As provost marshal of the division, as well as commander of the Headquarters Battalion, I could not represent him myself, but I did call in an excellent trial lawyer, Lieutenant-Colonel Carlton Fisher, well-known in civilian life, to defend him. It was the week before Christmas and we were combat loading at the time for our first operation against the Marshalls.

After the trial, Carl came to my headquarters and gave me a report. "We settled for Christmas," he said, and then he told me the story. The courtroom, which was used as a recreation center when court was not in session, was hung with wreaths of holly, bulging Christmas stockings, and ropes of shining tinsel. "The atmosphere was good," Carl said. "The girl refused to say the four-letter words the defendant used, but said she would whisper them to the President of the Court, if allowed,—and she did, and the President indicated familiarity with the subject matter. When the accused took the stand, he broke into tears, and I cried too. By that time I found, to my relief, that at least one of the court had a teardrop in his eye, and when the wife of the accused began to sob, most of us joined in and I knew we had won the case."

Carl reached down and opened a package he had brought with him. It was a bottle of bourbon. "The colonel sent me a fee and since you were the forwarding attorney, I am splitting it with you." We broke the seal and had a drink.

"What about the facts of the case?" I asked.

"De minimis non curat lex," he replied. ("The law is not concerned with small things.")

★

12. Kwajalein

TEN DAYS LATER, the 4th Marine Division combat-loaded for its 4,500 mile overseas attack on the Marshall Islands. On the morning of New Year's Day, 1944, I called Helen on the top secret telephone at the pier. At the end of our conversation I said, "I'll be seeing you," which was our code, previously agreed upon. With a break in her voice she answered, "I'll be seeing you," and that was all.

The code name Flintlock had been bandied around the bars, but except for a few of us in the inner circle, no one in the division knew its significance, even after the final rehearsals at sea off the coast of California. Now, as the top secret plans for Operation Flintlock were delivered and opened on our command ship, U.S.S. *Appalachian,* we learned that our job was to seize, occupy, and defend the islands of Roi and Namur and the islets of Ennuebing, Mellu, Ennugarret, and some even smaller—all part of the atoll of Kwajalein.

An atoll may be described as an irregular circlet of islands around a deep-water lagoon. Many of them have both barrier reefs far out beyond the surf and fringing reefs, closer in, protecting the islands themselves. The Marines were the spearhead of the audacious Nimitz policy of building a series of stepping stones across the Pacific, leaving the occupied islands in between, to wither on the vine. We were about to take the first big step with the capture of Roi and Namur, the first prewar Japanese territory to be occupied by American forces after the longest overseas attack in military history.

The Marshalls were said to have been visited by a Spanish navigator, Alvoro de Savedra, in 1529, but they were named for a British sea captain, John Marshall, who stopped there in 1788. After the Franco-Prussian War in 1871 Germany, with the gleam of colonial expansion in its eye, bought the islands from Spain, but held them only until 1914 when the Japanese moved in and ruled under a League of Nations mandate. When the Japanese left the League in 1933, they declared the Marshalls Japanese territory and developed them as a naval base.

Kwajalein, at the heart of the complex, is the world's largest atoll, comprising 85 islands around the largest landlocked lagoon. Namur was the administrative center, with a dock and a naval supply depot. Roi had the principal airfield in the area. Each less than one square mile in area, the two islands bristled with de-defensive armaments—coast defense guns, heavy and medium anti-aircraft guns, rapid-fire machine guns of various calibers, heavily armed concrete pillboxes, antitank trenches, and rifle pits, all laced together with barbed wire.

As our great armada moved smoothly and inexorably toward its target, Evans Carlson came to me and said he wished to address the troops. A tall, slim, austere man, and an inveterate cigarette smoker—he carried a case holding 60 cigarettes and was seldom seen without one—he had been billeted in my stateroom, and although I was senior to him by date of commission, I had allowed him the upper berth in recognition of his outstanding services. One story told about him concerned a dinner he attended given by a great Chinese warlord. Seated at a banquet table loaded with exotic food, the general sliced off the succulent hindquarter of a suckling pig and began gorging himself. Glancing at Carlson, who had as yet eaten nothing, the general gestured at the platters and dishes before him and asked Carlson which he would like. Carlson replied, "Please, just a bowl of millet,"—a cereal popular among the peasantry. Silence fell. The other diners watched the general's face anxiously. With the table groaning under the General's lavish hospitality, Carlson's refusal to eat as the general ate might have been considered an insult, but when the little bowl of cereal was brought the contrast between it and the glazed Peking duck, suckling pig, sliced boiled kidneys, stewed pigeons, and saffron-steamed fish was so extreme that the Chinese sense of humor intervened. The general broke into a guffaw, and the moment passed. But as commanding officer of troops aboard the *Appalachian,* I was not sure that Carlson's idea to address the troops was so good.

"These boys have their squadleaders, who have their platoon leaders, who have their company commanders, who have their battalion commanders, all the way up the task force commander," I said. "Each has his own particular job to do, so why complicate a buck private's thinking with top level strategy? You'll befuddle him. Let him do his little job, the one in front of his eyes."

But Carlson still wanted to talk to them, and so I climbed to the bridge to see Rear Admiral Richard L. Connolly in his cabin. With him was his chief of staff and exec, Captain Charles Wellborn, Jr., now retired as a vice admiral. Both made me welcome, offering a seat and a cup of java, and after a discussion it was agreed that both Carlson and I would address the troops in the enlisted galley on the following morning after chow.

I told the boys about Kwajalein and the tremendous armada of which they were a part, the largest yet to be assembled in the Pacific. As I detailed the number of destroyers, the number of cruisers, the list of battleships, and finally the list of carriers in the Fast Carrier Force, their cheers and shouts turned to yells of approval and applause. Carlson then spoke on a broader plane of the fellowship between officers and men—we were one, and all walking and fighting together.

On July 31, 1944, General Underhill, in charge of the first phase of the operation, seized the Ennuebing pass into the lagoon, mounted his guns on the island, crossed the lagoon to the far side, and took three small islands, on which he landed the artillery, the 75s and the 105s of the 14th Marines. The stage was now set for the assault on the heart of the atoll.

The following morning the landings began on Roi and Namur, after a heavy bombardment. By noon Roi, with its airfield, had been taken. Namur where resistance was somewhat more determined, was secured the following day. Captain Carl W. Proehl, intelligence officer of the Division, and Master Technical Sergeant David Dempsey, combat correspondent with the 4th, wrote about the extraordinary concentration of fire power on the islands before the assault:

Then shortly after 1100, the assault units were waved over the line of Departure, 4000 yards from the shore. Naval gunfire began to hurl its final salvos against the beach; dive bombers plummeted down to drop 1,000-pound blockbusters on installations not yet completely demolished; fighter planes came over for strafing runs. It was the heaviest and most perfectly coordinated concentration of pre-landing bombardment yet seen in the Pacific.

Landing on Namur, we set up Headquarters and began to organize the shattered remains of the island. A couple of camouflaged pup tent shelter halves, covering the remains of a blasted pillbox, made a comfortable CP. A row of canteens, still in their covers, were regularly dipped in the sea and strung along the edges of the tent, to dry in the trade winds. The evaporation chilled the contents of the canteens, turning them into water coolers, tropical-style. I also brought some folding cots ashore for the brass and offered one to Carlson, but true to his philosophy, he preferred to sleep in the sand.

During our stay on Kwajalein, we organized the islands for defense from the air and began cleaning up the battlefield. The Japanese dead lay in windrows inside and out of the concrete blockhouse and had long since begun to putrify. While trying to hire natives to help, I met an individual known as the King of the Marshalls, whose regalia consisted of white shorts, an open white shirt, shoes, and a Panama hat. When he said he could provide the men, I offered them $1 a day. "Oh, no," the King protested. "They can't earn that much money a day." We finally settled on a pound of rice per head per day, and I paid them off in captured sacks of Japanese rice. The King, his assistants, and the interpreter all had yaws. When I swabbed their sores with iodine, they would join in a war dance from the bite of the medication, but two of them attached themselves to me, and helped around the CP, for which I most generously rewarded them with captured tubs of Japanese soy sauce, considered to be a great delicacy.

After the Mongols captured Bokhara and Samarkand, it was said that the stench of death was so unbearable that no bird would fly over the ravaged cities. On Namur we had the same problem, with several thousand decomposing bodies, growing more repulsive and obnoxious by the second in the equatorial heat. Wearing cloths over their faces, the Micronesians would drag the corpses into deep craters made by 18-inch naval shells, and these would then be bulldozed over, but the stench persisted even when the grisly work was finished. You couldn't get away from it—the stink was everywhere, in everything you touched or handled. The tropical insects, sweat bees, gnats, and flies, which swarmed wherever there was corruption, got into our food, and the spread of disease began.

One of the few prisoners taken, a small, almost completely nude and very unhappy little fellow, who had cried out "Chosen! Chosen!" to indicate that he was a Korean, had been picked up by me just after the landing. Some of our public relations people photographed this minor event, and the press, hungry for a victory picture, printed it from coast to coast. My sister Frankie wrote to say that she had seen the picture and recognized me, although no names were mentioned, and my father-in-law sent on a copy of *The Daily News* from New York with the same photo on the front page. A few weeks later I receive a second letter from Frankie asking, "Is that your favorite Jap that you carry along with you for publicity? We see you from time to time in the papers and always with that same little Jap. Some war!"

Some war indeed. After 11 days on Namur, we embarked on the S.S. *Robin Wentley* and sailed for Hawaii—just 24 hours before a Japanese air raid destroyed a large part of our supplies and ammunition on the island.

The S.S. *Robin Wentley,* one of the Robin Line Freighters charter-partied to the U.S. Naval Service for transport duty in the Pacific, approached the slip at Kahului, the port of Maui in the Hawaiians. The tow-headed Lithuanian captain, who that day had announced at the officers' mess that although he was not Jewish he could not eat butter with meat, had just completed a melancholy talk with the business representative of the Maritime Union. Because of the union 40-hour week, the crew had refused to unload the Marines' equipment.

Standing at the bow, one of its members heaved the loop hawser to the pier, where a Kanaka was waiting to bend it around the forward bit. Despite the screams of the skipper on the bridge, the line fell into the water and was hauled back to the deck. The ship reversed out of the slip and made a second approach. Again the lined missed, to the accompaniment of jeers and ribald comments from the Marines, preparing to unload. On the third try, the line was caught, made fast, and the stern line followed—the ship docked. It started to rain as we marched ashore with the first installment of the 1500 cases of dysentery brought back from Kwajalein.

In convoy from the pier, we drove in trucks past Spreckelsville and Lower Paia, past the rich red soil of the pineapple plantations, to our camp above Haiku, with its lines of squad tents dripping in the early evening shower. The slopshoots, canteens, and officers' clubs were soon jammed with sweating, steaming, boisterous customers. The 4th Marine Division, back from its first operation, had landed at Maui, its home base until the war was over.

Beautiful Maui, the Valley Isle, gave itself to the Marines. As I wrote home in a letter to my college-mate, M. Lincoln Schuster:

> Here is a varied climate. Tropical heat, both humid and dry, cooling breezes and hot winds, and in the evening a sharp drop in temperature. We sleep under blankets, and high above us, at a rest lodge, it's quite cool at night. The surroundings are reminiscent of our own Adirondacks with a dry atmosphere, occasional evergreens, and up in the hills we find strange combinations of fruits, such as apples and bananas, growing side by side in a single orchard.
>
> Speaking of chow, not that we were, but let us, have you ever tasted a ripe pineapple, grown in rich red soil, in the blazing tropical heat and watered by mountain dew and the wet mists of low hanging clouds? This is not your half-grown blue or green pine, ripened in the hold of a ship, or at the corner market. It is real fruit, a full-blown yellow, heavy with juice and meat. Off comes the spiny top and prickly sides, and in a moment you have in your hand a great golden chunk of dripping honey. That's pineapple, as in pineapple.
>
> Our present location might well be called the Place of Storms and Rainbows. It rains part of every day but we no longer find that difficult. It is merely a question of comfort,

which is a relative term. In bivouac, to lie on a piece of firm turf is more satisfactory than on a rocky ledge; but both are less desirable than a discarded stretcher whose rests give support to the canvas and almost equals a cot in comfort. With all the rain, there are nevertheless a few cases of colds among our personnel, either ashore or at sea. At other times we passed close to waterspouts, those dark whirling funnels of danger rising to the skies. All through the Pacific, the natives have a much broader vocabulary than our language offers for the description of the varying shades of difference in clouds, winds, and weather.

But the ever-present rainbows here are unbelievably beautiful. No day goes by without five or six of them, usually in concentric pairs, and their brilliance and the sharpness of the colors are breathtaking. This morning there was a beauty marking the entire northerly heavens, with its shadowy companion above it. Not difficult to understand is the biblical combination of the "Deluge and the Rainbow."

Though bloodied in battle, we began intensive combat training all over again—reveille at five, at 6, the field where we fired new weapons and drilled with new artillery. There were daily slogs to the boondocks, night training, rubberboat training—the eternal toughening process of heavy physical drill and hard labor, with inspections on Saturday mornings and then the blessed weekends to decompress. But even that respite went when we began to rehearse for the next show with live ammo, live grenades, live artillery firing, tank-infantry tactics, and finally air-strafing with pay loads.

Each day, as the sun crept slowly below the yardarm, the officers would repair to their slopshoot to drown their growls and gripes in 25-cent whiskey and 10-cent beer. Back of the bar were the usual pinups, including a delightful line of cancan dancers, black-gartered and stockinged, kicking high to reveal a froth of lace around the circular seal of our military censor: "Passed by the U.S. Naval Censor."

The talk, however, was all above the belt. As the training peaked, behind the scuttlebut was the continuing question, "Where do we go from here? And when?" Wake, which had been honorably and courageously defended to the last livable moment, was the first choice of the highchair seers at the bar. In the Central Pacific only 700 miles north of Kwajalein and directly in the Japanese defense line, Wake made good sense. But then so did the Palaus, not too distant from the strategic island of Yap, an important stepping stone for MacArthur's return to the Philippines. "Doug" was even now creeping up along the northerly coast of New Guinea. Truk was another favorite, the reputedly impregnable citadel in the Carolines which had to be neutralized to insure the success of our advances in both the Central and Southern Pacific.

Intelligence had filtered through that the Japanese were expecting our next attack from the northeast against the Palaus, but another possibility was Saipan in the Marianas, directly in the central fairway of the Pacific. Saipan was the mightily fortified headquarters of the Japanese Central Pacific Command, 1300 miles further west than we'd ever gone before, some 3400 miles from Maui and less than a four-hour flight from Tokyo. But since it was flanked by the heavily fortified Carolines and would take us into the jaws of the Japanese fleet, Saipan appeared to be the least attractive of the four possible objectives.

One evening a runner from Headquarters slipped into the bar and singled me out. I signed his book, read the message, and finished my drink. "See you at chow," I said to the adjutant, and plowed through the red mud to the duck boards leading to my tent. Seated on the field stool, I reread the message:

> All commanding officers will report to
> Headquarters at 1900.
>   By Order of the Commanding General

After evening chow I walked over the ravine to Division Headquarters, where a guard met me at the entrance, checked my name and rank, and passed me through into the low U-shaped wooden building constructed by the Seabees (one of my battalions). The Commanding General, the Chief of Staff and the Assistant Division Commander were seated behind a green-baize covered table. On the wall directly behind them was a covered map prepared by the 2 Section. On the table were a pile of square manila envelopes marked with the names of the commanding officers of the combat teams and the heads of the general and special sections.

The proceedings were short and to the point. "I need not tell you that everything we say here is of the highest classified importance," said the General. "On a date that we shall announce in due course, we sail in a great company to seize, occupy, and defend the fortified island of Saipan."

There was a muted cheer. The General smiled, and the adjutant passed among the assembled officers, handing each his bulky envelope of secret orders, annexes, maps, and overlays. We were then excused.

Despite the highest security, the word got around. Maui knew about the impending attack long before the division combat-loaded for battle and left, on May 13, 1944, for a week of rehearsals off Maalea Bay. It was just three months after our arrival from Kwajalein.

Maalea Bay is a cove near the settlement of Kihei, which together with Kahului, forms the squeezed-in waist of Maui, between the massive swelling heights of Haleakala and the gentle uplift of the West Mountains—two separate islands in prehistoric times. The bay, with its rocky shore line, was a favorite spot with the natives for octopus hunting. Their technique was fascinating. When pierced by a spear, the creature would twine its tentacles around the long shaft. The Kanaka would then disable his catch by calmly putting his lips against the eye of the octopus and biting sharply into the soft flesh of its temple. The first time I saw this I thought of the sign above my sergeant major's desk: "Isn't there a harder way to do it?"

Rehearsals over, we sailed for the Central Pacific. We would let Wake wither on the vine. We would forego the Palau Islands, where the Japanese were furiously fortifying Peliliu in anticipation of our expected assault to help MacArthur, and we would bypass Truk, the heart of the Carolines. That massive fortress would be on our left flank all the way, threatening our supply lines, but the die was cast—we were on our way as ordered, to seize, occupy, and defend Saipan.

13. *Saipan*

THE 4TH MARINE DIVISION joined the task force at Eniwetok. Aboard the combat transport U.S.S. *Leonard Wood,* we entered the great lagoon and anchored amid a mighty company of ships waiting to allow the slow-moving LCTs and LCMs to get well ahead of the main body. The fast-sailing combat transports were giving them three days' start.

A group of us went ashore in a small boat. Only a few weeks before, this atoll had been enemy territory. Now it sported miniature windmills which operated clothes-washers, and *mirabile dictu,* there was even an officers' club. But the biggest surprise of all were the clotheslines strung close to the landing dock and decked with unmistakably feminine chemises, underpants, bras, and other dainty bits and pieces. We looked at each other, and hurried up the graveled path to the empty officers' club. Almost at once, a girl with a blonde forelock over her eye, wearing khaki slacks, tennis shoes, and a loose chambray shirt with silver bars on the collar, walked into the bar.

"What gives?" she asked.

I took a long look. "We just came ashore for a drink," I said. The others just kept looking.

"Warm beer, no ice," she replied. "Help yourself. And leave the change in the box behind the bar."

"What kind of an outfit is this?" I asked.

"We're an advance unit of the First Field Hospital," she said. "Ten nurse officers. Headquarters is at the other end of the island."

The warm beer was passed around. "You ladies certainly made

time," I said. "This island was only secured a few weeks ago. But the laundry service seems to be doing all right."

The girl smiled. "Take a look at Shantytown and see what the Seabees did for us."

They had built a street of shacks from scrap lumber, sheet iron, wooden battens, and sections of heavy crating, each with its own washing machine geared to a windmill, whirling in the trade winds. After another warm beer back at the club and a good-luck kiss from the nurse on watch, we returned in the ship's boat.

"What's that flying below the ensign?" I asked. As we got close, I realized that somebody had lost a pair of lace drawers.

On June 11 we sailed for the Marianas. During the day, with our sister transports, we regularly changed direction on command, to zigzag or to scatter formation. Scout planes occasionally flew overhead and as quickly disappeared; in all directions the eyes of the fleet were on watch. Below decks the tightly packed troop compartments were stifling and fetid despite the air funneled down from above, and nights offered no respite from the heat.

The decks were a maze of equipment and supplies—trucks loaded and tarpaulined, jeeps piled high with boxes, and metal-strapped pallets packed with G.I. cans of water, ammo, food, and medical supplies ready to be dragged ashore by the bull-dozers on landing. My favorite spot was at the point of the bow of the *Leonard Wood,* its knife edge cutting the black, rolling mass of the sea. I remember one night when the moon hid behind the clouds and only the phosphorescent feathers of the wavecrests lightened the blackout of the sea and ship. Then the clouds broke, and dimly off the starboard bow appeared the North Star, while close to the horizon far to the south hung the Southern Cross with its four major stars. The darkness soon closed in again, but thinking I had found a way to beat the censor, I wrote home mentioning the stars I had seen. I found out later that my father had been convinced I was in Iceland.

Moving on relentlessly, the great armada reached its objective —and hit. On D-day, June 15, we stormed ashore. In the first line of armored amphibs, I gathered up the units of our advance command post, moved to a clump of coconut palms, and set up my signal axis, while on both flanks units were landing and forming a line. Issue had been joined with the enemy and would continue for 25 days of bitter fighting.

I wrote Max Schuster about it later:

The legendary Saipan was neither fable nor fancy to us. From the grinding crash as our amphib tore and wrenched its way across the reef on D-day, we lived in the moment. Saipan would have been difficult even as a training or rehearsal exercise, for our enemy was no less the terrain itself than the Japs. The beaches, protected by a reef and small in area, had to be pulled out of the sea and bent to our will. There was death and destruction all about us and the desperate attempts of the enemy to stop us at the water line was evident from many signs, not the least of which was his artillery, dragged down to the beaches for point-blank firing.

Saipan is an island of cliffs, caves, and ravines leavened by fairly sizeable patches under cultivation. Its sugarcane production is nowhere nearly so extensive as on Tinian, the smaller of the two islands, but we did find patches of taro, corn, cotton, and wild pineapple. The coconut and plantain palms are common, with here and there a breadfruit and pandanus tree. Papayas were everywhere, now heavy with their clusters of ripening fruit. Over all of this loomed Mt. Tapotchau, up the tangled craggy slopes of which we were to push our lines.

There were on occasions moments of leisure when we could listen to the Jap radio boast of how the invaders had been destroyed and the fleet dispersed; or perhaps enjoy a drink of captured Kirin or Asahi beer, the equal of anything in the States; or that blessed moment of deep relaxation and repose in the form of an ocean bath. How we relished and savored the comfort of that rare pleasure.

In this operation, the extraordinary became the commonplace. Each moment had its own highlights and there was an overtone in each for the one who could listen. What comes to mind is not an organized chronological procession of facts, but rather an assortment of unrelated incidents which rush back with an emotional sweep; toiling up a craggy hillside at the head of our scouts attacking an enemy group holed up near the summit; the sickening stench of the dead, which strangely enough we have come to anticipate and associate with our victories; preparing a tiny fire in a discarded can to heat the bitter black coffee that was nectar to a hungry, thirsty, dirty Marine; lavender morning twilight breaking through the heavy blackness of the night; bathing and dressing the hideous wounds of a little child, assisted by a geisha girl who, miraculously, in all that welter of blood and dirt, kept clean and neat; advancing across a field covered with enemy dead just after his counterattacking columns had been slaughtered; moving out to a position in front of the lines just before an attack and watching our tanks and infantry come up and pass through into the enemy's positions. These were the order of the day and it was only the routine, the dull, or the drab that was extraordinary.

As the Marines moved ahead, they confronted the high ground at Fina Susu and Lake Susupe. This was the challenge. The Chief of Staff called me on the field telephone. "Report to Division Headquarters," he said, and hung up, even before I said, "Aye, aye, sir." When Rogers took that tone, it was either "up for a shoot" or a toughie of some kind.

Division Headquarters had been established in the shambles of a high-explosive shell hole back of a tiny hillock. A tarpaulin, spread between the trunks of two clumps of palms and camouflaged with fronds, extended the working space. In the same area, general and special sections had picked their locations and CP personnel had wired them in, setting up a message center. The artillery commander, Colonel Louis DeHaven, the bravest of the brave, was holding a canteen cup of instant coffee over a tiny fire contained in a punctured bean can. He offered me a sip. Then I stooped, drew aside the shelter half serving as a curtain and entered the heart of the command post. The General sat, Buddha-like, in a field armchair close to the battle map, silent and serious. The strain was showing.

Rogers began, "We want this Headquarters moved at once!

Make a reconnaissance in this area—he pointed to square 42A on the battle map—"and set up the command post." I looked at the area on the division map, then reached in my despatch case to check it on my map. Unlike positional warfare, a front line in a meeting engagement is never marked with any real precision. Small firing groups are irregularly placed along what is recognized as the line of furthest advance, their positions being fixed by points of military importance, such as woods, hill, cuts, draws, streams, and the like. The coordinates of these positions would be telephoned or radioed back to the division command post and set up on all the maps. And according to *my* map, the location of the proposed CP was in enemy hands.

"May I say something to the colonel?" I said. "That area, sir, I believe, is Jap territory."

The Chief of Staff, smarting because of a hold-up at Fina Susu, boiled over. "Colonel," he snapped, "if ever I need your advice as to the front line, which I doubt, you'll know about it. Men are being killed in this division. Move out!"

I saluted and returned to my own command post, where I quickly organized a small patrol consisting of the MP commander, Captain Dunn, a signalman, and a runner. Moving on a northerly course to Charan-Kanoa, the second largest village on the island, we changed direction to the northeast and moved down what was left of the main street. The splintered tinderbox houses were just piles of rubble, charred, shattered, and spilling into the road. An enormous bull, killed in the first attack, was covered by a blanket of green flies. The only living thing in sight was a fouled, thirsty hog, licking the maggots from the face of a decomposing Japanese sergeant. The body was lying below the raised floor of a shattered temple—its sacred purple and black draperies dragged in the scattered white ashes of the military dead, spilled when the shelling broke open the boxes prepared for shipment to the bereaved families.

I ordered the patrol to split and use the cover on both sides of the road, for the crazily slanting coconut palms, the broken pandanus and breadfruit trees offered some small measure of protection as we advanced. After the heavy shelling and the grinding traffic, the white, coral-based roads turned into pockmarked dust. With each step sending up clouds of pulverized stone, the four of us were soon covered with a film of white powder, and so I ordered the patrol into the fields on each side. Slowly, alert to every movement, we edged toward the area picked by the Chief of Staff.

The firing had increased. Shells from long-distance enemy artillery probing the rear areas keened overhead. The staccato rattle of machine guns joined the tearing crack of mortar bursts. Far to the south, groups of Marines could be seen advancing into the cane, the dust kicked up by jeeps and trucks adding to the pall over the terrain. The enemy's field artillery had begun to range the road. I ordered a change of direction by arm signal and we moved toward a handful of Marines digging in behind a broken coral rock fence line. Up ahead the fire continued. We flopped down and took cover.

"What outfit is this?" I asked the nearest Marine.

"First Battalion, Twenty-fourth Marines."

"Where's the CO?"

The Marine waved in the direction of a large naval shell hole. I walked over and sat down with Lieutenant Colonel Schultz.

"What are you doing here, post trooper?" he asked with a smile.

"Something new has been added," I said. "we're setting up the Division Command post in 42A behind the Jap front lines."

"That's nice. I've got two companies out ahead—about 200 yards—and that's the front front. Don't be unhappy," he added slyly. "There's a full Jap regiment out there for you to play with."

We shook hands and I signalled the patrol to get moving. The mortar fire increased as we inched ahead along the roadway, advancing from cover to cover, greeting and passing Schultz's front-line companies. The Japs had been hitting both sides of the road and were now on the beam. Out in front of the two companies on the line, the colonel had set up listening posts to pass back word of enemy ground movements. We passed these, and my little group was now past the front front line, in Japanese territory and under blazing sniper fire.

Reaching 42A, we waited behind a thick clump of pandanus. On my knees, I scanned the ground through glasses and saw nothing but groups of civilians scurrying toward the Jap positions in the hills. Then a mortar shell swished and swooped down on us, exploding squarely on the road. As my helmet rang with the shock, I felt a hit. A small fragment had cut through my despatch case, mashed a pack of Chesterfields, and been stopped by the metal tube of an anti-chap stick issued to protect the face and lips against the heat of the tropics. Reaching under my left arm into the case, I picked out the sizable metal splinter and held it up to the goggle-eyed patrol. "Still hot!" I said, and put it in my pocket. (I still have it.)

Clearly, 42A was no place for a command post. We picked our way back to the First Battalion command. The official report had the story.

> On D-plus-1 a reconnaissance party consisting of the Headquarters Commandant, Commanding Officer, Military Police Company and Executive Officer of the Fourth Signal Company, made a reconnaissance for a new CP in a location indicated after a map reconnaissance by the Chief of Staff, northeast of the first CP. This was found occupied by enemy troops. The reconnaissance party was under fire in that location at all times and on its return passed the CP of the 1st Battalion, 24th Marines, which had just had several casualties.

The enemy had put down a tight barrage on Division Headquarters during our absence. Dead and wounded were being evacuated and communication personnel were repairing the wires. When I reported to the Chief of Staff that 42A was held by a Jap regiment, all I got was a tight answer: "You sure had a break while you were up there. We took a lot of shelling at this CP."

A double break, I thought, reaching into my pocket to finger the shell splinter.

As the days went by, the last pockets of resistance began to crumble and Marpi point could be seen from the cliffs at Makunsha. Crushed into this enclave to the northeast of Karaberra were hordes of refugees retreating from the battle with what was left of their Japanese defenders. Then came the final, unforgettable horror of the entire campaign. Helpless, hopeless, and hapless, herded together in unbelievable misery, these poor, terrified civilians were murdered in cold blood by the remaining Japanese troops. Men, women, and children were shot, knifed or flung over the cliffs onto the rocks below.

All this took place in sight of the Marines, who cried to them to stop, repeating the Japanese words they had learned for contact with the civilians:"Shimpae Shinae"—"Don't be afraid." It was to no avail. Watching from high ground, powerless to help, I wondered what kind of military would deliberately murder its own civilians to prevent them falling into our hands as internees or prisoners of war.

The butchery was complete. Nothing was left but the clothing and personal possessions carried so trustingly to the end. Fluttering along the ground, they were carried out to sea by the breeze.

After 38 days on Saipan, tired to the marrow, reduced by battle casualties and a growing sick list, we were ordered to seize and defend the perilous beaches of Tinian to prepare the way for our sister division, the Second, to go ashore and take the island.

This we did.

President Roosevelt presented the Fourth Marine Division with the following citation:

> For outstanding performance in combat during the seizure of the Japanese-held islands of Saipan and Tinian in the Marianas from June 15 to August 1, 1944. Valiantly storming the mighty fortifications of Saipan on June 15, the Fourth Division, Reinforced, blasted the stubborn defense of the enemy in an undeviating advance over the perilously rugged terrain. Unflinching despite heavy casualties, this gallant group pursued the Japanese relentlessly across the entire length of the island, pressing on against bitter opposition for 25 days to crush all resistance in their zone of action. With but a brief rest period in which to reorganize and re-equip, the Division hurled its full fighting power against the dangerously narrow beaches of Tinian on July 24 and rapidly expanded the beachheads for the continued landing of troops, supplies and artillery. Unchecked by either natural obstacles or hostile fire, these indomitable men spearheaded a merciless attack which swept Japanese forces before it and ravaged all opposition within eight days to add Tinian to our record of conquests in these strategically vital islands.

14. Iwo Jima

BLOODY THOUGH IT WAS, Saipan was but the prelude to Iwo Jima. We were sitting in the skipper's cabin aboard the U.S.S. *Sanborn.* It was February 15th, 1945, and D-day was to be the 19th. Seated around the dinner table were the ship's captain, Commander Huguenin, Lieutenant Colonel J. M. Chambers, Lieutenant Colonel Hollis V. Mustain, and myself.

Mustain, who had come aboard from the U.S.S. *Nepa,* where his troops were embarked, was our guest for the evening. A great fighter, squarely built, rugged, and hard-headed, he was in command of the first battalion of the 25th, an appointment he had earned by distinguishing himself in the service in the line in the Saipan, Tinian, and Marshalls campaigns. We were talking about Saipan and he was ribbing Jo Chambers about Hill 500, where Mustain had called down, "Come Up, Jumping Jo." A grateful Congress was to award Jo a Medal of Honor for what he would do the next few days.

I was particularly happy to have Mustain aboard. In fact, we felt faint with pleasure, making it necessary to break out the liquor, in accordance with regulations, to preserve the health and strength of the command. There was indeed a marked improvement in strength and morale afterwards, once again proving the wisdom of the Navy Medical Corps.

After the main course, the sentry at the door poked his head between the curtains and said, "First Cook Stuart McCawley would like to speak to the colonel."

"What is it?" I asked. The sentry didn't have time to answer. McCawley himself appeared through the doorway bearing on a platter a mound of broiled peaches, oranges, and pineapples. Rich

118

juices formed a moat around the smoking heap, from which issued a most delectable fragrance. "This is my favorite dessert," McCawley volunteered. "The mess always asks for it and I thought you'd like it to top off the *despedido." Despedido* means "farewell party."

We fell upon it. Nothing like that platter, with warm natural flavors of the juices and fruit meats, had come our way in months.

"Hey, post trooper," said Chambers. "How about transferring that cook to a good outfit?"

"If," I answered loftily, "by a good outfit you mean yours, there isn't a Chinaman's chance." Mustain didn't say a word, but I decided privately that when we were all back at Maui, I'd ask McCawley if he'd like to serve with Colonel Mustain, and if so, transfer him over.

The drinks, the warm companionship, and the good food had eased the tension we had all grown used to on the eve of a major operation. Our last rehearsal had been completed and we would sail before dawn. The decks were again loaded down with the paraphernalia of war. Except for the hatch covers and a small space kept clear around the rails, every available square inch was covered with vehicles, preloaded pallets covered by tarpaulins, jeeps waterproofed and stripped for action, and every other kind of battle supplies.

Quiet, self-effacing, with the dignity and strength of greatness, Hollis Mustain was to take his men ashore, lead them to their objective, and then join the Corps' sublime band of those who, face to face with the enemy, gave their lives for their country. But that was still ahead. Supper over, we walked to the gangway, at the foot of which a small boat, fended from the ladder, danced on the water. Mustain saluted the colors and said, "So long, Mel." I called after him, "See you on the high ground." He smiled back over his shoulder and was gone.

With the morning our great armada, reaching to the horizon in every direction, stood out to sea in waters that had been Japanese for a century.

In the early hours of the 19th, this majestic company lay off the rock of Iwo Jima. On the vast expanse of shimmering waters there was no sound save the soft muted murmur of the waves cut by the bows of the transport, and no light beyond the feathery phosphorescence of the wavecrests to mark the progress of the fleet. In the darkness, only the masses of more solid blackness showed the presence of our neighbors in the convoy.

Deep in the center of the task force, protected by the fighting ships, the combat-loaded Marines were clambering down the cargo nets and into the waiting landing craft. Having rendezvous'd for control, they then moved to assembly areas, awaiting the signal to line up for the final approach to the line of departure. By then the first light of D-day morning had appeared, and high on the *Sanborn,* Huguenin had taken his place on the bridge, wearing blues and with his ribbons and decorations shining in the growing light. My command post had been set up on the sky bridge, the topmost station on the ship, where signalmen were logging all the messages coming through, so as to keep me informed of what was going on.

At H hour, the Marines began to hit the beach. And all went according to plan until the first three waves were ashore and moving up the heights to the airfield.

> Then came trouble—in large quantities. As the naval gunfire lifted, the Japanese opened up with every weapon they had, and soon a solid sheet of fire was pouring down on the beaches and incoming waves. It was the heaviest mortar and artillery fire yet seen in any operation. Boats were hit; they broached and clogged the beaches. Casualties mounted rapidly. Vehicles ashore found the sandy volcanic ash and the first terrace (with its 40 per cent grade) nearly impassable. Even tanks bogged down. Every move they made was under direct observation by the Japanese on top of the cliffline on the right flank and on Mt. Suribachi on the left.[1]

By noon the first casualties were coming aboard. For the rest of the afternoon, there was one recurrent call from the deck— "Stand by to receive wounded." On the quarterdeck, a senior medical officer was receiving the wounded over the rail, classifying them according to their medical needs and assigning them to the

[1] Division Report on Iwo Section III, Fourth Marine Division, Historical Division, U.S.M.C.

quarters best equipped to deal with their respective wounds. Even as one boat load was processed, the cry would come again to stand by and another dripping boatload would be hauled up to the rail on the davit cables. Amid all the noise and fog of battle, the litters would be lifted tenderly over the rail to waiting hands. The red wash slapping up the perpendicular sides of the LCVP with each roll of the ship would then be baled out, and the craft would be lowered to the water for another round trip to the beach.

Commander Bill Johnson was at the rail receiving the wounded when I approached. A new batch had just been deposited on the deck. "That one," he said, pointing to a head wound, "reload him and take him to the *Bayfield*. They have a head man there." Two corpsmen picked up the handles of the stretcher and lifted it, with the precision of long practice, over the rail and into the boat still hanging from the davits.

"That one," he continued, "take below into the officers' wardroom. We'll operate on him at once." "He'll come along nicely," he added, turning to me. The patient, a sturdy Seabee, took this in with no show of interest, and later in the wardroom, when I saw the surgeon cutting away some of the destroyed tissue of the sailor's leg with a pair of surgical scissors, he still seemed remarkably calm—as well as fully conscious. The doctor explained and the Seabee confirmed that he couldn't feel a thing.

Meanwhile in that ordered confusion on deck, two bloodied litters had remained untouched, their occupants gray and motionless. I asked Bill about them and he turned from his examination of a new batch of wounded. "This one," he said, pointing, "is dead." "That one," pointing to the other, "will die in about 10 minutes." He turned away and walked wearily to the next line of stretchers.

I looked at the silent form of the boy who had only 10 minutes to live. He was a sergeant. He was gray-faced, his eyes were staring, and his jaw had dropped. The stretcher was a bloodied mess. And suddenly I made up my mind he wasn't going to die—I'd be damned if I was just going to let him lie there and die. "I'll take this fellow out of your way," I told Johnson, beckoning over a black seaman who had come up from the engine room for a breath of air. We each took an end of the stretcher and somehow got him below to my room, just aft of the wardroom. A trail of blood had followed us across the deck and down the ladder; but in a moment I had Commander Reuben Sharpe, Medical Corps, there to attend him. Rube had been operating all afternoon, but he looked like a million dollars to me, butcher's apron and all.

"How about this man?" I asked. "Can you keep him going?"

Bloodied to the armpits, he kneeled down without a moment's hesitation, read the card attached to the stretcher, and made a quick deft examination.

"A sucking wound," he muttered, shaking his head, with a deep sigh. "He's very bad. "I'll give him plasma and later some whole blood if he can take it." He left and came back with a pharmacist's mate to set up the plasma transfusion. Satisfied now that everything possible was being done for him, I noticed that the 10 minutes had already passed and my sergeant was still alive.

An hour later he seemed to be holding his own. His card showed him to be Sergeant T. Hanley, 25th Marines, and it might have been my imagination, but it seemed to me that a touch of color had returned to the ashen pallor of his face.

I was back in my CP on the sky bridge when, shortly after sundown, the order came for the ship to disengage from the enemy and prepare for the expected Kamikaze attacks from Tokyo, two hours away—flying time. As night fell the neighboring ships faded into the gathering gloom, breaking off contact with the shore and fanning out by prearranged plan. Carrying our precious burden of wounded and of troops not yet put ashore, we moved to our night station, hatches battened down and observing the strictest blackout. Below decks the ship was a blaze of light, with seven operating tables going full blast in the wardroom and the ship's infirmary. No officer slept in his bunk that night, and every man's strength and resolution were concentrated on tending the wounded. When Air Express from Tokyo arrived in the early hours, they found no one home.

As the *Sanborn* had not yet landed the officers and men of the 4th Medical Battalion, the ship was blessed with more than its fair share of trained medical personnel. Although calls from the shore and other ships in the task force had reduced our roster, long before midnight every casualty had been processed, even cases requiring major operations.

Preparing for the next day kept me busy until just before dawn, when I checked on my sergeant again, as I had done several times during the night. He stirred restlessly. The whole blood had now given him a definite touch of color, and his condition, although still desperate, had improved in the nine hours since he had been brought aboard. The doctors told me he was actually breathing through a jagged opening in his back and the problem was that his lungs were filling up. I began to think that my hope for the sergeant was a triumph of optimism over experience. There was nothing more they could do except watch him closely for the next few hours. A premature operation in his condition might extinguish the flickering spark.

At dawn, we moved again to the attack. With a sandwich in one hand and a canteen cup of black coffee in the other, I saw the sun come up from the bridge. It had been a hard night for the valiant men ashore, and the morning was no better. The Marines had taken the airfield and were moving slowly ahead. My command post, on the alert all day, waited in vain for the order to set up ashore, and at sunset we again disengaged and moved out into the darkness of the night. In our division alone, the casualties of the first two days had been in excess of 2000.

Sergeant Hanley was still desperately sick. I watched him during the night and was at last rewarded when he turned his head toward me and murmured, "Want a priest." But we had no priest aboard —our Catholic chaplain had gone ashore early in the attack with troops of the 25th Marines. The only man available was Lieutenant Earl Dean Sneary, a Protestant minister, and I decided to ask the doctors if I couldn't pretend to Hanley that Chaplain Sneary was a priest. They consented and I led the minister over to the sergeant. "This is Father Sneary," I said. "He wants to bring you a good word of comfort."

The Chaplain, a giant of a man, leaned over the bunk. Placing a hand gently on the boy's brow and his lips close to his ear, he read the words of a Catholic prayer from a card concealed in his hand. When he finished, the sergeant turned his head and said, "Thank you, Father." I leaned over the bed and whispered to him, "You're among good friends, Tommy," and a teardrop rolled down his cheek.

Chaplain Sneary and I shook hands, resolving that if human

care could save that boy, he would indeed be saved. The next day, when I went in to see him, he was again conscious, though still in the Valley of the Shadow. "Tommy," I said, in a clumsy effort to appear casual, "You're doing grand. You'll be back in the old slopshoot drinking beer with the gang before you know it." "Colonel," he whispered, still terribly weak, "I'm only sorry I couldn't do more." This time a teardrop damn near rolled down my own cheek.

Then at last we went ashore and set up our command post. On February 28, 1945, I wrote to my friend Max Schuster:

> We storm the island of Iwo. This mighty fortress, only a pin point on the map, is half ours. Slowly but surely the Marines move ahead, with the flag flying from Suribachi to the rear.
>
> I am sitting on a wrecked Jap plane with Japanese characters on the tail and arabic numerals painted on its nose. Close by is a concrete pill box pierced by a 14" naval shell. In the wreckage of the gun are parts of its crew.
>
> Every inch of this ground has been contested. I can think of no more strongly fortified place under the sun. Heavy masonry and concrete have been used to strengthen even the smallest rifle pits and gun emplacements. We still look in awe at the beaches and ridges seized by Marine foot troops. I truly believe no fighting man in the history of the world could have done more.
>
> My CP is located close to the airstrip above the beach approaches to this ridge where Marines died facing a withering, murderous fire from the north, west, and south. The bravery of that assault against the high ground to the west has never been surpassed in my recollection. There was no cover, the ground was deep, shifting sands, and there is an increase in elevation of almost 200 feet from the water line to the airfield. All through the approaches to the field, deeply hidden in the sand and perfectly camouflaged were pill boxes and gun emplacements. Further up and along the ridge are concrete dugouts and block-houses, some of which to this moment are still undamaged even by our air support and heavy gun fire. To the north were the rugged cliffs and quarries enfilading the lines from that direction and to the south loomed the citadel of Suribachi, the volcano, a rocky height honeycombed with gun and mortar emplacements. Through that torrent of plunging fires, the Marines moved to the assault and took the ridge. Here again on the blazing frontier, courage was brightly written.

The battle for Iwo was far from over.

One morning, Brigadier General Walter Rogers, Corps chief of staff, sporting a shiny new gunboat star on his collar, drove by the Divisional CP, leaned out of his jeep cowboy fashion without slowing up, saluted, and called a greeting to the division commander, Major General Cliff Cates, a future Commandant of the Corps, who stood with Frank Hart, his ADC, near the field galley, drinking bitter, black coffee. The daily push was on and no news had as yet filtered back to Headquarters. We were awaiting a report from Walter Wensinger's 23rd Marines, who had been steadily pushing ahead. We were all members of the Forty-Niners, a highly select group of old-timers, whose only qualifications were a minimum age limit of 49 and combat on Iwo. Others, less charitable, called us the Metallic Brigade—gold in our teeth, silver in our hair, and lead in our asses—but for me, history was repeating itself. Twenty-seven years earlier, I had served with Lieutenant Cates and Sergeant Rogers at Belleau Wood.

The General and the assistant division commander stooped low and entered the concrete operation dugout, which two weeks before had been the Japanese signal center for the airfield defenses. I sat down to wait, took off my helmet, and let the early morning trades dry my sweaty head. But almost at once a runner popped out of the dugout looking for me.

"Sir, the General wants to see you at once," he said. I mopped my head, put on my tin hat and crawled on all fours along the low narrow passageway into the operations room of the 3 Section. General Cates minced no words.

"I want you to make up a combat battalion from among the units of your Support Group, and take it into the line before dark," he said. "You will set up on the left flank of the division and will extend to the O1 line. Call in as soon as you set up your command post."

I said, "Aye, aye sir."

That was all. Organize a brand new unit out of support battalions in the midst of a desperate battle, administer it, supply it, arm it, and before dark, lead it to a position which, although a reserve line, was forward of two other combat battalions. Every unit was far below strength. Although spirit was 100 percent strong, the flesh was 50 percent weak.

Four hundred yards from the O1 line loomed the high ground, the ruins of Minami with its perilous amphitheatre, scene of the bloodiest fighting of the engagement. Our frontline troops were almost 800 yards beyond this, but the area was under continuous enemy sniper and mortar fire. This was the high ground where Mustain had died and Chambers had earned his Medal of Honor. My job was to mop it up.

I left the dugout with General Hart and called a conference of my battalion commanders, all part of the support group. They had guessed what was coming and were already mulling over possible answers to demands on their strength. But at the first sign of a complaint, a blast from the General brought complete silence, and I began to pick their bones for my new outfit. They were going to be spread even thinner by the time I had taken what we had to have for the Fourth Provisional Battalion.

Rosters in hand, the battalion commanders sat in a circle on the shifting volcanic ash as I called out what I needed from each.

"Engineer Battalion, 1 officer, 20 men." Their CO Lieutenant Colonel Nelson Brown looked at me like a pioneer mother seeing her children taken by the redskins.

"Tank battalion, 2 officers, 25 men." Dickie Schmidt, CO, glanced at me sideways, and I could almost hear the words forming on his lips. But hell's bells, it wasn't the first time I had been called an SOB.

"Armored Amphibs, 2 officers, 10 men." The suave, cultured Howath, getting off lightly, said nothing.

"Headquarters Battalion, 5 officers, 40 men." Bert Fay, the only spread eagle colonel in my outfit, gave me the pick of his unit.

"Motor Transport Battalion, 3 officers, 10 machine gunners." Ralph Schiesswohl, the commanding officer, was a Forty-Niner and one of the few on Iwo who had fought at Belleau Wood.

"Service Battalion, 4 officers, 50 men." Jack Fondahl, the CO, looked at me in despair. A reserve officer and inspector of police in the nation's capital, he had over the years become inured to emergencies, but gutting his battalion was almost more than he could bear. And yet his only comment was, "I have 400 Marines awaiting burial." When I made a point of taking no one from his graves registration and burial details, he sent me a swell quartermaster and hornswoggled a bulldozer for me to set up my supply dump.

And so down the line I went. Rube Sharpe organized the Medical Section. Dutch Schatzel, division signal officer, assigned me an outstanding signal detail. The 4 Section armed us. When the conference broke up, Vannell, my runner, and I shuffled through the ash to our support group command post, where we found quite a crowd at the entrance to the sandbagged hut. Vannell pushed through and came back with the news.

"Those fellows want to go along with you, sir. And everyone knows more about the new job than I do," he added dryly.

At the head of the line, I noted, was McCawley, the cook, maestro of the broiled fruit aboard the *Sanborn*. There were now no signs of the galley about that Marine. "Colonel, take me along with you," he pleaded. "I qualified as an expert!" Here was someone more valuable than the ordinary rifleman, but I could not approve his request. "It's up to your battalion commander, Mac," I told him. "I can't go over his head."

When the detail from his battalion reported to my adjutant, McCawley was in command, saluting with a sly smile. "The salt of the earth," I said to myself.

The next two hours were a battle in themselves, setting up, under cover, a brand new battalion, assigning officers, and getting the noncoms acquainted with their men. Then, as my supplies began to arrive, I turned the outfit over to Lt.-Col. Treitel, my exec, and left to set up the command post, which I had selected after a map reconnaisance. It was close to airfield No. 2, with the 23rd and 24th Regimental CPs behind us on the west, and to the south, the 3rd Battalion of the 23rd in reserve. That done, Treitel came up soon after with the troops. We had made excellent time.

By 2 P.M., my wires were in, and I reported to the chief of staff. Colonel Al Pollock, now retired as a four-star general, answered the field phone.

"Fremont reporting," I said. The signal section had assigned me that word as my code name.

"Who in the hell is Fremont?" demanded the colonel. Very much deflated, I identified myself.

"Mel's Marauders," he replied. "Where are you?" I gave him the coordinates, and he added, "On the high ground."

We cleared up the area—and what a world of understatement that encompasses. On one of the early patrols, Baker Company called in, "We've had a little trouble over at Crossroads 249. We smoked out a big snipers' nest. We lost a man." "Who was it?" I asked. And I felt a dead weight sink into the pit of my stomach when he replied, "McCawley." No end to the toll of the high ground.

On the night of March 15–16, a final attempt was made by the enemy to break out of the corner into which they had been driven. They were repulsed, and the island was secured the following day. I received two messages that afternoon.

The first read, "The Commanding General of the Fifth Amphibious Corps has announced that all organized resistance on Iwo Jima has ceased." I was ordered to return with my troops and detach them back to their respective battalions.

The second message came from the U.S.S. *Sanborn* at sea: "Your sergeant has been transferred to the hospital ship. Medical officers advise he will live."

I felt good. My sergeant would live. The spell of the high ground was finally broken. His 10-minute allotment on the quarterdeck of the *Sanborn* would now grow into a long life. I sent the message by runner to Chaplain Sneary.

The previous day I had written to Schuster:

> Today we dedicate our Division cemetery, and though yesterday the flag was raised with all due ceremony, the guns are still firing and our operation orders still go out. The island has been secured except for a small strip at the northerly tip. The barbarous, uncivilized Jap is still a good soldier.
>
> We have built a bridge of graves across the Pacific and to the doorstep of Japan. On the sandspit we called Aqua Pura, between Roi and Namur on Kwajalein Atoll, we set up our first cemetery and dedicated it with all the fresh emotion of our christening in battle. Strangely enough our next was merely a section of the cemetery on the island of Oahu not too far from where Kamehameha, King Of Hawaii, destroyed the army of his rival, the King of Oahu, and forced the survivors off the high cliffs at Nuuanu Pali, to become,

in 1795, the first King of all the Hawaiian Islands. In that service cemetery we buried some Marines and Navy who were lost in an explosion and fire which destroyed several of our ships at Pearl Harbor.

On Saipan we dedicated our Memorial to a great host of comrades and again on Tinian. Today at Iwo the three religions will bless, with their prayers, this multitude of white headboards, measuring the Fourth Division's share in this battle. Even while we prepare the cemetery for the event the crash of gunfire continues, and overhead, the heavies whistle on their way from Suribachi to the north end. The dead are still coming in.

This morning at daybreak, I walked through our position. Most of the men, with the exception of the security detachments, were still asleep. The air was cool but not chilled and a pair of strange little brown and gray birds played in the first light. They ran along the sand, much in the way of our sandpiper and seemed not to mind the heavy gunfire from batteries only a short distance away. I paused for a moment to examine a little clump of scrub and in it found four distinct varieties of flowers; a baby poinsettia, a dwarfed marigold, a twisted violet and a cloud of tiny, plum-colored buds. The flowers here are all in miniature. There is an inevitable spring which no battle can restrain. . . .

Four years later, I was in the officers' club at Camp Lejeune in North Carolina. Spring had come again—in a riot of azaleas, spreading beauty and peace over the countryside. As I walked by a warrant officer sitting with his family at a table on the aisle, he stood up.

"I'd like you to meet my wife and my son, sir," he said. He turned and spoke to his boy. "Mel, meet the Colonel." I took his little paw and bowed to the lady.

"Tommy has told us all about you and the *Sanborn* and the attack on Iwo when he was a sergeant," said Mrs. Hanley. Her eyes were eloquent. "We've named our boy for you," she said.

Official war bond poster issued in 1943 to sell war bonds.

"Acting Jack" Krulewitch, drill instructor, 12th Drill Co. F. 1917.

The taking of Namur Island on Kwajalein atoll in the Marshall Islands, 1944.

Krulewitch at Seagirt, New Jersey, 1932.

Ten minutes after landing on Namur Island the Japanese ammunition cache explodes, 1944.

(top) Fighting across the cane fields of Saipan, Mariana Islands.
(below) Tanks leading the assault. (1944)

Raising the flag February 23, 1945 on Iwo Jima.

(Official U.S. Marine Corps photograph.)

Marines inching their way to the airfield on Iwo Jima, 1945.

Krulewitch, Chairman of the U.S.O. Campaign Commission, awarding the 1961 Woman of the Year to Mary Martin with Richard Rodgers adding the magic touch.

Krulewitch outnumbered by Mary Martin, Sophie Tucker and Hedda Hopper, 1966.

Krulewitch with Governor
Nelson Rockefeller at
Pocantico Hills, N.Y.

Krulewitch with Ingemar
Johansson, World Heavy-
weight Champion of 1959.

N.Y. Boxing Commissioner Krulewitch with Jack Dempsey,
Mickey Walker and Gene Tunney, 1963.

(top) Krulewitch presenting the U.S.O. Gold Medal Award to Bob Hope, 1963.
(bottom) Krulewitch presenting his Antiquarian Law book collection to Dean Michael Sovern, Columbia Law School, 1970.

★

15. Court Martial

THE RAIN HAD STOPPED, and I decided to adjourn the general court martial in which I was sitting as president. We had convened in a small tent shack, back of Division Headquarters, on Maui, not far from the head, and what with counsel, guards for the prisoner, clerks, and members of the court, we were pretty cramped for space. It was 4 o'clock, a good time to quit, although I had sat until 5 o'clock the previous day, hoping to be done with it.

I just wasn't satisfied with the case. I didn't care for the attitude of the members of the court, and I felt unpleasantly disquieted by the charge and specifications against the prisoner—cowardice in the face of the enemy. I called the judge advocate and counsel up to the bench, a muddy, badly scored table, knocked together by the maintenance platoon, and with a nod to the members of the court sitting on both sides of me, announced that we would recess until tomorrow. The prisoner, Private Lon Chapman, was removed to the brig, the clerks and assistants collected their papers together, and I walked out to my jeep.

Vannell, my driver, was asleep. He awoke with a start, rolled an apologetic eye, jumped out, and opened the door. "Division wine mess," I said, for I really needed a drink, a drink as far away as possible from the gossip of my own unit bar. Between operations, the drudgery of administrative detail in a rest area bore down heavily on a unit geared for combat.

We drove down through the ancient pineapple field in which we had set up our camp, past the deep gulch to the west, past Buster Burnett's chicken farm on the right, and then to the wine mess, close to the little town of Haiku. This beautiful club had been

130

built for us by Carl Fisher, our legal officer, now a Supreme Court justice in Erie County, New York, and Bill Anderson, the engineer major, while we were away from camp on our last expedition. At this time of day, it was particularly restful, because few, if any, of the outfit were free then to enjoy the cool shadowed *lanai* with its banks of tropical flowers and ferns, the long, brilliantly polished bar, and the spacious dining room with its neat bamboo tables and chairs. In fact, the bar had not opened yet for cocktail traffic, but as president of the mess I thought I might manage to wangle a drink.

Swords, the warrant officer in charge, had heard us drive up. By the time I had walked around to his shack in the rear of the bar, he had pulled a shirt over his head and rubbed the sleep out of his eyes. He could see I was in no mood for conversation, and after a generous shot of Scotch, for which I laid down the regular price, 20 cents, on the bar, I waved him good-bye and went to look for Vannell in the parking lot. He was not asleep this time. Hanging over the side of our jeep were two attractive Filipino girls, gay and animated as a pair of humming birds, who vanished at my approach.

I told Vannell I was going for a walk. He was to go back to camp, get his chow, and meet me back at the wine mess at 6 o'clock. He knew I'd miss chow at the officers' mess and I could almost see him disapprove, but he knew something was up and did as he was told without a word.

I wanted to walk this case out of my system. There were seven members of the court, and five of us would decide our verdict. Instinct told me that three of them would vote for the death penalty and that two were wavering and might vote with the others. With far more courtroom experience than any of them, I could see how the case was going and I wanted to find a way to save that boy's life if I could. He was an inarticulate hillbilly from Kentucky, and I had never found a white feather on any of his sort. After 20 years at the bar, and having sat in judgment in many cases, I was deeply convinced that this was no case for the death penalty, nor for life imprisonment.

The boy was one of the crew of an amphibious tractor bringing in troops to storm the beach at Iwo Jima. He had dropped his pack overboard as the vehicle beached and gone after it. Heavy casualties had been sustained in the amphibs, and half the crew of that tractor had been lost in the operation. Three days later he had turned himself in and been brought back to Maui for trial.

Lieutenant Charles McCane, who had been assigned to defend him, was no legal firebrand. Courteous and gentlemanly in manner, he had put in little or no defense other than character testimony, including the fact that the accused had been awarded a Silver Star for gallantry on Saipan. This was more like evidence in mitigation than evidence in defense, but I had allowed it.

The accused was a total stranger to me, but I had once known a Marine named Newhouse who had been charged with a similar offense and held for trial. When we combat-loaded for Saipan, the General decided to take all the prisoners along and show them that life wasn't one continual round of pleasure in the brig. Newhouse was turned over to me and from the moment he came aboard my ship, I had trouble. It got so that every morning, after receiving the reports of the unit commanders, I would ask about him, particularly if I hadn't had a complaint for a day. I was quite sure that when we landed, I would have to put him in irons, lug him ashore, and detail a fighting Marine to guard him during the battle.

As it turned out, I took him ashore without the irons and assigned him to a sergeant in charge of a work detail for Division Headquarters. But as a result of all this attention, Newhouse had begun to think of himself as something special, and I found him under foot all day long. On D-plus-1, our CP was shelled and I made arrangements to throw out a scout net about 1000 yards in front—just in case. We set up the picket line, and then the real heavy stuff came over, with a lot of close-in mortar fire. Everybody had gone underground except Newhouse, who had followed me around as I scouted the area, and I'm frank to say I welcomed him. He was good company, and fearless when the chips were down.

He was one of the three men I took with me when General Rogers ordered a reconnaissance of map square 42A as a possible new location for Division Headquarters on Saipan. And he was there when the piece of mortar shell hit my map case, tore through the heavy webbing and inside canvas partitions, and finally came to rest against the metal tube of an anti-chap grease lipstick—anti-chap, stock No. 29-L-300. (Many a time we had laughed at these white lipsticks. I had even asked Commander Reuben L. Sharpe, of the Navy Medical Corps, our senior line doctor, when he planned to issue the rest of the compact, but I've been a tropical lipstick fan ever since.) General Harry Schmidt, the CG, marked my fitness report "courageous and conscientious" largely because of what happened on that patrol, and since Newhouse was right along with me and had thus earned the same commendation, I decided to give him a letter to take the curse off his sentence when he came up for trial. It sprung him, and he was with me on Iwo.

Thinking about this and about Private Chapman, I suddenly realized it was getting late. A mongoose skipped across the road in front of me, a little furry animal with sharp eyes, a small weasel-like head, and a long, bushy tail. This was Rikki-Tikki-Tavi, immortalized by Kipling as the greatest of all fighters—a killer who would never quit. This little fellow loves to play, but like all the Newhouses, when the chips are down, he finds himself.

I turned back towards the club. I would go over my notes of the evidence and see what I could do. In my mind's eye, I was back in my law office analysing the evidence, the character of the witnesses, the plans for the next day's trial, the points of law that had come up, and preparing my answers to them—I was back, indeed, to everything I had left years before on becoming active again in the Corps.

Those who sit on a court martial are forbidden by law to originate evidence. For the court to do so, says the book, "lays it open to animadversion and must be scrupulously avoided." But I was also mindful of a section of *Naval Courts and Boards* which permits us, "with a view to a more thorough investigation of the case," to hear certain evidence not introduced by either party, to adjourn for a reasonable time, and to require the judge advocate, who is the military prosecuting attorney, to procure such evidence.

I wanted to know what the accused had been doing after he had jumped from the amphib and what he had done in the three days before he surrendered himself to the naval authorities. Grim and tight-lipped, the accused had persisted in his refusal to state where he'd been during the three days. All the defense, or prosecution, could get out of him was that he had "stayed around till the whole comp'ny was ashore," and then he had joined it.

Vannell was waiting for me at the division mess and I climbed aboard. I felt good again. Even without further evidence, I knew that in our deliberations, after the court had been cleared and we were preparing to vote, I could present a persuasive argument against the death penalty or a life sentence. There would be a fight, but in the end I was pretty sure they'd go along. The court would find Chapman guilty and sentence him to a term at hard labor in a naval prison, but justice would be served and I'd have no sleepless nights over a doubtful death sentence.

"We'll go up to Kokomo for some rum and a steak," I told Vannell. He smiled broadly, sensing my change of mood. We drove up the hill, through the camp, past the old *haole* burying ground, which the natives used to call the "English-speaking cemetery," and through the village to the restaurant. Nodding to friends at the tables, I moved to the bar, where Kung, the Chinese-Hawaiian boy, was waiting for me with a broad grin, and Commander Miller, an old Chinaphile, was shaking the box.

"Kameroon for the drinks?" he asked.

"Big and little," I answered, "start rolling."

"A large rum," I ordered, as Miller rolled a little Kameroon. "And a steak for me."

"I know," Kung said. "Big dish tonight."

Next morning, I entered the shack, reconvened the court, and had the record of proceedings of the previous day read and approved. As the defense was about to rest I spoke for the court:

> Pursuant to Section 252 of *Naval Courts and Boards,* the court desires to hear evidence not introduced by either party, with a view to a more thorough investigation of the case, with regard to the acts of the accused during the three days before he surrendered himself to naval authority. The judge advocate is called upon to procure such evidence, if practicable.

The court then adjourned until the following afternoon, and at my nod, the judge advocate came to the bench.

"Get going on those three days," I said. "Find out from his

CO what he has on it, and talk to the accused with him. Find out who was on the beach in the vicinity of where the amphib landed, what outfit was holding the line, and what happened on the beach. Get me all the dope and put it in legal form."

Rudi Jacobsen, the judge advocate, saluted, about-faced, and marched off. He was a tall, serious, slow-moving westerner, a patient, middle-of-the-road guy, who had been admitted to the bar in his home state, and after joining the Corps, had been shanghaied into the legal office. Surprised by the court's intervention, he now found his open-and-shut case tossed back into his lap, and worse still, with a great deal of work to do.

Next morning there were a dozen unemployed Marines hanging around the shack. As the door opened, they moved into court and sat on the benches against the walls. Lieutenant McCane began the proceedings. "If the court pleases, I'd like to call the accused."

Private Chapman was duly sworn as a witness in his own behalf, after various sections of *Naval Courts and Boards* had been fully explained to him in protection of his rights. His only comment was, "Ah didn't want to say nuthin' but Mr. McCane, he says for me to do hit, so ah'm here."

Counsel began to question him. "What did you do when your amphibious tractor hit the beach?"

"Ah jumped down an' picked up ma pack fum the sand."

"What did you see on the beach?"

"They wuz afirin' plenty, thar. Ah didn't purtically cyar fo' it but ah wasn't afeered, like the paper says. Ah didn't run away, but ah will say that Sergeant Porter did say for me to come back to the 'phib'. Ah didn't go back and purty soon it shoved off. But ah wuz way up the hill then."

"What hill was that?" the Lieutenant asked.

"That wuz the big hill," Chapman answered. "That wuz a fort in the middle of the hill lookin' out awn the airfield and Lieutenant Chapman was fightin' with the others right in front of it."

At the name of Lieutenant Marion Chapman, all in the courtroom felt a common bond of pride. Almost single-handedly, that officer had taken one of the vital pill-boxes on the beach side of the slope up to the airfield. His name was a benediction in our outfit.

"Did you know Lieutenant Chapman?" McCane continued. "Yes," replied the accused. "He come fum ma part o' the country."

"What did you do when you saw him up on the hill?"

"Ah run up to side him."

To all who had been on Iwo, the picture was a vivid canvas— a searing torrent of fire showering every inch of the hillside to the airfield, churning up the volcanic ash and every living thing in its path since H-Hour. This boy had seen Lieutenant Chapman heavily engaged in the desperate fight for the airfield and through that curtain of blazing hell had "run up to side him." There was a lump in my throat as I thought of what we had almost done to that boy.

"What happened then?" Counsel continued.

The accused shrugged. "Ah said to the Lieutenant, here ah am, and ah started firin'. We kept awn untel he says, 'Hol' up. Ah'm goin' in there, and if it's OK, we'll all go in.' He come out right away and says for us to come in. It was real nice and quiet inside all concrete and steel, nothing but a few dead Japs. The firin' was heavy outside but it shor wuz fine inside."

"What did you do after that?"

"Stayed along until we went up on the airfield that evenin'. More troops came up the next two days. Ah stayed with him all the time until he was wounded." The boy gulped and faltered. "They tuk him away."

"What did you do after that?"

"Ah come down and found my platoon. They tol' me ah wuz in trouble, and ah guess ah am. Marion tol' me the same thing befo' they tuk him away."

We were all thinking of that great Marine hero and fighter, who had contributed so much to the seizure of the airfield and to the success of the operation. Posthumously decorated, his name added luster to the roster of Marine immortals.

Counsel turned the witness over for cross-examination but the judge advocate had no desire to question him.

"I should like to call Captain Thomas Barry, Medical Corps, United States Navy," said Lieutenant McCane.

Duly sworn in as a witness for the accused, Captain Barry agreed that he knew Lieutenant Marion Chapman.

"Dr. Barry, did you ever have a conversation with him?" asked McCane. "And if so, will you state the substance of it?"

"I attended Lieutenant Chapman when he was brought to the first aid station on Iwo Jima," the doctor replied. "He had been shot through the lungs and the spine and we did what we could for him. He could not talk when he was brought in, but before he died he was able to say a few words."

"What did he say to you about the fight, if anything?"

"He tried to give me a message but up until last night I didn't understand it. He said something about taking care of Lon—he said, 'He was with me all the way up the hill.' "

The accused leaned forward across the table and buried his face in his arms. His shoulders shook with deep, heavy sobs—the first sign of emotion he had shown.

"Did you know who the party was to whom the Lieutenant referred as Lon?" McCane asked the doctor.

"No," he answered, "not until last night. I was going over the Lieutenant's medical record book and was making the final closing"—he cleared his throat—"final closing entries, when I came across the name of his next of kin."

"And who was that?"

"His brother," said the doctor. "Private Lon Chapman, the accused."

And so the court was cleared to deliberate on the boy who had disobeyed orders and left the comparative security of the tractor for an assault through a curtain of fire up the slopes of Iwo Jima to stand at his brother's side in that fight—a boy who, even on trial for his life before a general court martial, could not bring himself to mention his brother's name lest it be tainted by his own arrest.

Our deliberations did not take long. The prisoner was brought before us with his counsel and I spoke for the court, acquitting him of all charges and specifications.

I was grim and unsmiling as I walked to the door. We had damn near blown the case. Corporal Newhouse, clerk of the court martial, shined, shaved, and in clean khaki, snapped to attention as I passed. Saluting, he broke into a smile from ear to ear. And did I notice a wink?

I shrugged it off, returned his salute, and left.

★

16. *Dewey or Do We Not*

BACK FROM THE WAR at the end of 1945, I drove Helen and the kids to New York City, where eventually we found an apartment in Gramercy Park, settled the children in school, and set about picking up the threads of civilian life. For me, that meant politics and law. Accordingly, I enrolled in the Tenth, later called the First, District Republican Club, and accepted an invitation to join the firm of Baker, Obermeier & Rosner as a paying guest— I paid rent, used their legal and secretarial staff, and split my fees.

Personal friends on the bench got me away to a good start, passing on references, receiverships, and trusteeships. Supreme Court Justice William C. Hecht, Jr., son of the celebrated Republican leader and federal marshal, for instance, appointed me a trustee of one of the New York Title Mortgage issues. Considering that my law practice had been in cold storage for almost five years of soldiering, we were doing all right.

My new firm was the successor to Baker & Obermeier. Baker, a good lawyer and head of The Jewish Memorial Hospital in Brooklyn, had passed from the scene and the action in the outfit lay between Rosner and Leonard J. Obermeier, whom I had first met back in the early days of the Roaring Twenties when he was chairman of the County Republican Law Committee and I was one of its members. Obermeier in those days had been a gifted orator, capable of crushing all opposition into stunned silence by the violence, volume, and fluent obscenity he would occasionally unleash in the Republican clubhouse and at the office. Obermeier was German and proud of it. He delighted in being called a squarehead because he could then balance a law book on the flat surface of his bald head, and bellow, "Try to do this,

138

you hunkie." Many a courteous gentleman of the old school who dared to oppose Leonard, in public *or* private, had been reduced to nerveless paralysis by his verbal onslaught.

Politically, the Republicans were in good shape in New York. Governor Tom Dewey had been in the driver's seat at Albany for four years and was a seasoned campaigner. In 1946, however, there appeared on the Republican horizon for the first time a possible contender for leadership in the shape of "Wild Bill" Donovan, former chief of the wartime O.S.S. Already engaged in the long haul to the presidential race in 1948, Dewey was a shoo-in for re-election; but a new and important Republican figure on the local scene, particularly someone from upstate New York, who might be considered for the United States Senate, was a complication he could do without. Donovan had served gloriously in two wars, and was now the head of a great Wall Street law firm.

Recognizing the danger for 1948, Dewey got busy. There was no time to lose, because important party members had already thrown their support to Bill Donovan—George Sibley, long a confidant of Dewey, a successful businessman, and a long-time leader in New York City politics; John S. McCloy, former Assistant Secretary of the Navy and a prominent figure in world politics and banking; and Archie Dawson, a close personal friend of Dewey and one of his campaign managers in 1942.

Alarmed by this, King Dewey called for his Herbert Brownell, later Attorney General of the United States, and chairman of the Republican National Committee; he called for his Al Chapman, his gubernatorial campaign manager and chairman of the State Tax Commission; and he called for his Tom Curran, New York Secretary of State and chairman of the Republican County Committee of New York. These were King Dewey's fiddlers three, and all were personal friends of mine.

Tom Curran, a veteran himself of World War I, was my district leader in the old Tenth. Herb Brownell, the power behind the throne in the Gramercy Park district, which had once spawned a President in the person of district leader Chester A. Arthur, was a neighbor whom I had gotten to know well through our respective broods of children, all of whom went to Friends Seminary, the Quaker School on Rutherford Place. And Al Chapman, the forceful yet courteous director of the Dewey campaigns, I had known for years.

Called into executive session at the Hotel Roosevelt to stop the Donovan boom from spreading, these fiddlers three, as I later learned, suggested Krulewitch to start the ball rolling with a rival candidate for the Senate, one Hugh A. Drum, Lieutenant General, U.S.A., Retired. With a distinguished military background in the regulars, Drum had been appointed by Dewey as commander of the New York National Guard and had succeeded to the late Al Smith's job in the management of the Empire State Building.

On Sunday, August 25th, I was up at Rolling Acres, my sister's place near Danbury, when I was called to the phone, "It's for you, Mel," Helen said. "The Governor wants to talk to you."

I was a bit skeptical about this, but it was indeed Tom Dewey on the line. "Hi, Mel," he began. "I'd like to talk to you about the campaign." I'd known Tom from the days when he'd run for district attorney. As his campaign chairman in the Thirteenth Assembly District, I'd helped him carry the district.

Next morning I met him at the Roosevelt with Al Chapman. The first thing he wanted to know was if I knew Drum. When I answered, "Yes," Dewey smiled. "That's at least something," he said, and then asked Al to outline the plan. I was to form a committee of veterans to support Drum for the Republican nomination for United States Senator, which would be acted upon at the Republican State Convention at Saratoga Springs on Tuesday, September 3rd. No mention was made of Donovan.

I went back to the office and got to work. Having met General Drum just once at a veterans' reception at the Waldorf, I knew little about him other than his public record. A telephone call to the Republican State Committee put that right, producing a fat folder of biographical and other material. Then I called up pals of mine in Brooklyn, the Bronx, and Queens, made them vice chairmen of my committee and asked them to get me the names of fellow-travelers who would serve on a committee for Drum. By Monday night, August 26th, I not only had all the names I needed but was besieged with calls from upstate veterans volunteering their services. By then, I had drafted a news release, and as cautioned by Dewey, checked it with Herb Brownell. It went out on the morning of the 27th, making headlines that night and for days afterward.

FROM: Office of   (Release for P. M. Papers
Melvin L. Krulewitch   Tuesday, August 27th, 1946)
285 Madison Avenue, NYC

Declaring that Lieut. General Hugh A. Drum, U.S.A., (retired) "is the outstanding man to be found in this State for the Republican nomination for United States Senate," and that he "will bring to the Senate a far-reaching background in national and international affairs," Col. Melvin L. Krulewitch, Marine veteran of both World Wars, announced today (Tues.) organization of a Veterans' Committee to urge the drafting of General Drum for the United States Senate nomination at the Republican Convention in Saratoga Springs, on September 3rd and 4th next.

Col. Krulewitch, who made the announcement of the formation of the Veterans' Committee for General Drum from his offices at 285 Madison Avenue, said that "while organization of the Veterans' Committee for the General was confined to New York County at the moment, it will be extended to the five counties of the Greater City, and upstate as well.

In his announcement, Col. Krulewitch said, in part: "Republican veterans of this State are in favor of drafting General Hugh A. Drum for their next United States Senator.

"General Drum has lived, not for days or weeks, but years of his life in many parts of the world. China, the Philippines, Hawaii, England, France, Germany, the Mediterranean and all of the Far East are well-known to him. As a result, he is intimately familiar with the affairs of these countries and the problems involved in our relationships with them— which must be translated into terms of treaties, world peace, and world trade."

After outlining Drum's career, the statement went on:

The Veterans for General Drum Committee is aware that the name of General William J. Donovan has been advanced as Republican candidate for United States Senator. Our Veterans' Committee is of the opinion that General Donovan is a fine gentleman, a gallant soldier and an honest, most reputable member of the Bar. The Committee believes, however, General Donovan's talents appear to be more responsive to the field of corporation law than to politics.

In the days that followed, we had a friendly press under such headlines as:

VETS FOR DRUM   **DRUM FOR SENATOR**
UNITS GROWING   **MOVEMENT GAINING**

DRUM BACKERS   **DRUM DRIVE FOR SENATE**
FLY TO ALBANY   **WINS SUPPORT**

VETS IN BRONX
BACK DRUM

Binghamton, Buffalo, Oneida, Ithaca, Newburgh, Troy, and Yonkers, all gave our committee a big spread while Dewey kept up the pretence of being an innocent bystander. We received droves of volunteers, and promises of financial aid when necessary. The Governor was reported to be in New York on purely "private business," and Paul E. Lockwood, the Governor's secretary, insisted that "Mr. Dewey was not taking a personal hand in the Senate battle."

How personal could you get? Only in the *New York Post,* a voice crying in the wilderness, was there a Doubting Thomas.

Bob Spivack wrote:

OUST DONOVAN COMMAND ISSUED TO DEWEY AIDS

Gov. Dewey's political lieutenants, ranging from ex-GOP National Chairman Brownell and Nassau County Boss Sprague to the lowliest district captains, were under strict orders today to knock Maj. Gen. Donovan out of the U. S. Senate race before the Republican State Convention opens Tuesday.

The penalty for any leader who steps out of line was to be the immediate withdrawal of all State patronage.

While his associates in the 62 counties were telegraphing and phoning delegates, Dewey himself professed to be a mere sidelines observer and made no comment on the heated Senate fight.

The *Buffalo News* then came out with a story about the big "b'ys," as Obermeier used to call the backroom powers, looking about in a case of a possible stalemate. Speaker of the Assembly Irving M. Ives was mentioned as a compromise candidate, as was my present law-office associate, Hon. Nathaniel L. Goldstein, then the Attorney General of the State. Able, sincere, and hardworking, Nat was always the one watching the help and the bank balance in every outfit he joined.

Despite the secrecy of the Dewey plan, the true story got around. Pulitzer Prize winner Westbrook Pegler, no shrinking daisy in the realm of the controversial, had the picture exactly right when he wrote:

> The Governor is about as sure a thing for re-election as we ever find in politics and he figures that if he can elect a Senator who would owe everything to him it would be folly to let the convention nominate Donovan, who then would stand alone and not in Dewey's shadow. Nobody ever heard of Drum in politics until a few days ago.
>
> This opposition to Donovan is all Dewey's doing and it demonstrates a personal characteristic that Tom's friends as well as his opponents have noted. He is unwilling to risk the presence on the ticket of a big man.
>
> Gov. Dewey's record as Governor has been so fine and his exploitation of that record so skillful that, as I say, he can't fail to be re-elected unless he drops dead. But, as to the Presidential nomination in 1948, he has done himself harm rather than good because he indicates that he would place personal subservience and loyalty above ability and independence in order to maintain himself on an eminence.

Then suddenly it was all over. Except for the one occasion I had mentioned to the Governor, I had never met General Drum, and when John Mooney of the Gannett News Service asked me about it, I told him so. He reported, "Colonel Krulewitch said he hadn't talked with General Drum, didn't know whether he would accept, and has been trying to locate Drum, who is vacationing in the Canadian wilds."

Perhaps because of this, Drum flattened out like a pancake and withdrew from the race without a warning. He announced that he had never aspired to political office and had not sought, and was not seeking, this or any other nomination. "Veterans for Drum" folded its tents and silently proceeded to Saratoga the following Tuesday, September 3rd, where Irving Ives was nominated as Republican candidate for the United States Senate, a race he won that November. Again Dewey had triumphed, and no future competitor loomed on the political horizon. The road was cleared to 1948 and the close one with Harry Truman.

But for me that was not quite the end of the story. It had been made known to Dewey by Tom Curran that Krulewitch would accept appointment to the Public Service Commission, where a vacancy existed. This job required knowledge of a very specialized branch of law, involving the regulation of the rates and services of the public utilities operating in the state of New York. I was experienced in this area, having been special counsel to the New York Commission, consultant to the New Jersey Commission, and counsel to the Westchester County Board of Supervisors in utility matters. Tom had also mentioned to Dewey, certain political matters in which I had been helpful as counsel to the Republican County Committee, as a party worker in a successful campaign for district attorney, and so on. A Commissioner of the Public Service Commission had real power, a real opportunity to serve the public, and Tom Curran was optimistic. He had explained this to Paul Lockwood, who was well disposed toward my appointment and was pushing it.

The following morning, I received a telegram from Lockwood asking me to meet the Governor at the Roosevelt Hotel:

Governor Dewey will be happy to have you call on him at his apartment 1527 Hotel Roosevelt, New York City, on Thursday, January 13th, at 4:30 P.M. Will you kindly confirm to me at The Roosevelt by wire or telephone MUrray Hill 4-6623. Thanks and regards—

Paul E. Lockwood

Obermeier, whose experience in the political arena went back to the early 1900s, suggested a formal approach and that I should address Dewey as "your excellency." He even asked me if I had a cutaway to wear.

When I met Paul Lockwood in the foyer of the Governor's offices, he said—promisingly, I thought—"The Governor has something very nice to say to you. I'll take you right in."

This was it. I walked into the large office and behind the desk was a smiling Tom Dewey. We shook hands and the Governor was most cordial. "Mel," he said, "you've been a great soldier and patriot and I am going to confer upon you the State's highest decoration for bravery." The floor swayed under me. My guts turned to water at this perfidy. Was this the payoff? Dewey continued, "Would you please meet me at the Plaza at 12:30?"

It was then 12 noon. Bewildered, I took a cab to the Plaza Hotel and joined Senator Herbert Lehman, formerly Governor, in the Baroque Suite. When Dewey arrived, Lockwood lined the two of us up in front of the Governor, who read some words from a paper and pinned on the bosom of the weeping Senator Lehman the Silver Cross posthumously awarded to his son killed in the service. Then he pinned the same order on me. I coldly shook hands with him, embraced Lehman, and repaired to that ancient bar behind the Appellate Division which was once palindromically known as "Reviver" and was frequented by Chester A. Arthur before and after, though not during, his residence in the White House.

The following Monday morning, Governor Thomas E. Dewey announced the appointment of Paul Lockwood as a Public Service Commissioner.

★

17. The Unconquered

THIS IS A STORY of Palestine, the land of Israel, with its shining cities of Jerusalem, Haifa, and Tel Aviv; its ancient settlements of Bethlehem, Hebron, and Jericho; its swift-flowing, muddy Jordan and its somber Dead Sea; its green valleys and lakes of Galilee; its hosts of settlements in the good lands and in the desert.

This is a story of a road to Jerusalem winding its tortuous way from the teeming cities of Tel Aviv and Jaffa on the sparkling coast, through the rich flatlands of olive and orange groves, to the yawning mouth of the Bab-el-Wad, inviting the unwary into the foothills beneath the mountain passes leading to the Holy City. Over all looms the natural fortress of Mount Castel (Quastal), which dominates the road. For centuries, it has been said that "he who takes Castel sleeps in Jerusalem," and the grim, unyielding mountain that has heard the tread of every army of the earth still stands keeper of the road. Throughout history, standing as the guardian of the Holy City, Mount Castel has held the keys to the kingdom.

Arab and Jew, Christian and infidel, Mongol and Turk—each has felt the call of the land, and each has tarried for his appointed time and gone his way, or remained to sleep forever in the watered vineyards or in the barren wastes of ancient glories. Here for thousands of years Arab and Jew have lived together as brothers of the soil with no distress save where the greedy or the wicked have sought to shake the loyalty of each to the other.

There were Jewish settlements for centuries in Egypt, even after the Exodus. In the Arabic-speaking areas of West Asia, from Baghdad to Alexandretta to the Nile, despite constant wars and revolutions, two great creeds evolved from the basic monotheism

146

of the Jew. But in the past 200 years, the Jew brought something new into this milieu—an element lacking in the Arab world. He brought with him the rub-off of European cultures, acquired during his wanderings over the face of the earth, and this was the line of difference. The Jew had become a world product.

The Arab historically settled his differences by the sword. The battle cry, "The Koran or the sword," after the Hegira, was the call to arms for the swarming hordes of "true believers," through the Near East, North Africa, and Europe. The choice was between the sword or the word, and to this day the insignia of Pax Arabia can be seen in the green and white national flag of Saudi Arabia, which carries both a sword and an excerpt from the Koran: "There is no god but God, and Mohammed is his prophet."

We sat in Colonel Harry Henshel's vice-presidential office in the magnificent Radio City suite of the Bulova Watch Company. A powerhouse in the New York community, he rated a plush magnificence of polished walnut—shiny black onyx desk and table furnishings, high-piled, fawn-colored rugs, hard seated, straight-backed chairs, thank God, and shiny leather chaises for afternoon siestas. The walls were lined with community and military awards and framed acknowledgments to him as the fall-guy guest of honor for innumerable fund-raising projects.

A member of the Bulova family, Harry had served under General of the Army Omar N. Bradley in the European theatre and had invited him upon his retirement from active military service in 1953 to take a job with the firm as research and development chairman. The General had accepted and five years later had become chairman of the board of the parent organization. Shortly after Omar's return to the States as a General of the Army, Harry had introduced me to him in Washington. Never backward in taking a crack at the Marines, à la Truman (and I hasten to add, with as little success as that President), Harry had slyly remarked to Brad, "Our war in Europe didn't need the Marines." Rising to the bait, I told him, "You had all you needed for that show— a Marine lieutenant and a platoon. The others were busy." This did not go over big with the General.

But our meeting that day in February, 1948, was with Teddy Kollek, a brilliant young Austrian operating out of 14 East 60th

Street, the Jewish underground headquarters adjoining the Copacabana and the Harmonie Club, and across the street from J. P. Morgan and Spruille Braden's Metropolitan Club. From that completely visible hideaway, he was busily organizing the flow of men and arms into Palestine. Now the versatile, progressive mayor of Jerusalem, Teddy must certainly have read his Alice. We spoke of shoes (provided by the U.J.A.), and ships (LSTs, postwar surplus), and sealing wax (sealed documents in diplomatic pouches carried by international couriers), of cabbages (developments in the food-raising *kibbutzim*) and kings (Teddy was always a brilliant king-maker).

With his German accent and faultless grammar, he filled in the Palestine picture with machine-gun speed and clarity. "We've got 700,000 lives there and we're up against a situation that will worsen. The British are slated to pull out and leave the country in a few weeks. Around us are thirty million enemies and we stand like the English in 1941. We need your help."

This tow-headed, Aryan-looking, fast-talking Jew, blue-eyed and smiling, was one of that eternally unconquerable breed, cast out of many countries and consumed by fire, only to rise and rise again, phoenixlike, from its own ashes and bare bones. He described the Haganah, the home-defense militia organized with a cadre of some 6000 former British officers and noncoms, operating both aboveground and underground and winked at by the British. To the two terrorist organizations known as the IZL and the Stern Gang, he referred only in terms of disavowal and disgust.

As an officer of the U.S.A. Armed Forces, a colonel on ready reserve of the Marines, with a division staff command, I decided I would go to Washington and request limited military approval "for travel outside the continental limits." I was anxious to see the situation at firsthand, and Harry agreed to go with me if I obtained permission.

Cliff Cates, my lifetime comrade-in-arms from Belleau Wood to Iwo Jima, was Commandant of the Corps then and well-disposed to my request. The situation was tense in Palestine—Headquarters was watchful and waiting. Major General M. C. "Jack" Horner, a pal in many a landing, had G-2'd the picture at HQ and spoke knowledgeably of the Yarkon, the Jordan, Galilee, and the Bab-el-Wad. In the end I agreed to go commercial, at my own expense, without pay or allowances, and with no involvement of the U.S. I was to contact our consul general in Jerusalem and our military attaché there and keep in touch.

Helen and I were not Zionists. I had finished four long years away from home; we were dug in at Gramercy Park; the children were at Friends Seminary around the corner and Helen was happy as a clam. We were at peace. But when we spoke of the Near East on my return from Washington, her radar sensed a new development.

"When do you leave?" she asked suddenly.

"In a week," I replied. "I spoke to Cliff Cates and he says OK as long as we don't involve the U. S."

"Go with God," said my darling.

On March 31, 1948, Harry Henshel and I flew to Palestine in an Air France four-motored DC4, a rattling good job, and after an eight-hour wait at Orly, in Paris, landed at Lydda at 2:30 A.M. —the last plane in before the field closed down. With Scots in full regalia guarding the airport, we rubbed elbows in the customs house with groups of hooded Arabs—the men shrouded in jellabas and burnooses and wearing the *kaffiah,* the women veiled—and with Yemenite Jews in yellow and black striped robes and twisted turbans, their pitch-black screw curls over each ear, talking earnestly to the Scots, who blankly saw no evil, heard no evil, and spoke no evil. On the surface it was like a travel poster—except for the wanted notices on the customs house walls, showing pictures of British deserters and announcing procedures for their capture and return.

Harry and I went through customs and stepped outside to the tarmac bordering the airfield. In the predawn twilight the shadowy masses to the east vaguely outlined the long ridge between Ramallah and Hebron, with the heights of Jerusalem between.

"Harry," I said, "we are on the holy soil of Palestine. How about asking for a blessing?"

"You know about that," he answered. "I don't know the words. Go ahead."

So I recited the ancient blessing in classical Hebrew and then translated it into English for Harry:

> Blessed art thou, O Lord our God, King of the
> Universe, who has kept us in life and has preserved
> us and enabled us to reach this moment.

"That's fine," said Harry. "The last time I said a Hebrew word, I found myself married."[1]

We waited there for the Haganah to contact us as arranged, and eventually a small single-motored Cub landed in the reeds on the edge of the airfield. We helped the Jewish pilot, an ex-RAF flyer, pull the tail out of the brush, then crawled into the fuselage and stretched out flat in the space behind the pilot's seat. Flying at 1500 feet on the 20-kilometer hop to Tel Aviv, we passed over a green tropical landscape split by ragged outcrops of brown-white stone, with occasional strings of camels lazing and bobbing along. Swooping over valleys and villages, we landed on an airstrip at the beach close by the Gat Rimon Hotel, where we were to stay. The hotel faced the Jaffa Road, and its windows and sashes on the south side were pockmarked and scarred by sniper fire from that direction.

Tel Aviv was a happy city, full of bright, gay, laughing crowds, young men and women enjoying themselves on the beach, bars going full tilt, hibiscus and oleander flowering everywhere, juke boxes blaring, soft drinks and ices being served under umbrellas. Where was the war? It reminded me rather of Havana. Harry said the Bronx, and there was indeed a New York feeling about it.

That night, right across the way, the Café Maxim, a gambling joint, was going full tilt. In a hot *chemin-de-fer* game, the crowd around the table, some wearing yarmulkes, shouted the bets in Hebrew, although the big one was always in Monte Carlo language— *Banco*. Next door was the Café Pilz, a night club with blond, Persian-lamb coiffured Menahem, the M.C. of the cabaret—the lion, or should I say, lioness of the evening. All very normal and American.

Instead of joining the festivities, we were briefed by Shlomo

---

[1] It is the custom in a Jewish religious marriage for the groom to recite in Hebrew, the covenant when he places the ring on the bride's finger, "Behold thou art consecrated unto me by this ring according to the law of Moses and Israel." The bride does not answer.

Schmeir, a Haganah commander, and Moshe Dayan. Right at
the outset, I told these Jewish leaders that all the military information obtained would go back to Washington; we had no intention
of sailing under false colors. They understood this and respected
our position. With the announced abandonment of the mandate by
Great Britain, opinion was divided over the future of Israel. Many
people of the highest standing in the Palestine Jewish community
were against independence; some favored dual nationality with
the Arabs, others a commonwealth status as part of Great Britain
or even France.

These differing points of view were exemplified by the two great
Jewish women of the era: Golda Meir and Henrietta Szold. Golda,
the granite–faced politician and leader of her people, was for
complete independence—then as now—and brushed off any
attempt to dilute this position. She was determined to hold the line
and settle for nothing short of peace with security, no matter what
or how long it took. Less dogmatically certain of the wisdom of
this was Henrietta, the beautiful, sensitive, classically educated
American who created Hadassah, the nonsectarian medical and
nursing service in Israel, and was the matriarch of Youth Aliyah,
which brought in and trained a new generation of young colonists.
Like Dr. Judah Magnes, President of the Hebrew University, and
many others, she had not felt the moment was ripe for complete
independence.

But under their inspired leaders, the younger survivors of the
European charnel houses, the men and women who had been
degraded and reviled and whose families had been murdered and
tortured, yearned for a home rather than another temporary
peace. They pushed the movement, in torrents of emotion, toward
the objective of a Jewish homeland, the land of Israel—*Eretz
avowtaynu,* "the land of our fathers." The Jewish communities of
America, the British Commonwealth, Europe, and elsewhere
generally endorsed this dream, and worked for it, too—with
money, arms, and political support.

All this came into focus in the person of David Ben Gurion,
the leader of the Jewish state. There were other world-
famous Jews closely identified with Israel, like Chaim Weizmann,
its first President, but Ben Gurion was the head of the Jewish

Agency, which ran the country. Upon that broad head, with its bushy clumps of white hair, fell the responsibility for the country, its government, and its war.

A meeting with him had been arranged for us. The missus answered the door, shrieked that she wasn't dressed, clutched her robe around her, and invited us in. Harry, Shlomo Shmeir, Moshe Dayan, and I walked through to his office, which was lined with books to the ceiling and filled with the fragrance of orange blossoms.

Small and animated, he greeted us: *"Sholom, Sholom. . . ."* We spoke of the States and the recent World War. He blamed the British for their favoritism to the Arabs, and discussed his military situation. I was clear on it after my talks at Marine Corps Headquarters in Washington and surprised him by mentioning places of strategic importance.

"You've been here before," he said. "When were you here last?"

"I haven't been here for 2000 years," I answered, poker-faced.

He roared and opened up about some of his problems. "Most of us here speak Hebrew, Arabic, and English, and some even more. The Arabs know English and some Hebrew and so we have trouble with communications. How did you do it in the Pacific?"

"We used talkers," I said. "Navajos in pairs—one at the front and his partner at headquarters. Nobody could wiretap that language."

"A wonderful idea," he said, slapping his thigh. "We'll use Circassians. Nobody can understand them, sometimes not even themselves."

He spoke to us of his hopes and dreams in terms reminiscent of Winston Churchill. "We will go on. We will go ahead. We will fight."

That was the only meeting we had with Ben Gurion, but we were to spend a great deal of time with Moshe Dayan, now Israeli Secretary of Defense.

I reported to my Headquarters as follows:

The first phase of the war in Palestine opened with a general Arab guerilla offensive after the 29 November 1947

United Nations decision, to partition the country and set up separate Jewish and Arab states. Jewish settlements and outposts throughout the country were attacked by irregular bands, augmented by trained soldiers—Arab infiltrees from Iraq, Syria, Transjordan, a sprinkling of Nazi prisoners of war, Yugoslav Moslems, and British police and army deserters. Haganah's policy seems to have been to reorganize itself, transforming its force from a clandestine underground army into a modern militia, the Jewish army of Palestine. In this phase the scattered Jewish settlements stood their ground and repelled attacks against superior firepower and numbers.

The Haganah was the quasi-official Israeli defense force in Palestine, but at the same time, and often in opposition to it, there were two underground terrorist groups, one calling itself IZL[2] and the other known in our press as the Stern Gang, an offshoot of the Irgun. While the Haganah had spent years in patient, unglamorous, day-by-day, bread-and-butter defense of peaceful agricultural Jewish settlements, the terrorists had sought notoriety at any cost and in any quarter.

Our report continued:

Phase two opened at the end of March, 1948, when Haganah went over to the offensive, operating as a national army, with a general staff, planned operations, good supply techniques, well-trained combat troops and good field commanders. Although the Arab Liberation Army possessed superior firepower, it functioned without a coherent central command, its fighters were untrained in modern battle techniques, and it suffered from poor communications, ill-organized supply lines and poor liaison with other sectors of the front.

The military situation was deeply confused. The British, who had announced their impending departure with the decision of the United Nations, were striking at both sides, but generally and patently in support of the Arabs. The Arab League and the Mufti had declared war on Jewish Palestine, and the Irgun was at war against any opposition to its existence. After the British executed Irgun members captured in an assault on the Ramat Gan police

---

[2] *Irgun Zwei Leumi*, which it translated as National Military organization.

station and the citadel of Acre, the Irgun had captured two policemen at the swimming pool of Ramat Gan for execution in reprisal.
Through the efforts of Haganah, these prisoners were rescued. But
after the trial and executions following the Acre attack, two
British sergeants were captured by the Irgun and hanged in cold
blood. Shades of Hitler, Stalin, and Eichmann!

A typical terrorist action was the capture and destruction of the
village of Deir Yassin, an incident which aroused the Palestine
Jewish community against the Irgun. The massacre of women and
children aroused violent antagonism to the Jewish cause around
the world. The Jewish Agency, of which Ben Gurion was chairman, publicly expressed its horror and disgust and Kol Hamegen
Haivri, the broadcasting service of the Haganah, announced on
April 10, 1948:

> After the outrageous action of the dissidents in displaying
> in the streets of Jerusalem Arab women and children
> brought from Deir Yassin yesterday afternoon, the Haganah
> took these women and children from the hands of the dissi-
> dents and brought them to the security zone, where they
> handed them over to the Government security forces.

Harry and I were not present at this miniature Roman victory
procession; we were observing the troop training in Jerusalem,
which was under virtual siege. But we knew of it, and saw in the
badly damaged Hadassah emergency clinic, opposite the bombed
out building of *The Palestine Post,* two dreadfully wounded Yemenite Jews—Irgunists. By coincidence, in the same ward two little
baby boys, one with the stump of the umbilical cord still tied
off, lay in wicker baskets on the floor.

The best account of this atrocity was given by John Roy
Carlson.

> . . . But before we left Jerusalem two outrages—one Jewish,
> the other Arab—shocked the conscience of every decent Jew,
> Christian, and Moslem. The first occurred at Deir Yassin, a
> small Arab village on the outskirts of Jerusalem. For years
> the Arabs there had lived at peace with the Jews. Then sud-
> denly the Arabs began to snipe and stage vicious attacks on
> isolated Jewish settlements. After several warnings the Stern

group told the Arabs to evacuate their women and children because it intended to retaliate in kind. The Arabs refused, counting on the presence of women and children to prevent the Jews from attacking. The Sternists, in turn, believing the families had been evacuated, staged an all-out attack, determined to silence those Arabs who had been massacring Jews for weeks.

When the Arabs put up stiff resistance, the Sternists called in the Irgun, whereupon the Arab warriors fled. In the melee, the innocent suffered: the women, the children, the aged. The slaughter reached a toll of 150. Bodies were piled on street corners. Others were thrown into wells. Despite the heat of war, the massacre was as senseless as it was hideous. Every Jew I met was horrified and ashamed. The fact that this was the only instance of its kind in the history of Jewish-Arab relations, or that the Arab leaders of Deir Yassin had been warned to evacuate their women and children, does not excuse its vindictiveness. . . .[3]

The Arab reprisal was not long in coming. Carlson goes on:

On April 13, a convoy of nurses, doctors, medical students and scholars set out for the Hebrew University and the Hadassah Hospital on Mount Scopus, above Jerusalem. The British had been duly informed of the non-military nature of the convoy, and the Jews had requested their protection. But instead of the British, the Arabs came—hundreds of veterans of Nebi Daniel and Mount Castel. First they set up roadblocks, then they knocked out the first in the convoy of four armored buses. For seven hours the Arabs battered the helpless victims with grenades, Bren guns, Molotov cocktails. They set two cars on fire, shooting down those who crawled out. Among the seventy-seven who perished were men eminent in Palestine science: Dr. Chaim Yasky, director of the Hadassah Hospital; Dr. Mizurky, cancer specialist; Dr. Benjamin Klar, philologist; Dr. Abraham Freimann, authority on Jewish law; Doljansky and Ben-David of the Faculty of Medicine, who had treated many Arabs.

British police watched as the slaughter went on. When it was nearly over, they laid down a smoke screen, drove off the Arabs, and arranged for a truce. Then they carried off the survivors—28 out of 105![4]

---

[3] *Cairo to Damascus,* Alfred A. Knopf, p. 181.
[4] Ibid., pp. 181–182.

We discussed the terrorists—or dissidents—with commanders of Haganah. "We can put down the Irgun and the Stern," they said, "but this would result in a civil war here."

Haganah and Irgun were announced enemies—but were they? Arms and ammo were stolen from Haganah by Irgun, we were informed, but both were receiving financial support from American Jews. Seeking world press coverage at the expense of Haganah, the Irgun used the Arab alibi, "He beat me and he cried. He ran ahead of me and complained." The Irgun's propaganda methods, impartial observers felt, consisted of the repeated, the repeated, the repeated big lie. But the terrorism continued. When Count Folke Bernadotte, United Nations mediator, was murdered in Palestine on September 17, 1948, the world automatically assumed that it was the act of Jewish terrorists.

The Hotel Eden, where Harry and I were staying, was near the American Consulate and the King David Hotel, not too far from Zion Square and Ben Yehuda Street, which had been bombed by the British. It was also close to the Jewish Agency, where one morning, we noticed a crowd had gathered—all men and many of them wearing *tallit* and *yarmulke*. One was even wearing a large, cubical, polished black *tefilin* phylactery on his head, and all were praying together, bending forward and back in a religious frenzy, with their side curls swinging in unison.

We asked our guide what it was all about.

"They don' wan' women to bade in de same wadder as mens," he laughed. It was the local method of protesting against women's liberation in the Holy Land. Young men and women commonly swam together from the beach in Tel Aviv and in the plush pools of private villas. This protest by orthodox Jews was novel to me, although I knew that each day the orthodox male Jew thanks and blesses God, as part of his morning prayers, for not making him a woman! Now that women have crossed all frontiers previously open only to the male, I question the necessity for ecclesiastical mandates barring them from complete religious equality under Jewish law. Ordinances requiring a woman to take a bath at least once a month seem a gratuitous affront, as do those barring her from being counted as one of the minimum number of congregants required to constitute a lawful religious service and requiring her to be separated by a balcony or screen from the congregation.

The Eden was an excellent hotel—small, clean, and well-furnished—with good views of the old walled city. Its standard of catering, however, was dependent on the ebb and flow of the war. Although most of the food was prepared according to the demands of *Kashruth* (Kosher), there were no ironclad prohibitions against other foods in the city, and bacon and eggs and similar non-Kosher dishes were also available. Least desirable was dried Australian rabbit. Provided you made sure the hotel cat was safely asleep in the kitchen, even the rabbit wasn't bad when potted and stewed and served with black bread and chicory coffee. And there was no lack of Palestinian wine to help it down.

Alma, our chambermaid at the Eden, was in a class by herself. About 5 feet 4 inches tall, with shining black hair parted in the center, a creamy pink-tinted complexion, cherry-red lips, flashing luminous dark eyes, pert tilted nose, and milk-white even teeth, she had an alluring figure as well—high, full breasts, a dainty waist, and hips that rippled under her white singlet, which if not a mini, was near enough. She doubled as bellboy, busboy, laundress, and char. Without a word, she took my tropical green skivvies, shirts and sox, and sewed into each her own private code of identification in red thread.

At the back of the wide hotel lobby was a grand *escalier* in polished stone leading up to a mezzanine landing, and where it divided to the right and left, and continued to the second floor. Alma's job each morning at 7 was to wash and polish this stairway. She would first fasten the brush to one of her shoes, and then, dancing back and forth, would scrub the landing. Next came the stairs, where she would return to hand scrubbing. Bending to her task, she would disclose to the Alma-watchers gathered at the foot of the stairway a rippling, twinkling, dimpling behind and a thin, transparent G–string. As she worked her way down the steps, the angle of vision lessened—and so did her audience. One day I saw Alma bending over to help change a tire on the hotel's beat-up jalopy. The sidewalk audience was eight men deep!

In front of the hotel across the street was an open space where squads of young Jews, boys and girls, were learning field skirmishing and scouting. The familiar commands for the prone, sitting, and squatting positions and advancing by files brought back memories of Parris Island in 1917—although admittedly, with some slight differences. These agile, eager girls in line with the men were something new, as were the shouting, bearded, Yeshiva *bochurs,* wearing skull caps and going through every movement of the Schools of the Soldier and the Squad as set out in military regulations. They came from all over the world. There were Hungarians, Poles, Italians, Rumanians, Bulgars, Czechs, Moroccans, Algerians, Russians—even Circassians, who as Ben Gurion had said, were the most difficult to understand. Nearby were the medical examination rooms for recruits, and the line of young women I saw waiting to go in for the physical check stands out for me as an example of devotion and dedication at its highest: blonde and blue-eyed *sabras,* dark-skinned Spanish, Portuguese, Italian, North African, and Yemenite women all marching on to war.

These people were no longer a single ethnic strain. Over the centuries, with the infusion of blood lines from Northern Europe and Ethiopia, from Barbary Coast pirates and from Hindustan, from Celt and Greek, from Mongol and Muscovite, and from the American melting pot, there had evolved a new, tough breed that would no longer bemoan its fate and wail, but when the issue was joined, would attack and attack again, with a grim unyielding determination to enforce its will on the enemy. Here in Israel there were no regulation uniforms and no insignia, except the Palmach pin worn by a special group of commandos—an olive branch twined around a sword. Ordnance was you-name-it. In the ranks were British Lee Enfields, French Lebels, a few Springfield models 1898 and 1903, and Skoda rifles built on the Manlicher base, much like our Springfield's '03. A buck private had to be a part-time expert in arms and ammo.

The drill instructor hinted that these recruits would be in the line that night, adding dryly, "Training in the front lines, they learn quickly."

The last time I saw Alma was on a call to arms early one evening during the siege. All employees lined up in front of the hotel in their work clothes—clerks, waiters, cooks, kitchen workers, and maintenance men. And there was that beautiful girl, proud and unafraid, taking her weapons as they were handed out. Her abbreviated detail then moved to a position on the line between the Old and New Cities, which had become a battleground with the Jewish quarter of Jerusalem under siege. We too were under siege in our part of the New City, but some supplies were coming in from settlements along the coast.

Between the Eden and the U.S. Consulate, just north of the Kind David Hotel and the YMCA, sporadic firing had been heard, but we encountered no difficulty when we paid our official call on Consul General Thomas C. Wasson. The building was strongly built of Palestinian stone with street level administration offices approached through a walled garden court. The main reception room was one flight up, with sleeping and living quarters on that floor and above. The consulate staff wore European dress, and it was impossible to distinguish between *Aravi* and *Yahudi,* who were about equally represented. Almost the only sign of the emergency was a quiet American on duty in the garden, wearing a navy blue suit, OD shirt, and a revolver, holster, and belt. The walls had been sand-bagged and wired, however, and we made some suggestions for beefing up these defenses.

Wasson, a polished diplomat, tall, spare, and smiling, gave us a run-down on the situation. "The Jews will sweep through the Arabs because they are like the Americans—self-reliant," he said. "The Arab leaders want to disarm the Jews and then prohibit immigration, but no suggestion has been made about disarming the Arabs." He spoke warmly of Dr. Judah Magnes, President of the Hebrew University and one-time Rabbi of Temple Emanuel, the great Jewish synagogue in New York. "He sat on that very couch," he said, pointing to the couch on which Harry and I were seated, "and we spoke together of the future of this land. He's a better Christian than I am." Forty-three years before, Magnes, a handsome young rabbi, had marched up Broadway in New York City, protesting the Russian pogroms against the Jews.

The consul general escorted us to the gate, through an office besieged with American citizens vainly trying to get back to "God's Country." Returning across No Man's Land to the Hotel Eden, Harry and I were accused on arrival of gross recklessness;

for during our absence, two Jews had been shot in the area and were in the Hadassah clinic. We had been lucky. Shortly after we returned to New York, Consul General Wasson was killed in cold blood by a sniper not far from the hotel.

From Jerusalem, we went back to Tel Aviv to observe the skirmishing around the city and north towards Haifa. The Arab Legion had crossed the Jordan to the Mediterranean coast and had been in action against the line of settlement to the west. Before leaving for Haifa we visited the recently abandoned village of a Sheik Emunus, the only truly Arab settlement that we examined in detail. Most of the inhabitants had gone, and it was patrolled by units of the Haganah. The filth and degradation were overpowering. The rough, unpaved streets between the windowless mud huts were graded downward to a shallow, open sewer for garbage and human soil. What looked like a tiny human embryo in a half parchment sac lay in the ditch with the rotting sewage.

It was very like the village described by John Roy Carlson in *Cairo to Damascus*.

> The people about us lived with their animals, went to bed with them, and woke up at the same hour with them. Nearly every native was barefooted, and went to bed unwashed, got up the next morning and went through the grime of the streets, and then went to bed again without ever bathing his body or feet, until the dirt and dung caked on them and formed a leathery protective coating. I was convinced that soap and water alone could never remove it. . . .
>
> All day long, adults urinated against the walls, while children and teenagers splotched their excrement anywhere, usually near the base of the walls, so that it was positively unsafe to walk anywhere but in the middle of the street. Even though the dung soon dried in the intense heat of the day, swarms of green-black flies always festered there, especially when someone stepped on the mounds. Garbage was cast indiscriminately in the streets. Ma'alesh!
>
> Hordes of children played among the refuse, and the inevitable droppings of donkeys, dogs, cats, chickens, camels and horses. Pitiful, scab-covered, undersized children with running eyes scurried about, sores untreated, hair uncombed week after week till it was matted like the underside of a pig. . . .
>
> As for the women, they seemed to be the main repository of

filth. Whenever they washed—usually in a contaminated river—they went into the water dressed, and in groups, washing their dirty clothes and dirty bodies at the same time. Clay or a piece of soft wood usually served as soap. In many villages the women never washed thoroughly except on the occasion of their marriage and once a year at the feast of Bairam. . . .[5]

The one decent building was the sheik's green and white marble mansion with an empty pool in the courtyard. On guard in front of the entrance was a husky Haganah girl in very well-filled dark blue slacks and brief leather jerkin, holding under her arm a Thompson .45 caliber submachine gun, a rare weapon in these parts.

We drove up to Haifa with Shlomo Shmeir and Irene Broza of the Haganah, Shlomo hiding his gun in a specially contrived drop in back of the glove compartment. After passing through farmlands owned by Jews and Arabs, one of whom was ploughing his field with a camel, we hit a battle-scarred section on the outskirts of Mishmar Ha'Emek and found ourselves in the midst of a line of troop carriers jammed with green-bereted Jordan Legion troops, uniformed, well-armed, healthy-looking, and of every skin-tone from cream white to pitch black.

The reluctant British mingled uncertainly with the Arabs. The rank and file did not understand why they were there, since the mandate was about to end, and understood even less this new Jewish element which had complicated their historically supercilious attitude toward the East, Far and Near, and its peoples. Bewildered and confused, the British brass could not realize that thousands of men were engaged in an impudent war right under their noses; they could not understand, and therefore ignored, Jewish appeals to reason and humanitarian sympathy.

The day's action in the Emek had been won by the Jews. *The Palestine Post* recorded the victory:

MISHMAR HA'EMEK HURLS ARABS BACK

Farmers Defeat Army of Arab Attackers

[5] 1951, Alfred A. Knopf.

HAIFA: Monday—Mishmar Ha'Emek is standing by. The settlement fought a bitter battle yesterday, beating back an Arab assault in which a gang of over 1,000 had tried again and again to advance on it. The settlers engaged the aggressors for seven hours, from 5 P.M. till midnight, and thrust them back. . . .

The attackers . . . covered their advance with 25-pounders. . . .

The sniping and occasional rattle of musketry continued as we arrived at a British command post on the road. A blond sergeant in field fatigues, beret, gat, and a scrubby mustache, his soup plate helmet hanging from his belt, came up to inspect our papers. Harry pulled out his ID card and announced, "Americans." The sergeant shouted to his detail, "Thank God. The Yanks are coming." They all laughed and a few, lying in the grass on the roadside, struggled up to take a look. We didn't dally, however, and returned to our car, which was now surrounded by curious Arab legionnaires, who had come up to second the Iraqis in the attack.

We reached Haifa that evening. The city, with its beautiful, curving harbor, was the leading port in the Levant, and was doubly important because of its oil refinery and heavy industries. The mayor, Shaptai Levy, an expert political tight-rope walker, had arranged a meeting for us with the Druses, Arabs who sided with the Jews. After drinking thick, syrupy, black coffee with them until 2 A.M. the others left for the hotel and I walked alone down the hill to the waterfront, enjoying the seeming peace and beauty of the setting under the shadow of Mt. Carmel.

Carmel, fortified by the Haganah, commanded the approaches to the city, and we climbed the heights at dawn in company with two officers of Haganah. As we drew near the barbed-wire entanglement, a young man stepped out and stood at the point of the hill, watching our every move as we approached. Clutching a grenade in each hand, with the breeze rustling through his open shirt, he looked like a Haganah version of the Winged Victory—blue-eyed, black-bearded, head high, fearless, and unconquerable.

I remember, months later, meeting my old friend Manchester Body, publisher of the *Los Angeles News,* in New York. He had just returned from Palestine with a group of American correspondents, and he shook his head sadly over the plight of the Jews and their impending destruction. "This will be another Forty Days of Musa Dagh," he said, referring to the massacre of the Armenians by the Turks. A vision of that Jewish soldier at the point of Mt. Carmel flashed back to mind. "That will never happen," I prophesied, and quoted him the Biblical words of hope:

> Not by my might nor my power but
> by my spirit, said the Lord.[6]

From Haifa, Harry and I returned to Jerusalem, enroute to Jericho and Bet Harava, the House in the Desert, close by the potash and salt works of the Dead Sea, a thousand feet below sea level. From the air, we gained a new perspective of place and distance. To the north, we glimpsed Mt. Hermon, its snow-covered summit declining to the south and west into cultivated terraces and thousands of draws—ideal ambush country. As we neared the Dead Sea, the land broke up into bare, knobbed *wadis,* mesas like New Mexico's, and gullies and ravines, all barren and desolate.

We landed at the potash works after a half-hour flight. This was a big business operation with a huge plant and heavy machinery, its drying pans gleaming with chemicals. But the jewel of the desert was Bet Harava. Its patient people had literally washed the salt, potash, and other chemicals out of the sands and had made the desert bloom with fruit trees, flower gardens, and palms. Across the nearby border in Jordan was desolation, yet this village had a tree-bordered pool of fresh water where carp were raised to provide fresh fish for the settlers in the midst of the desert!

The *muktar,* the Jewish mayor of the town, was a tall, slim, serious–looking man, wearing spectacles and dressed in khaki. As we stood at the barbed-wire entanglements looking across at Jericho, we wondered what he had to say about his opposite number, the Arab *muktar* in Jericho, a well-known trading center for arms.

"Do you ever see him to talk to?" I asked.

[6] Zechariah 4. 11. 6.

"Yes," he replied. "We met late last night over coffee. He will not harm us. We're friends."

I looked over at Jericho and wondered. A month later Carlson visited this site in company with units of the Arab Legion:

> Photographing as I went along, I saw, with Torkom, a sight that sickened me. The huge plant, stretching over many acres, with its generators, transformers, pumps, and a thousand and one irreplaceable items of machinery—transported at tremendous cost from England and the United States—was systematically being looted and destroyed: building by building, machine by machine, board by board. Hundreds of Arab scavengers, working with teams of donkeys, mules, and trucks, had already stripped away most of the vital working parts, and were now tearing at the corrugated tin, pipes, wire, boards, and small machines. What they could not take apart they smashed with sledge hammers. Instead of utilizing the giant plant, or at least expropriating some of the equipment for constructive purposes—in a land so desperately in need of lumber, glass, ironwork and all else that was in such abundance here—they were destroying everything, ruthlessly, cold-bloodedly, insanely.
>
> The plant already looked like a miniature Hiroshima, minus the ravages of fire. And this wanton destruction was more or less officially sanctioned by Trans-Jordan officials. A dozen Arab Legion guards were on hand to keep law and order among the looters.
>
> About a mile away I saw what was left of Beth Harava, a settlement founded by the Jews, who had brought water there to make the desert bloom, so that trees and flowers grew 1,300 feet below sea level.[7]

We returned to Jerusalem in a convoy of three cars, two of them British weapon carriers each with four troops. In our thinly armored potash truck were Moshe Dayan, Harry, myself, and the truck driver, a Polish immigrant named Shimshon (Samson), whose broad smile disclosed four shining, gold front teeth. Shimshon at once informed us that he had five grandchildren. "I don't look fifty three, do I?" We dutifully answered, "No." He nodded his head at the two military vehicles, "See?" he said. "We have

---

[7] Ibid, pp. 363–4.

guards. The Arabs don't have guards. Nobody attacks them. Only us they attack. The British and Jews are partners in the potash company so we get good guards."

For a time, the only disturbance of the peace was the sound of troops firing at inanimate targets for practice. But as we neared Sheik Jarrah, between Mount Scopus and the New City, we were suddenly running the gauntlet through violent crowds lining the streets, who fired upon and stoned the convoy. At each hit, the iron plates armoring the truck clanged like a fire bell. Then a sleek black limousine skirted the road and passed us.

"Arabs or Jews?" I asked Shimshon.

"Arabs," he answered. *Die sind die reiche nit die schmutzigeh,* he added in Yiddish. ("These are the rich, not the dirty ones.")

The important village of Sheik Jarrah had been reduced by artillery fire to a pile of rubble—at the top of one heap, miraculously, the lintel of a blue doorway and the door itself remained standing.

"Here is where we used to stop for lemonade," Shimshon said sadly, "But now it's closed."

The heat in the truck was unbearable. I recalled an ancient Hebrew prayer dating from the early days of the Jewish Kingdom, and repeated it—*Moshiv Horuah* ("May the winds blow"), hoping for a breeze in the truck. Moshe and Shimshon howled.

The crowds had now become very menacing, but they melted away when the limey lieutenant fired a few rounds, and we reached the Hotel Eden with no further trouble. But the siege was still on. There was no contact with the coast. The Tel Aviv road was blocked and so was the road to Jerusalem. At Haganah Headquarters we met the leaders of all the units in the Jerusalem sector. Something was in the air, and the officers and men had gathered for final briefing. It was obvious that an assault was impending and that the objective was Mt. Castel, which had changed hands several times during the last fortnight. The relief of the city and the opening of the road was contingent on taking and holding the hill.

That night, there was a party in the large underground basement of a storage warehouse that was also used as a drill hall— a party reminiscent of the hot chow, slum, white bread, and ser-

geant-major coffee on the night before our attacks in World War
I. A young Yemenite girl on guard at the entrance, armed with an
ancient French Chauchat, let us through at a word from Moshe.
It was like a pioneer hoedown in full blast, with music and intermittent stamping of the *hora*. The star of the evening was Mayme
Richardson, a dramatic soprano whom we had met in the consul's
office. She sang Handel's Hallelujah, arias from Scarlatti and
Verdi, a group of creole songs, and then, moving the audience
most deeply, the old Negro spiritual of Jericho, so much a part
of ancient Jewish history:

> Joshua fit de battle ob Jericho
> Joshua fit de battle ob Jericho
> An' de walls came tumblin' down.
>
> Up to de walls ob Jericho
> He marched with spear in han'
> "Go blow dem ram horns" Joshua cried
> Kose de battle am in my han'
>
> Joshua fit de battle ob Jericho, Jericho, Jericho
> Joshua fit de battle ob Jericho
> An' de walls come tumblin' down.

At daylight the Haganah would mount the final attack on
Mount Castel from the north, south, and west, to lift the siege of
Jerusalem. Successful ambushes of Jewish convoys on the outskirts
of the city had led the Arab commander, Abdul Kader el Husseini, to storm the hill and invade the New City, the backbone
of the Jewish community. For 5 days, Castel had changed hands
in bitter fighting—no quarter asked or given—and at the end the
Arabs were still in possession.

We left the party and walked down the silent streets to Haganah
headquarters on the western edge of town. H-hour was the twilight just before dawn, and long lines of ghostly forms were moving
into assembly areas for the jump-off. At the foot of the hill troops
had already moved into their positions, the citadel looming high
above with little or no cover for the attacking waves.

The Arabs opened fire, but there was no answer from the

Haganah. As the twilight broke into a deep purple flush in the sky, the shrill piercing call to arms on the *shofar,* the ram's horn, sounded the attack. On three sides of the hill, men and women resolutely beat their way up and up under fire, leaving their wounded and dead behind.

Meanwhile, convoys from the coast were waiting at Rehovot, Richon-le-Zion, Hulda, Petah Tikva, Aqir, and Tel Litwinsky, the trucks loaded with sacks of flour, bread, fruit, vegetables, oil, cheese, butter, freshly slaughtered cattle, medical supplies, ammo, and water. Forty miles from the battle, awaiting the signal that Castel had been taken, the Palmach, or Jewish commandos, were ready to run the first convoy through the Bab-el-Wad seven miles from Castel, past the hill, and into the city.

We were across the road on the north side observing the fighting through our field glasses. There was nothing new in the attack. The crimson and gold shell bursts, the staccato rattle of automatic weapons, the clouds of dust and smoke, the penetrating stink of cordite—all this was a throwback to Iwo Jima and the spell of the high ground. Again it was "seize, occupy, and defend," but this time it was Semite brothers who were cutting each other's throats and dying side by side.

Then, suddenly the hill was taken. As Harry and I drove our jeep back to headquarters, the word was passed again and again, "The road is open," and in the streets, the gathering crowds cried out, "The road is open!" At the communications center, a young Jewish matron, heavily pregnant, pressed her belly close to the combination transmitter and receiver set. The news began to come through. Contact had been made with the convoy master, and the news electrified the throng closing in on her. "The convoy, three hundred trucks, is on its way from Hulda."

In the streets, crowds began to form around public loudspeakers. "The convoy has passed Latrun and is 15 miles away." "The convoy has entered the Bab-el-Wad defile."

A hushed silence greeted the last announcement. Bab-el-Wad, the graveyard of many a Jewish convoy, seven miles from Castel, was littered with the rusted skeletons of burned-out trucks, buses, cars, and military vehicles.

"The convoy has passed through the Bab-el-Wad on its way

to Castel." Shouts, cries, prayers, and sobbing filled the city and a motorcycle detail left to meet the convoy and escort it home.

"The convoy is entering the city."

Jerusalem knew no limit to prayers and tears of thanksgiving. With the convoy master in the lead, the long line of trucks, buses, armored cars, and autos made its way down Ben Yehuda Street to Zion Square, Haganah men and women perched on top of each truck. The shrieks and cries of welcome were especially fervent when the trucks loaded with milch cows came to a halt at the Hadassah clinic—the sick and the children would drink milk again that night.

The Palestine Post of April 12, 1948, reported the Arab reason for the loss of Castel:

TACTICAL ERROR

The Jews were able to reoccupy Mount Castel because the Arab fighters had left the area to attend the funeral on Friday of the commander Abdul Kader el Husseini', the Arab daily *Falastin* **reported yesterday.**

Having observed this victory, we prepared to leave Palestine, a land not at that moment flowing with milk and honey. The nation of Israel was being torn from a hostile land, in the face of an unfriendly world, and I believe now, as I believed then, that the Jews will hold it against any odds. Part of my report to head-quarters read as follows:

My judgment, based on personal observation, is that while some of the Jewish outposts and settlements may be lost in an all-out Arab invasion, Haganah will successfully defend itself against the main attacks. If it acquires heavy weapons and planes, it can win an offensive war against any combination of its enemies.

I paid a farewell call on Ben Gurion. We met in his garden at night—this time the fragrance of jasmine was added to the ever-present perfume of orange blossoms. He took my arm as we walked to the gate, and his parting words were, "Do not forget us. Our future and our lot is with America." At the airport, Moshe

Dayan handed me a gift, remarking dryly, "General Husseini gave it to me." It was a black leather pistol holster and shoulder belt, embroidered in silver braid with the crescent and the sword.

Lowell Limpus of the *New York Daily News,* hungry for a story, met us on our arrival at LaGuardia (Idlewild would not open until July). That night he headlined his interview:

JEWS CAN BEAT ARABS ALONE, 2 U.S. VETERANS CONVINCED.

We do not have the final answer yet. The fortified line along the Suez Canal, where Israel sleeps on its arms, is still a battlefront. After the mad rush for conquest in 1967, Israel occupies, by virtue of an inconclusive armistice dictated by the balance of power between East and West, twice as much territory as it had in 1948. Diplomatic necessity may require, even command, a return of some of these occupied territories, for while Israel must grow, it cannot do so where it exists at the vital expense of its neighbors. Surrounded by 90 million enemies, Israel must aim for peace with security, within its frontiers.

Did Thomas Paine have the answer when he wrote his *American Crisis* about another democracy in swaddling clothes, almost two hundred years ago? "I have as little superstition in me as any man living, but my secret opinion has ever been, and still is, that God Almighty will not give up a people to military destruction or leave them unsupported to perish, who have so earnestly and so repeatedly sought to avoid the calamities of war, by every decent method which wisdom could invent."

18. Korea

ON MY RETURN from Jerusalem, I reported to Cliff Cates, Commandant of the Marine Corps, and gave him a beautiful silver and jeweled Arab dagger as a souvenir. Very seriously, he reached into his pocket and paid me a traditional penny for the knife—"He who gives a knife to a friend, cuts friendship"—and we settled down to talk of the Israeli army and its weapons manufacture, the guerrilla groups, the Arab Legion, and our Consul General Thomas C. Wasson, who had been dry-gulched in front of the Consulate.

We discussed the much talked-of plan to send U.S. Marines to Palestine. I argued strongly against it. Harry Henshel and I presented the same arguments later that day and in the days following to representatives of the Senate and the House, and we won out—the Marines were not sent to Israel. At Cates' suggestion I also talked to Bill Riley, a brigadier general who was about to receive his order as chief of staff to Count Folke Bernadotte, the representative of the United Nations in its first Arab-Israeli truce negotiations.

After that, there was little or no Marine Corps activity for me—except for selection boards, policy boards, and two-week summer training—until 1950, when the situation changed with the United Nations' intervention in Korea. President Truman's statement was carried in *The New York Times* of Wednesday, June 28:

> In Korea the Government forces, which were armed to prevent border raids and to preserve internal security, were attacked by invading forces from North Korea. The Security Council of the United Nations called upon the invading troops to cease hostilities and to withdraw to the Thirty-

eighth Parallel. This they have not done, but on the contrary have pressed the attack. The Security Council called upon all members of the United Nations to render every assistance to the United Nations in the execution of this resolution.

In these circumstances I have ordered United States air and sea forces to give the Korean Government troops cover and support.

The attack upon Korea makes it plain beyond all doubt that Communism has passed beyond the use of subversion to conquer independent nations and will now use armed invasion and war. . . .

On December 16, 1952, I was ordered to Korea. The situation I found there has been described in Bob Leckie's book *The War in Korea.*

By year's end, Van Fleet had 16 divisions manning a line resembling the old bunker-and-trench battlefronts of World War II. This force consisted of ROK divisions, one British Commonwealth division and one U.S. Marine and three U.S. Army divisions, with one ROK and three U.S. Army divisions in reserve. Attached to the American divisions were all those battalions and brigades from the other United Nations members with troops in Korea, and there was a regiment of South Korean Marines attached to the U.S. Marine division. . . .

Between the onset of winter in November-December of 1952 and the arrival of the spring of 1953, the Korean battlefront was characterized by artillery exchanges, sporadic small-scale fighting, constant patrolling, and a propaganda war carried on through loudspeakers set up at the front by both sides. On one side, the Chinese and North Koreans occupied their honeycombed hillsides, on the other United Nations troops sat out the winter in bunkers or in the trenches of the outposts. Both sides sent out patrols to see what the other side was doing.[1]

The activity at the front by the Chinese Communist forces was also designed to provide material for the truce talks at Panmunjon and perhaps better their bargaining position.

[1] Random House, 1963, pp. 361–362, 366.

> Winning new dominating hill or ridge positions adjacent to
> the Marine Main Line of Resistance, or that uneasy No-
> Man's-Land buffer zone between the Communist Chinese
> Forces and United Nations lines, would be both militarily
> and psychologically advantageous to the Communists. Any
> new yardage or victory, no matter how small, could be ex-
> ploited as leverage against the 'Wall Street capitalists'
> when truce talks resumed at the Panmunjon bargaining
> table.[2]

Most of the attacks on both sides centered on the outposts
later named for three Nevada cities, Carson, Reno, and Vegas—
key positions over which there had been extensive disagreement
during the 1952 summer truce talks. Vegas was the highest of
them, offering excellent observation of the Chinese supply route,
and was usually manned by a reinforced rifle platoon. Because of
its importance and the continuous tension of heavy shelling, the
Vegas detachments were relieved and replaced every few days.

I reported by chopper to General Al Pollock, my friend as far
back as the late Twenties and now Commanding General of the
1st Marine Division in Korea. Al had assigned me to Headquarters,
located near the railhead at Munson-ne, as a sort of assistant to
Bill Buse, his chief of staff. I drew combat equipment, including
armor, was quartered in a small trailer heated spasmodically by
a GI can of oil which was carbureted through a coil to a pathetic
flame that went out more often than not.

Al greeted me warmly with a quart of I. W. Harper, bourbon
being the Marine Corps' traditional drink (although scotch has
crept in with later generations). Jim Lucas, Pulitzer Prize
winner and Scripps–Howard correspondent, joined me as bottle in
hand, I made for my trailer. There we relaxed and talked of Saipan and Iwo Jima. The bourbon dropped as our spirits rose. Al
stopped by for a visit, eyed the diminished level in the bottle, and
when Jim left, expressed some misgivings about his prize-winning
articles on Korea—a display of pessimism which I attributed to
the imminent failure of our bourbon supply. Outside there were
three flagpoles, flags snapping in the breeze in front of the administration shack—the blue United Nations flag at the highest peak
in the center, with our own on each side below it. I had never

[2] U.S. Marine Operations in Korea, 1950-1953, Volume V, p. VII:27.

before seen the Stars and Stripes flying in combat below the level of another color. It was the tide of the times, and it looked good to me.

My first duty was to inspect the main line of resistance (MLR) positions held by units of three combat regiments—the 1st, 5th, and 7th—which were defending their respective fronts with field fortifications consisting of wire, trenches, bunkers, and caves cut into the rock of the hillside. Down in the plains between the scattered hamlets were rice paddies, some frozen over, where die-hard Koreans maintained the threadbare routines of civilian life. Little groups of men and women would visit their broken-down temple; there were occasional weddings or burial processions, the peasants in bright colors, white and pink, wearing typical polished leather opera hats with short brims and tiny projecting crowns. In the villages, hopeful groups of farmers' wives still squatted behind a semicircle of baskets holding cabbages, radishes, onions, garlic, and a form of pepper unknown in the States—all necessary ingredients for the fermentation and pickling of an unearthly concoction called *kimchi,* a tidbit known throughout Korea and which gives rise to a national fragrance and an eye-watering, stomach-turning stench equaled only by the local "honey" wagons, which spray human soil on the rice and vegetable paddies. The effect of both became more poignant as the thermometer rose.

Throughout this area, Colonel Loren E. Haffner, CO of the 7th Marines, had set up posters of the American gopher or prairie dog with the slogan:

DIG TO LIVE,
LIVE TO FIGHT.

The efficacy of this advertising message among the craggy rocks of his positions in the 1st Marine Division support line is not recorded, but it was very reminiscent of the trench warfare of World War I. Four-star General Lew Walt, at that time the colonel commanding the 5th Marines in Korea, took me for a walk through his MLR area. We were being slightly shelled at the time, and I picked up the nose cap of a mortar shell with a Russian inscription: АПЯИН . Though I wore armor, Lew took care of the elderly, and shunted me into a foxhole with the remark, "This is no place for a Belleau Wood veteran."

The big event of my tour, however, was a visit to Colonel Hewett D. Adams in 1st Marines' front lines on the occasion of the rotation of the personnel of the Vegas outpost.

> The outpost detachment stood nighttime posts on a 50 per cent basis and remained within the several living bunkers or other shelters during daylight hours because of heavy shelling and sniper fire. Incessent enemy pressure at the exposed outpost made it expedient to rotate infantry Marines at Vegas every three days and observers, at the end of four or five days.[3]

The front came alive at night. Hundreds of Marines patrolled the 1st Marine Division sector, mostly for reconnaissance or security, but also for combat with Chinese patrols either by plan or by mischance. The Chinese would keep our dead frozen solid in grotesque, misshapen lumps in full view of our MLR and outposts, a horror picture for new replacements at the front. The propaganda battle was also in full bloom with loudspeakers on both sides and Communist signs in English, "Go Home" being a favorite theme.

On our side, the enemy dead received an honorable military burial, and their wounded, full medical and hospital treatment. It was ironic to note in the prisoner wards that a blood transfusion for a Chinese prisoner might have come from a patriotic New England schoolmarm or a Hollywood starlet.

Colonel Adams invited me to the assembly point of the patrols. Every precaution had been taken against sound or light by muffling and blanketing all equipment. The war diary gives the regimental picture:

> In early January, 1953, 1st Marines (Col. H. D. Adams) manned the right regtl sector of 1st Mar Div front. 2/1 and 3/1 were on line, in left and right MLR battalion positions, respectively. 7th Marines (Col. Loren E. Haffner) on MLR in center regtl sector.
>   On night of 6-7 January, 3/1 relieved on line by 1/1.
>   Beginning on 20 January, 5th Marines elements began a phased relief of 1st Marines in right sector. (This got

[3] U.S. Marine Operations in Korea, 1950-1953, Volume V, p. VII:27.

underway on 20 January when 2/5 relieved part of the
1/1 force at Combat Outposts #19 (Berlin) and #19A
(East Berlin).

Regimental relief completed on 25 January when 5th Marines (Col. Lewis W. Walt) assumed operational responsibility for right sector.

A relevant excerpt about COP Vegas appeared in the Jan '53
3/1 command diary (page 1), for the 1-6 Jan '53 period:

> . . . . In addition to MLR positions, personnel of the battalion *occupied three permanent combat outposts.* Hills 19
> and 19A were manned by personnel of How Company. Hill
> 21 [i.e., Vegas] was manned by Item Company. The latter
> COP is unique in that it was under the administrative control of this battalion, but under the operational control of
> the MLR battalion on our left flank. Hill 21 is mutually
> supporting with the two permanent outposts of that unit
> [i.e., Carson, Reno] and they were, therefore, given operational control of the entire group.

Also, for the 6-22 Jan period,

> 3/1 dispatched a reinforced platoon each night to Dog Company, 2nd Battalion, 1st Marines, to occupy a position on
> the MLR vacated by a platoon of that company which occupied a blocking position [i.e., the Reno Block] each night.
> This reinforced platoon was under the operational control
> of the 2nd Bn. It returned the following morning and reverted to parent control.

I joined the group at the assembly point and we all moved away
in a darkened, silenced line to the outpost. Adams had gone off
somewhere else, and I instinctively followed those only a few feet
ahead and invisible to sight, though close enough to touch, as we
stumped down the craggy heights toward the valley between the
Main Line and Vegas.

Though not part of the relief, I found myself moving along in
Indian file toward the black mass outlined in the distance—the
Chinese lines. Then I stopped for a moment to find out who was
behind me, and I was lost. It was like a bad dream of No Man's
Land, except that here it was for real. In the distance I could hear
the faint rustle of moving bodies, but whether they were Chinese

or not, I could not tell. Even in 15-below-zero weather I had begun to sweat in my long johns, field uniform, and parka, and a black terror took hold of me. The shuffling came closer, and now I could detect the smell of American sweat and the muttering of English. Three Marines approached; they were returning from Vegas but had gotten lost in all the twisting and turning, confused by the black, starless night and bitter cold. After a whispered word of identification, we joined forces, a colonel and three privates in a valley that could easily spell death for the four of us.

Lost in the icy rocks and scrub, we clawed our way back up the hill towards the main line of the 5th Marines. The going was very hard, and as we approached the limits of endurance in the freezing weather, we knew that only vigorous movement could save us. The temperature had dropped to 17 degrees below, and we fought that rugged, craggy, perilous terrain with the cold clawing at our guts, our hearts, and our breath. We sobbed as we struggled up the steep, bitter, bruising pitch of the hill, very close now to the stumbling, tripping, cursing limit of our strength.

Snow began to fall. It looked like the end. The three Marines collapsed and could go no further. Reaching out to them, I found myself calling, urging, wheedling, even begging them to get up—not a colonel now, but a sergeant again, using a sergeant's language, pulling the men forward to safety and away from certain death. Splinters of icy rubble slid beneath our boots as we pushed on. In my mouth was the sour vomit taste of exhaustion. We found ourselves, the four of us, holding each other up as we moved over the last stretch to the high ground. A hoarse faltering voice—was it mine?—called, "Come on, Marines," as together we lurched and blundered over the crest into waiting arms, warmth, the bunkers, and the nectar of black coffee. It was a while before I realized that the gasping, wrenching, heavy breathing was mine.

I returned to Division Headquarters after dawn and went to the officers' galley for still more coffee, pitch black, bitter, and hot. The General was up. They were bringing him his eye-opener and a bucket of hot water for his bath and shave. When he saw me, he called out, "Hi, Mel. Everything OK?"

"Aye, aye, sir," I replied.

19. Liquor

CANDY IS DANDY, BUT
LIQUOR IS QUICKER

—Ogden Nash

U.S.S. *Bayfield*

23 January, 1945

TO: **ALL HANDS**

REFERENCE: *Navy Regulations Art. 13 and 118*

1. Above regulations are quoted:
Distilled spirits shall be admitted on board of vessel of war only upon the order and under the control of the medical officers of such vessels, and to be used only for medical purposes. (R. S. Sec. 1624, art. 13).

(a) Alcoholic liquors shall not be admitted or used on board any ship or aircraft of the Navy, except as authorized for medical purposes.

(b) The introduction, possession, or use of alcoholic liquors for drinking purposes or for sale is prohibited within navy yards, marine barracks, naval stations and other places ashore under the jurisdiction of the Navy Department which are located in States, Territories or insular possessions in which the possession or use of such liquors for drinking purposes is not permitted by law.

177

(c) No person in the naval service shall possess or use any narcotic substance on board ships or aircraft of the Navy or within navy yards, marine barracks, naval stations, or other places under the jurisdiction of the Navy Department, except as authorized for medical purposes (C.N.R. 16, art. 118).

2. C.O. of troops will inform all Marine Corps personnel of this bulletin—officers and enlisted men.

3. O.D. will inspect all packages, leaving or coming on board, carried by any officer or man, Navy, Marine Corps, or Coast Guard, and confiscate any unauthorized article, reporting your action to the Commanding Officer.

Distribution:
    All Officers Ship & Staff
    O.D. File
    Marines—10
    Flag Office—10
    All Bulletin Boards.

In spite of this directive, which was standard operating procedure for all ships of the Fourth Marine Division flotilla, the young wives' tale, "If it's there, the Marines will find it," applied to liquor as well as to sex. President Wilson's Secretary of the Navy had issued the order in 1914, making the Navy dry, but it was no more universally observed than the civilian law of the land during the bootleg and speakeasy era.

You brought to the officers' slopshoot all your domestic problems—the oh-so-friendly wife or, even worse, the silent drinker; the son who hated the service; the daughter who stayed out late and couldn't be handled; and a fluctuating bank balance. For years after World War I, the large hump in the captains' list presented problems of promotion; a Marine officer at that time was happy to retire on a captain's pay, while a major's allowance was almost beyond hope. Some even retired as first lieutenants, but the blessing of the high octane oblivion could always wipe the slate clean for the moment. With World War II, liquor became as much a part of the Marine Corps' divisional staff life as the chow line did on the headquarters combat transport. Drinking was not openly permitted, however, and one Coast Guard skipper aboard the U.S.S. *Leonard Wood* was hell on wheels against drinking and gambling. The story is told, and later became popular in night spots back home, of how he pussy-footed around officers' compartments, searching out victims, and finally during the happy hour after 5 P.M., he pushed open the door of the chaplains' office and found the three holy men sitting around an empty card table with a detectable odor of *spiritus frumenti* in the air.

"I've caught you," howled the skipper, pointing to the Catholic priest. "You were drinking and gambling." The priest, hesitating only a moment for a silent prayer for forgiveness, answered, "No, sir." The captain turned to the Protestant chaplain and, looking at him eye to eye, said, "But you were drinking." The minister, begging the Father of all under his breath for forgiveness, replied, "No, sir." The captain turned to the Jewish chaplain and said, "Then you were the one drinking and gambling, weren't you?"

"With whom, sir?" the rabbi replied.

From LSTs to battleships, in every craft I set foot on, liquor was always in the picture. Brandy was available for medicinal purposes from every medical detachment, afloat or ashore, and our senior medical officer, a full captain in rank, always issued brandy to the senior officers "for medical use ashore for the enlisted in the case of an emergency," or before we made a landing in the face of the enemy.

On our way to Saipan in the Marianas, we lay off the Aloha Tower, on Sand Island at Honolulu awaiting orders to sail. Our Burial Officer, Captain Lew Nutting, had gone over to check on some of our heavy LSTs in Pearl Harbor, and while he was there, from some spark or flame, the source of which was never determined, five combat-loaded ships caught fire and a disastrous chain of explosions followed. Overcome by the havoc and destruction, Lew reported in by phone and came back to the *Leonard Wood* weeping and hysterical. I hurried him down to the sick bay, pushed through the waiting room where one dull-looking Marine was sitting apathetically waiting for the Medical Corps man, and got him into the doctor's office. The lieutenant, M.C., opened the safe, took out a sealed flat pint of bourbon, called in a corpsman, and ordered him to give the patient a drink. We sat discussing the catastrophe and waited, but no drink was forthcoming. The doctor called for the attendant again and asked about the drink. "Sir, I gave him the drink," he replied, "and he left." "Who did you give it to?" thundered the doctor. "I gave it to the Marine in the waiting room," the corpsman faltered.

We looked at each other and howled. "Bring me the bottle and glasses," the doctor snapped. Then he turned to me with a shrug, and said, as though some precious life-restoring potion were involved, "The Marine outside was waiting for a dose of salts."

Liquor was produced ashore from the most unexpected hiding places. One highly placed officer, now in retirement, had it in a rubber bladder suspended under his shirt around his neck. He sipped the liquor through a tube, similar to those for the emergency inflation of life jackets. Robert Sherrod, editor-at-large of *The Saturday Evening Post* and long-time combat correspondent, once found himself meandering along near the beach on Saipan with Frank Kelly, of the Paris edition of the *New York Herald Tribune,* and Hamm, the A.P. photographer. We had just secured the landing and extended our perimeter about 800 yards, with a good defense, and for the moment, all was quiet in our sector although we were expecting a counter-attack, and the Jap snipers were busy. All of us had dug in and I had, when I could get it, in the manner of Belleau Wood, dug deep. As Bob and his companions walked toward my command post, the alert was passed "Condition Red," which meant an air attack. "Let's go," I said, and we flopped down, the four of us in a dugout with no overhead shelter except a camouflaged poncho as the planes came over. I had a bottle of Schenley's Black Label, nicknamed "Black Death," but only one tin cup. But we passed it around and eventually climbed out of the dugout when both the Jap planes and the whiskey had disappeared. In his *Green Beach Landing,* Bob mentioned the incident. "When the word Condition Red was passed (meaning that Jap planes were on their way) Kelly and I, slow diggers, found refuge in a poncho-covered foxhole with the division Provost Marshal, Lieut. Colonel Melvin Krulewitch of

Albany, New York. The Colonel found—of all things—a bottle of bourbon."

I had a good friend in Chaplain Roderick Hurley, a Catholic priest attached to the 25th Marines. Tall, tough, with shaggy dark hair, he was usually at the front in helmet and combat fatigues, radiating companionship and comfort to all. He could drink most Marines under the table but carried no liquor or food, living on the hospitality of the troops. On Saipan during the battle, I met him once on one of my surveys and fortunately had provided for such an emergency by carrying with me a large can of Japanese crab and a bottle of rum. I also had a soup spoon, and so we ate the crab, passing the spoon back and forth and wetting the food down with rum. We were at ease, close to the front with our guns shelling the enemy position. I quoted to Father Hurley the maxim, "Who sups with the Devil must use a long spoon," from Aesop's Fables, and we often laughed about the incident, although we could never agree on who was the Devil, the Catholic or the Jew.

Liquor flowed wherever there were Marines, and the definition of an alcoholic was, "Someone who drinks more than you do." There were all kinds of strange native homebrews in the Pacific, but sake was the most obtainable field drink—often by the case and the price was right! There was also plenty of beer ashore, the Asahi and Kirin brews being the equal of the best Stateside beer. Drinking it was prohibited, of course, but only if you were caught in the act.

In Saipan, the next cheapest drink available was bourbon. I remember a moment during the early days of the landings when the beach was the usual crash-jammed, cluttered bedlam of troops, landing craft, dozers dragging loaded pallets of water, medical supplies, ammo and rations, disabled tanks, and a miserable clutch of half-crazed natives. Scattered about in this chaos were hospital corpsmen attending the wounded amid a continuous staccatto crackle of rifle and machine gun fire, with the distant boom and close crashing thunderburst of artillery—truly the smoke and fog of war. And through the shattered trunks and fronds of coconut palms, the tropical sun poured down its burning heat on the Japanese dead sprawled about every strong point and wrecked embankment along the shore. After two days of naval gunfire and bombing, the smell of putrefaction was everywhere. Whisky alone took the taste out of your mouth.

The Officers' Club of the 4th Marine Division had been financed, on leaving the States, by a voluntary stock subscription. It proved an excellent gamble and we all got our money back when the Division was disbanded. It was a beautiful bottle club tastefully decorated in the Hawaiian motif, and run by Lieutenant Colonel Armand Jacobsen, attached to the Service Battalion. After Iwo Jima, Okinawa, Hiroshima, and V.J. Day, Arnie had his problems. He had operated the Club so well that he hardly knew what to do with the surplus stocks of whisky, gin, and rum, left over after all the stockholders had been paid off. First, he extended the Happy Hour to two hours and then to the whole evening, reducing his prices to 15 cents a drink. Then it was further lowered to 10 cents and although this made a dent in the supply, there was still a surplus. Arnie called a final meeting of the Board and his recommendation was passed unanimously—indeed with a rising voice vote. From then on, while the supply lasted, drinks were free.

The days of hard drinking in the Corps are now gone. They weren't good and they weren't bad. We grew up with liquor during the speakeasy era; it hardened us and, in the service, gave us the only relief we had from the curse of unsatisfied ambition and the slings and arrows of recurring crises. After 30 years of drinking Jack London wrote:

> It was my unmitigated and absolute good fortune, good luck, chance, call it what you will, that brought me through the fires of John Barleycorn. My life, my career, my joy in living, have not been destroyed. They have been scorched, it is true; but, like the survivors of forlorn hopes, they have by unthinkably miraculous ways come through the fight to marvel at the tally of the slain.

So, perhaps, it was with me.

★

20. *Vox Populi, Vox Dei*

AFTER THE KOREAN armistice, it was back again to New York, the law, and politics, but now life was increasingly overshadowed by the illness of my beloved Helen. Beginning in 1954, the illness continued through '55 and '56, and in '57 Helen lapsed into a six-months' coma from which she never recovered. On June 15, 1957, Republican County Chairman Bob Curran called me down to his office for a chat, and I was glad of the diversion.

"Mel, how's Helen?" he asked. I answered despondently that she was about the same. Then he sprang it on me.

"We'd like you to run for borough president of New York," he said. "You know the score, Mel. Bob Wagner's a strong candidate for mayor, but you'd be running against a black man and lightning might strike. Do you think you could get a Liberal endorsement?"

Thinking of some of my friends who had been generous supporters of the Liberal Party, I hesitated. "I don't know," I said.

"Listen," he said. "If you want to, you can decline the nomination within the time limit. And it won't cost you a dime," he added, rising to his feet. "Come to the County Committee this afternoon at four."

And so it came to pass. I was nominated as Republican candidate for borough president of New York County, petitions were duly sent to all district clubs for signing by registered Republicans, and I began my campaign against one Hulan Jack with the slogan, "Who you foolin', Hewlin?"

"It won't cost you a dime," Tom Curran had said. First of all, we had to have a press director, and we were lucky to get an experienced newspaperman to take the job for $1250 for the campaign. Fortunately, I had a close personal friend in long-time writer and editor Lou Ruppel, a former executive editor of Hearst publications and recently editor of *Collier's* and of course Lou worked for free throughout the campaign. Though we had plenty of good publicity, there was not much money available for the vital political necessities of campaign literature, press advertising, and radio and television messages. And there was little or no help from disappearing Bob Christenberry, Republican candidate for mayor. On some engagements of more than casual importance, *I* had to make the major address for the ticket in place of Bob, who was unavoidably detained elsewhere.

The happiest part of the campaign was the turnout of old friends, in every walk of city life, from the Marine Corps to the various service and benevolent agencies with which I had been associated over the years. Milton Weill, President of the Federation of Jewish Philanthropies, was my campaign chairman. Co-chairman was Ed Chinlund, treasurer of Macy's. Ralph Horgan was one of my directors, and he got me the *Irish Echo*. After listing all the Irish names on my committee with their parish and Catholic affiliations, the story continued:

> Colonel Horgan points out that it is only fitting that General Krulewitch receive the support of so many Manhattan Irish inasmuch as back in 1935, the then Captain Krulewitch commanded the 19th Marine Reserve Regiment, affectionately known as "The Irish Marines" because of the predominance of the Sons of Erin in its ranks.

Some of the Irish support was not for Krulewitch, but against Krulewitch's opponent. A Krulewitch parade in Yorkville, organized by my niece Marjorie Kogan, passed 86th Street and Third Avenue, where I was mingling unrecognized with the bystanders. One Irishman, smoking a blackened clay pipe, announced to everyone in earshot, "I ain't voting for no nigger. I hear this Polack is a good Catholic." I quietly slipped away.

The campaign had barely begun, however, when I was called at 2 A.M. one morning to the Medical Center on Washington Heights, where my wife had been a patient of Dr. Lawrence Poole, the chief neurosurgeon at the hospital. I had visited Helen there that very afternooon. "Your wife has expired," I was told. Alone, I said good-bye to my beloved—my thoughts with my children in the shock of our loss.

The newspapers carried the story—it was worth a few more lines in view of the campaign—and my friends gathered at the Park Avenue Synagogue for the services. There were so many of them that the supply of black cloth caps, required to be worn at a conservative service, ran out, and a hurried call brought black tissue-paper ones. The sight of so many of my Marine buddies and friends, wearing these caps, canted Marine fashion, relieved for a moment some of the acute bitterness of this tragedy. Mayor Wagner and some of the other Democrats campaigning for the election attended the services, but my opponent, Hulan Jack, did not.

I toured the County from Spuyten Duyvil to the Battery, and from the East River to the Hudson, not forgetting Harlem, my opponent's stronghold, where I was welcomed on occasions by such remarks as, "Here's a man who's not afraid to come up to Harlem." I even spoke in Adam Clayton Powell's church and met his associate, an assistant pastor by the name of Likerish. His only political remark to me after the meeting, which strangely enough was not too controversial, was, "Lincoln freed us, and Roosevelt fed us." This was enough to show which way the wind blew, and would keep blowing, in Harlem. My hopes for the Liberal endorsement proved fruitless, although the Citizens Union marked me "preferred" and gave me a plug "as a man of occupational ability, integrity, and high ideals of public service." My good friend Jack Kaplan, identified with many a benevolent activity and a long-time contributor to innumerable liberal causes, spoke to Liberal Party boss Alex Rose in my behalf, but because race was an issue, Rose passed the word that his party could not switch to the right in this election. Jack sent a generous contribution as a consolation prize. I had the Chinese press, the Jewish press, and the Greek press, but still the campaign lagged. What I didn't have were the dyed-in-the-wool Democratic party voters who wouldn't split for a Republican, for love or money. The days when you could buy votes were long gone.

Nicholas Murray Butler, who was a member of our old club in what was once called Manhattanville, used to tell the story of

Sam, who was met on election day by the Democratic captain with a bundle of printed ballots in his hand. (In those days, each party printed its own ballots and distributed them to the voters.) The Democratic captain gave Sam a ballot and a $5 bill. A bit farther on, Sam then met the Republican captain, who gave him a Republican ballot and a $10 bill. Sam accepted the ballot and the money and entered the voting booth. Since the ballots were printed in different colors, it was easy to see which ballot was voted. Sam voted Democrat and was immediately buttonholed by the wrathful Republican captain. "Sam," he shouted, "How come you voted the Democratic ballot? He only gave you $5 and I gave you $10." Sam thought for a moment, and answered, "I voted his because he was the least corrupt."

Since I was running against a black man, the question of civil rights in housing was frequently raised. Stanley Isaacs, the great liberal leader who was a member of my committee, a previous borough president and the Republican minority leader of the City Council, had long advocated equal rights in this area, and I went along with him. In answer to a question at a meeting in Harlem, I stated that I would rather have a clean, God-fearing, law-abiding black family as next-door neighbors than a millionaire Mafioso. This pleased absolutely nobody. The blacks said that "clean" was an aspersion, suggesting that all blacks were not clean, and that "law-abiding" implied that they were not all law-abiding; and an Italian group wrote in to say that there was no such thing as the Mafia, and that my statement was another slur on law-abiding citizens of Italian origin. Each day, we batted them out as they were pitched.

In October I received orders from the Marine Corps which placed me on active duty for 10 days in Washington. The publicity was useful—there were pictures of me in uniform saying good-bye to the kids—and the break was a welcome relief from a sluggish campaign. But the wise guys in both parties knew I couldn't win. And I didn't. Election Day came and went, and *mirabile dictu,* I carried two assembly districts, but in the black districts I didn't even receive the usual miserable Republican pittance. Still, I received many congratulatory messages, even from people I had never met, like Herbert Bayard Swope, the world-renowned American Pulitzer Prize-winning journalist and public official. A truly comforting letter came from Harold Riegelman, who had made a great run for mayor four years before, and although defeated, had carried two counties and almost won a third. He wrote:

Dear Mel:

You lost the election but you won the campaign. I am sure you will enjoy the fruits of that victory for the rest of what I hope will be a long life: an intimate knowledge of our county and the rich pattern of communities it embraces; new friends and a far wider circle of people who have come to know a fine, humane citizen with a stout fighting heart; a keen appreciation of the fascinating problems of government and the rewarding memory of a clean fight well fought.

These are wonderful satisfactions which will grow with the passing years. You have richly earned them all.

Sincerely,
Harold

Shortly after the election, my successful opponent Hulan "Who yuh foolin'?" Jack was indicted for fraud, convicted, and thrown out of office.

21. *Operation Nan*

SPRING HAD COME to the Potomac, and to me as well. I had shuttled down to Washington on Eastern, hopped a cab to the Navy Annex at Arlington, waved to the guard box at the entrance, and stepped out in front of Headquarters, United States Marine Corps. The day was warm, sunny, and dry, the shrubs well-leafed, the trees spreading shade. The air was fresh and I felt at home.

The Marine at the information desk took my name, whispered into his phone, and I was on my way to the Commandant's office, where I reported to his ADC and sat down to wait, glancing again at the rows of framed portraits of the Commandants, as I had done so many times before. There was General George Barnett, who had signed my warrant as corporal in 1917. The first graduate of the Naval Academy at Annapolis to become Commandant of the Marines, he had hobnobbed with politicians and businessmen who were important in the Democratic administration of Woodrow Wilson, and in the end, political pressures had brought him down before his term.

Next to him was General John Archer Lejeune, who had a quality rare in a fighting man—a combination of all the virtues that made you like him for himself. Without fear and without reproach, he would be known as "Johnny the Good."

Then came Wendell Cushing Neville, Lejeune's segundo, known as Buck Neville, who commanded the Marine Brigade in 1918 from Soissons to Germany. He succeeded Lejeune and died in office. After him came Ben Hebard Fuller, appointed from one-star rank, and not even the senior brigadier at the time when major generals were available for appointment. Fuller, a great officer, had lost his son at Belleau Wood.

188

John Henry Russell, Jr., was the only Commandant I never met personally from 1917 to date. A Navy brat, he graduated from the Academy, as did his father, and both he and his father retired as two-star flag officers. Then Thomas Holcomb, who had commanded my battalion at Belleau Wood (one of the four future commandants of the Corps who served in France with the 4th Marine Brigade). It was he who finally broke down and sent me to the Pacific in 1943. Next, Archie Vandergrift, who achieved world fame as the successful commanding general of the 1st Marine Division at Guadalcanal, and then Cliff Cates, the 19th Commandant of the Corps, known to me over a period of 50 years. Fearless in battle, gay and debonair, he gathered around him a host of loyal friends. Usually in the right place at the right moment, he was known as Lucky Cates.

Lem Shepherd succeeded him. A great human being, never a seeker of publicity or acclaim, he was a God-fearing, humble man of highest quality, loyal to the small as well as the great. Randy Pate, whom I was waiting to see, had been recommended by General Shepherd as Commandant. A graduate, like Lem, of V.M.I., he had suffered a series of staff assignments and misfortunes, including a crash landing on a reef with no food or water. Seriously injured, he had spent six months in the hospital. His appointment as Commandant ended the hopes of a flock of senior generals.

His aide escorted me into the inner sanctuary, and he rose to greet me. He didn't look at all well. There was a sallow cast to his usual ruddy complexion and his eyes were pale and tired. Deeply etched in his face were lines of fatigue, and I could sense the strain. He had finished more than half his tour of duty as Commandant and the weight of responsibility showed. He smiled and motioned me to sit alongside his desk.

"Mel," he said, "I know what you've been through."

This nearly undid me. Helen had died the previous year, after three long years of agony. There seemed no limit to this shattering loss. Alcohol dulled it only for a moment, and work was not much help. It hurt to rattle around our home at Gramercy Park, where Luther, my houseman, would often say, "Ginral, you don't laugh much." There was no getting back into stride. The hard hit had come. I was still holding on, without tears, rolling with the punch, but staggering. Tightly sealed in, the loss and the bitter loneliness were a malignancy eating into my spirit.

"We've been thinking of you down here," Randy Pate continued. "That's why I had you come down." He shuffled some papers on the desk in front of him. "We'd like you to do a job for us. You'll be ordered to Europe for the record but you'll switch at Lages in the Azores and go to Morocco. Contact our ambassador, who'll know about you, get the lowdown on the French, Spanish, and American situations, and let us know if there's anything the Corps should know well in advance. We may be closing up shop there before long. Above all, don't involve us." He smiled. "Where necessary, be silent in the usual seven languages."

As he spoke, my mind reached behind his words. We had had many a drink together in Washington, New York, and Quantico, and it suddenly dawned on me that he had been helped to this invitation. The previous fall, when I had stood for borough president of Manhattan in a strongly Democratic constituency, "like Hitler running on Delancey Street," as one wag put it, Lou Ruppel, a Marine comrade-in-arms and editor-in-chief of *Collier's,* had helped direct the campaign. Behind Randy's bland exterior, I detected the fine Italian hand of Lou, that lovable rascal, long a welcome guest at the White House. I could even place the moment when he had planned this therapeutic escape for me from the Valley of Despond. Nan, my sugarplum, was at the Sorbonne in Paris, and Pete was getting ready for Columbia. Morocco, Paris, Sorbonne, Nan. It was all clear to me now.

We had been drinking in my place at Gramercy Park, and one of Pete's poetry books was open on the coffee table. There in front of me were the poems of Robert Burns:

> Auld Lang Syne
> Should auld acquaintance be forgot
> And never brought to mind?

I began to break and turned the page:

> My love is like a red, red rose
> That's newly sprung in June. . . .

> So fair art thou, my bonnie lass
> So deep in love am I. . . .

I had been racked with sorrow—a healthy, cleansing sadness. It was Lou Ruppel who had called the Commandant and set the wheels in motion for my visit to Headquarters and this talk with Randy Pate.

My authorization came through on April 4:

FROM: Commandant of the Marine Corps
  TO: Major General Melvin L. KRULEWITCH
          04303 USMCR (Ret)
          45 Gramercy Park, New York 10, New York

SUBJ: Authorization Orders

1. On or about 6 April 1958 you are authorized to proceed to Europe where you will carry out the instructions issued verbally by the Commandant of the Marine Corps.

*   *   *   *   *   *   *   *   *   *   *   *   *   *   *

4. Please effect the necessary passport and immunization requirements.

R. McC. PATE

Copy to:
MajGen Krulewitch—25

Floyd Bennett gave me a hop to Norfolk on a two-motored Beechcraft, a doubtful blessing—the Marine corporal sitting directly behind me had made himself a cornucopia of newspaper, and heaved into it continuously. The Navy transport waiting on the field with the two-star general's plate affixed to its nose made up for it though, as did the warm reception by the captain and co-pilot.

At the last moment, however, a noisy wailing party of four, a woman and three children, dragged and scrambled across the field to the plane, and unfortunately, made it. It turned out she was the wife of a civilian employee of the United States Army in Germany, and was returning after a visit to the States. Loudly vocal, her dark hair wildly unkempt, she arrived in a vaporous cloud of perspiration, wearing a tight, shining, black rayon shift without belt or buckles. Adding to the general air of abandon, the dress was cut so low in front that whenever she bent to attend to one of the children, she almost fell out of it. As we took off, she announced that her husband would never have forgiven her if she'd missed the plane. The captain and I exchanged glances. For most of the flight the children cried and cried. Her standard method of pacifying them was to stick a chocolate lollipop, of which she had a plentiful supply, into each gaping mouth. Because of her and the children, I spent a good part of the time with the pilots up forward in a small dressing room and bunk, directly aft of the cockpit. Most of the body of the plane was loaded with ammo and medical supplies, and the family had the free run of it.

On arrival at Lages Airport on Pico Island, where the happy little family party had to change planes for Germany, the steward opened the exit door as the passenger loading ramp was wheeled up. I stood there waiting to descend. With a whirl and a flourish, the lady and her brood forced themselves ahead of me. Turning, she pushed the youngest against my chest, saying, "Hold him," and proceeded down the ramp. The child was wet—or worse. On the tarmac the commandant of the airport was waiting; word of my arrival had been wired ahead. I handed back the child, and the CO smiled. "Glad to have you aboard, General. But we didn't expect your family."

"Bite your tongue," I lashed out at him.

After refueling, we continued on, blessedly alone, to Port Lyautey, a U.S. Naval base on the Atlantic coast of Morocco, named for General Louis H. G. Lyautey, the great colonizer and diplomatic Resident General of France. There I received, with the same never-ending surprise, the full red-carpet treatment, including the two-star flag at the yardarm. Colonel David W. Silvey, U.S. Marine Corps, and an honor guard were waiting to greet me, and I was then conducted to my quarters where I enjoyed a hot bath before adjourning to the cafeteria for lunch.

My official call on our ambassador, the Hon. Cavendish W.

Cannon, produced a gold mine of information. We were in the middle of a hot and cold diplomatic war between Morocco and Spain and Morocco and France. Vice President Nixon had visited the Sultan in the previous year, and in the fall, King Mohammed had visited Eisenhower in Washington, these meetings resulting in a healthy grant of $20 million to Morocco, followed by an additional $10 million in 1958. In the very week of my visit, the United States had helped calm the frontier tensions with Spain by sending a diplomatic note expressing Washington's hope that a peaceful solution could be found to the dispute.

Discussing our position, Ambassador Cannon reviewed the history of our friendship with Morocco, as far back as the landings of Operation Torch in 1943 and the meetings at Casablanca, when Roosevelt expressed his strong support of a free Morocco. Our intervention had produced some immediate, unexpected concessions; Spain had agreed to transfer what was called the Southern Protectorate of Morocco to King Mohammed's government, although this was a mixed blessing, since the Protectorate was a desert waste with a population of about two persons to the square mile.

More complicated were the claims against France, then inextricably enmeshed in the Algerian War. Morocco claimed territory as far south as the Senegal River, including portions of Algeria and Mauritania. Based to some extent on racial and religious grounds, these claims were not taken very seriously by the French side of the French-Moroccan boundary negotiating commission. The Moroccans, said the ambassador with the faintest of smiles, were not prepared to negotiate on a purely legalistic basis. "We want to keep the British and the French fully informed," he said. "They received advance notice of the President's intervention last week, and to complete the picture, they should know our analysis of the reaction of the Spanish and Moroccan interests as well as the diplomatic recommendations in our follow-up. And as you know, you Marines will be out of here before long."

This was the kind of confirmation General Pate needed in order to plan the Marine Corps' fiscal and personnel policies. Saying good-by to Lyautey, a cushy billet, would mean something to a few, from a personal point of view, but nothing in terms of

world perspective. After being invited by the ambassador to drop
in two days later, when he expected a visit from officers of the
Sixth Fleet, I left the embassy, and drove back to Kenitra and
my VIP quarters, where I found that my brown and black silk
dressing gown, resembling a jellaba, had been stolen. It looked too
much like the real thing for an Arab to pass up. Besides, someone
would achieve merit by stealing from an unbeliever.

Next day, the sleek, black limousine with its two American
flags rippling in the breeze hummed through the *medina* at Rabat.
We were on our way to visit the first secretary of the embassy,
the Hon. Ben Franklin Dixon, a Marine major and a comrade
during World War II, and for show I had taken on an additional
sergeant to sit up front with the driver. We passed the *souqs,*
crammed with every kind of shop—here a waterfall of shoes and
slippers, some of goatskin, painted brilliant crimson; there an open-
air teahouse or a carpet-weaver's workshop. Amid the smells and
the shouting, were shops for leather goods, musical instruments,
brass ware, and jewelry, all crowded with pointing and chattering
Berbers, Chlues, Tauregs, Bedouins, and foreigners. It was a fascinating sight—long white cloaks striped in gray, yellow, and purple
flowing jellabas, stiff white turbans, *kaffiahs, tarboosh,* fezzes, green
and yellow twisted headcloths, as well as every shade of complexion,
from coal black to creamy white. The streets wound in and around
the quarters and then into the *mella,* the Jewish district of the capital,
much like the *medina,* but separate and apart.

As we drove by, a small red-lettered sign high up on the front
of a gloomy-looking dive caught my eye. The letters were in
Hebrew: ‏כשר‎ ‏כשר‎ . You see them in New York, Paris,
and London, and they mean that the food is prepared in accordance with orthodox Jewish rituals. I ordered the driver to turn at
the next corner and come back around. We stopped in front of the
shop, the sergeants jumped out and stood at attention, and I went
into what turned out to be a small restaurant with a bar along the
side. People were eating at some six or eight tables and all looked
up as I entered, in uniform, with two sergeants behind me. Sitting
around relaxing with their own kind in a Jewish cafe, they looked
and looked again. Not a word was said, but their eyes spoke

volumes. It was an age-old questioning—Friend or foe? Life or death? For centuries, they had been caught in the middle.

The *patronne* came out of the kitchen, her face steamy-red from the cooking. She wiped her hands on her apron, and greeted me in French. Her concern was obvious, but when I announced, loud enough for all to hear, *a-no-chi-ivri* ("I am a Hebrew"), the tension broke. The group left their tables and crowded around, urging drinks or refreshments on us. One young man in a long linen coverall turned to the phone. *Il me faut telephoner mon père,* he said. ("I must telephone my father.") When we left I was escorted to the door by the entire group.

Ben Dixon, second in command at the Embassy, light complexioned, of middle height and build, had served in the Pacific when we both were attached to the 4th Marine Division. A military dandy with an attractive matinee-idol mustache, he had become a diplomat on leaving the service. We shot the breeze between drinks and refreshments. It was a touch of the Corps "in sunny tropic scenes." Then I returned to Port Lyautey for a scheduled dinner, stopping off at the base cafeteria for a cup of coffee.

The manager came over and asked if he could sit with me. I wondered why but answered that of course he could. He continued, *"Je serais très fier de vous joindre."* Again I wondered why and soon learned. Speaking in French he said that he had heard by telephone from Rabat that I was Jewish. His name was Fasi. He was Jewish too, he said, and it made him proud. He looked, spoke, and acted like an Arab, but he was Jewish. It was like turning up a Marine, as has so often happened, in a strange corner of the world.

We discussed the problems of Jews in Morocco. There was no emergency, if you didn't mind being insulted and reminded at every turn that you were a second-class citizen. Some 40,000 had emigrated to Israel but the important Jewish social, professional, and financial classes still remained to grace the business and residential sections of Casablanca and Rabat. A few, originally Jewish, had converted to Islam but still bore their Jewish names, such as El Kôhen, Beñ Jullûn. Others remained Jewish, such as Moshé Beñ-Attâr, Solomoñ Beñ-Arrôsh, and many more.

A bitter hatred for the Jew had spread like a cancerous growth throughout the Arab world. In his sweep from China to central Europe, Genghis Khan, had said, "The victor and the vanquished can never be friends." This was true, although in Morocco Jews had lived in peace for 600 years and more. Morocco had taken no part in the Vichy armistice of 1940 when France fell; on the contrary, the Sultan had actively protected his Jewish subjects in 1943 when the French Resident General, a Vichy loyalist, had ordered him to enforce the Nuremberg anti-Jewish laws. King Mohammed refused and is said to have told General Charles Noguès, who turned French guns against our North African landings in Operation Torch, "My Jewish subjects are as much under my protection as the Moslems."

During our talk the manager poured coffee, handed me the sugar and milk, straightened the dishes, and tried hard to serve me in every way possible. Then one of the long-robed Arab employees came running over, crying *"chergui, chergui,"* and pointing to the windows. The manager got up, shouting orders, and ran to the cashier's desk to secure the takings. At the steam tables, the food was covered over and carried to the reefers. All condiments, sugars, and spices on the tables were quickly removed to the kitchens.

Over the protests of the Arabs, I slipped outside to find the skies had darkened, blotting out the sun, and everyone was running for cover. As I sprinted for the car the first gritting particles of sand and dust penetrated my nose, ears, eyes, and mouth and found a way into my clothes, shoes, and headgear. It was a sandstorm, the *chergui,* rare in Morocco but not uncommon in North Africa.

I picked up a fluttering bit of dark golden yarn caught in the brambles of a red barberry bush. Someone had gone by in a hurry. The air was heavy—biting and burning. This type of sandstorm whirled like the inverted cone of the twisters I had seen at sea. I knew what was coming and could smell it. There was more than noise, heat, and wind. It put a choking, pressing, suffocating, mortally dangerous weight on the lungs. The hum grew louder, like the swarming of locusts. The whirling wind had pulled great waves of sand into the air, and we were about to get the full benefit.

To protect the car, I ordered the sergeant chauffeur to drive into the heart of the wind toward the hangar at the airfield. Its great gates were closing as we approached, but someone had seen us and held them open long enough for us to squeeze in under the wings of the Navy transport before they slid shut. Even in the shelter of the hangar the air had thickened. Getting out of the car would have been a struggle as the pressure mounted, so we lay back listening to the sand shift through the joints and air vents of the hangar's corrugated plates.

Hours seemed to pass, and then someone knocked at the hangar door and called out. It was Fasi. He had heard we were in the hangar, and since the storm had died down, had come to fetch us. We shook and shook ourselves, jumped up and down, and slapped our clothes to get rid of the sand, and then drove back to the cafeteria, where Fasi had arranged a mighty meal of *tagine* (roast lamb), *meshui,* couscous, and steaks, the best of Morocco and the U.S. Navy. We slept well that night. In the morning, I found that my West Indian St. John's Bay Rum had disappeared.

Next day, I reported to the Embassy and found Ambassador Cannon entertaining four officers from the Sixth Fleet who had dropped into Rabat, not only to pay their respects to our ambassador, but also because they had wangled leave and an invitation to visit Sandhurst, the British West Point. Their important diplomatic problem, with which they were patently bursting at the seams, was transportation. And all of them looked to me.

"Do you have any immediate plans?" asked the ambassador. "You have first call on the plane scheduled to leave tomorrow."

Sandhurst, London, Paris, the Sorbonne, and Nan, my sugarplum—the idea burst like a star shell, and Operation Nan unfolded like a rose. But it had to be handled with savvy—not too eager at first, then a gradual assent, as I allowed them to persuade me. After all, I had no authority to reserve a Government plane for my own personal use.

It worked. The officers were most grateful, the ambassador deeply appreciative, and I licked my chops.

We landed at Farnborough Airport in Hampshire, England,

where transportation was waiting to take us to Sandhurst. The plane was ordered to stand by.

The Royal Military College at Sandhurst was the result of a merger in 1947 of the Royal Military Academy, founded in Woolwich in 1741 for the technical training of officers in artillery, engineering, and communications, and affectionately nicknamed "The Shop," and the Royal Military College, founded in 1799 by Frederick, Duke of York, George III's favorite son. Freddie, the commander-in-chief of the army, had taken unto himself a gorgeous creature, Mary Ann Clarke, as his mistress, and set her up in Gloucester with an allowance of £1000 a year. In those days it was the practice in England to purchase commissions and a kind of price list had been established over the years, depending, of course, on rank and regiment. In 1798 a commission as lieutenant in the Grenadier Guards cost £1700, twice as much as a lieutenancy in a line regiment. The commission of a major or lieutenant colonel sold for as much as £4200 or £5400 or even higher.

Making use of her close connection with the commander-in-chief, Mary began to sell commissions at bargain rates, charging as little as £200 for an ensignship and £900 for a majority—less than half the going rate on the open market. Naturally there was a public outcry, and Parliament, although loath to involve the King's son in a scandal, ordered an inquiry. In 1809 Freddie was found guilty of corruption and he resigned as commander-in-chief. Mary Ann was still on the ball, however. Her collection of the Duke's love letters was ready for publication when an offer to suppress them in return for the sum of £10,000 was accepted.

Many gallant officers purchased commissions, however, and lived to have their names memorialized in the military annals of their country. Walking through Sandhurst's memorial chapel, we saw marble tablets chronicling a cross section of British history and devotion to duty: Crimea, Delhi, Lucknow, New Zealand, Zululand, Afghanistan, Egypt, Sudan, Manipur, Punjab, South Africa, Somaliland, Tibet, France, Cameroons, Mesopotamia, Gallipoli, Belgium, Palestine, Tobruk, Burma, Korea—all memorializing the awards of the Victoria Cross to alumni of Sandhurst. We breathed history.

Then I drove back alone to Farnborough, on the last lap to my objective. Nan, my sugarplum, my little girl, was living in a pension run by a genteel French couple, André Langes, a retired cryptographer for French intelligence, and motherly Mme. Langes. From Orly I took a taxi for the long ride to 50 Rue Ribera, off the avenue Mozart, south of the Eiffel Tower. The Langeses lived on the fifth floor of a six-story walk-up. I rang the bell. Nan's roommate, a blonde Swedish student, opened the door, looked at me, and called, "Nan!" My sugarplum came running. "Daddy, Daddy!"

Mission accomplished.

★

22. The $64,000 Question

WHEN JUSTICE BERNARD BOTEIN, now a practicing lawyer, was appointed presiding justice of the Appellate Division, Supreme Court, New York County, by Governor Averell Harriman, he also succeeded to the patronage of that office, which included such appointments as referee in disciplinary proceedings against lawyers, impartial designees in labor disputes, and the lush appointment of five (now ten) referees to audit and investigate the reports of committees for incompetents. Bernie's predecessor, Dave Peck, had appointed me one of those referees, and the job brought in about $30,000 a year.

I had known Bernie for years, more closely after 1946, when we became fellow trustees of the Park Avenue Synagogue, and we had many mutual friends. Tall, spare, serious, and with a crown of fluffy, white hair, he had spoken to me about the possibilities of his appointment as chief justice, after Judge Peck retired, adding before we parted that there was one Republican he would appoint as referee, and that would be Mel Krulewitch.

Bernie duly got the job, and I heard nothing further until February, 1958, came up—the month when referees were annually appointed. Then I received a telephone call from the judge asking me to come to see him, presumably about my reappointment since he had already appointed William J. Calise, a political figure, to one of the positions.

The judge indicated that he had other plans for the appointment.

I reached for my fountain pen. "I'll sign my resignation right now," I answered.

I waited only to close out a few pending matters and sent in

200

my resignation, without mentioning our conversation on the eve of his appointment. Judge Botein subsequently appointed to fill the position a gentleman with whom he had been friendly long years before.

Now that a Republican state organization had been returned to power, the scramble for office began. Pretty Caroline Simon, defeated in the Manhattan election for president of the Council, deftly and daintily got her foot in the door of the gold rush to be appointed secretary of state, a sinecure usually reserved for the New York County chairman of the successful political party. Bob Christenberry, who had run for mayor, was appointed postmaster of New York City, a position that Jacob Javits, United States Senator, had offered to me, only I just couldn't take it. Jim Lundy, the only member of the Republican state ticket to be defeated in that campaign (he lost to Arthur Leavitt), was appointed chairman of the Public Service Commission. Apparently the word was out to take care of Krulewitch, who had lost gracefully.

Having served both Republican and Democratic administrations as special counsel in utilities, I day-dreamed of a beautiful public career—public service commissioner, then attorney general and maybe lieutenant governor—or if not, counsel later on to the great utility combines. I dreamed well. I should have stayed at home.

The telephone rang. It was the Governor's office calling from Albany. "The Governor would like to speak to you," said a secretary's voice. "Can you make it tomorrow morning?" Would a dog eat cold turkey? I asked myself.

"I'm sure I can make it," said I, with visions of the long-sought appointment to the Public Service Commission dancing before me.

"Shall we send a car for you?"

"No," I replied grandly—for who turns down a hitch offered by the Governor? "I'll take the morning Empire, if you don't mind, and walk up from the station."

"Good enough," she said. "Shall we say 11:30?"

This was it.

I arrived in Albany on the Empire State and went to the Ten Eyck hotel to freshen up before meeting the Governor. In the

lobby I met former senator MacNeil Mitchell, and Bernard
Newman, then Republican County chairman, and later a justice
of the Supreme Court of the State of New York. Of middle height,
chunky, an athlete and boxer in his youth and still not averse to
a wrestling bout in his law office, Bernard had a disarming affa-
bility. He knew of my interest in an appointment as a Public
Service commissioner, and so did MacNeil Mitchell. In fact, Mac
had previously told me I would be appointed to the Public Service
Commission or his name was not Mitchell (it still is Mitchell).
MacNeil was the Republican district leader of the old Tenth
Assembly District, from which he had served in the state legislature for almost 30 years. He was slim, tallish, high-colored, and
every inch a professional politician, despite his Ivy League dress
and appearance.

With his support, it seemed that Bernie Newman had recommended me to the Governor as chairman of the State Athletic
Commission! Slightly stunned by the news, I left them in the lobby
and walked up to the Capitol.

The executive chambers in the early days of January, 1959,
were jammed with crowds of hopefuls, near-hopefuls and hoping-
against-hope hopefuls waiting in the lobbies. When my turn came,
a secretary ushered me into Rocky's beautiful office, and the
Governor stood to greet me, gracious, smiling, and animated.
Lieutenant Governor Malcolm Wilson was with him, and so was
Secretary of State Caroline Simon, After a general preliminary
chat, the Governor turned to me and said, "I want a strong man
for chairman of the Athletic Commission."

Caroline squealed, "Superb appointment," and Malcolm beamed
approval.

I told the Governor that my interests were in the law, particularly in public utility regulation, and that given a choice, I would
prefer *that* appointment. The Governor replied, however, that he
was not planning to do anything at the moment with the vacant
position of Public Service commissioner. Disappointed, I told the
Governor that I would like time to consider the matter, and he
agreed.

At that very moment, Dick Amper, the Governor's press officer,
came into the room and said, "The press have it." This had not

been planned, but the effect was the same. After a little more discussion, I weakened. "I shall never let you down," the Governor said. "That goes both ways," I replied.

Rockefeller never let me down—not once—during the almost seven and a half years I served as a member of his team. During one of my subsequent investigations into underworld influence on boxing, when the press was hinting darkly at a shakeup in the Commission, Rocky came to me during a dinner at the executive mansion in honor of a visiting princess of the Netherlands, and punching a forefinger into my chest, said, "I'm with you." That was just the support I needed, and I floated on air.

So it looked as though I was chairman of the Athletic Commission, although the swearing in required two additional visits to Albany. That evening after our talk, I ate a late snack, all alone at Keeler's. Then, finding there were no railroad connections, no planes, and no one I knew driving to New York, I went down to the bus terminal for the next bus to the city, which finally left at 11 P.M. Three hours later, tired, weary, disappointed, and disillusioned, I walked into my apartment at Gramercy Park. No one was home—the children were away at college—and all I wanted was a couple of shots of Dewar's and a hot tub. I unlocked the door to a clanging, jangling, shrilling chorus of telephones. All the extensions in this eight–room apartment were ringing and ringing and ringing.

I let them ring and took my tub. But some sadist had thought up the idea of phoning every five minutes, and sleep was out of the question. I finally gave in. Picking up the extension on my night table I asked, "Who is it?" A voice replied, "This is Jack Cuddy of United Press. I hope I'm not disturbing you."

"That's a masterpiece of understatement," I said curtly. "What's on your mind?"

Then he asked the $64,000 question. "Some of the boys at the office would like to know how you pronounce your name."

★

23. Iwo Jima Was Never Like This

As CHAIRMAN of the New York State Athletic Commission, I became the number one target for the sports press, although I had gotten used to taking it on the chin after a lifetime in the Marine Corps, some 30 years at the bar, and a losing campaign for borough president of Manhattan. For one thing, I knew little about the boxing game. I had watched a few bouts, had boxed at school, and had even seen Gentleman Jim Corbett go a couple of rounds with a sparring partner, skip rope, and sing "Knock Him Down McCloskey" at Hammerstein's Victoria—the same Jim Corbett who knocked out the fabulous John L. Sullivan on September 7th, 1892, to win the world's heavyweight title.

I also saw the Dempsey-Carpentier fight in July, 1921, at Boyle's Thirty Acres, in which the Frenchman was knocked out in the fourth round. And in 1923, I watched Luis Firpo, the Wild Bull of the Pampas, knock Dempsey out of the ring, and saw the boxing writers seated at ringside push him back in again. But all this had little to do with a sport which had by now fallen into the hands of a small sinister group against whom only a handful of die-hard lovers of the game were still fighting their losing battle.

Before I entered the chairman's office on West 47th Street, Marvin Kohn, who I discovered was the Commission's press secretary, press officer, press agent, and public information officer, had set up a press conference in my law office. Marvin was over 6 feet, and over 250 pounds—an honest, baby-faced bundle of nerves, who affected a cane and had an enviable gang of female satellites. Every noon at his favorite table in Sardi's West, backed against the wall, Marvin watched the action, not only in boxing, but in the fortunes of a long list of celebrities who swore by him.

That morning I ran the gauntlet of the press—and made it—by saying nothing and passing the buck, Army-style. Milt Gross, still running a sports column, got a break which he did not deserve, when I took him to the City Athletic Club for lunch. He asked me what I knew about Cus D'Amato, and I pronounced it in the proper way, against his "Deeamato." In his column next day, he claimed that Krulewitch knew nothing about boxing because he couldn't even pronounce "Deeamato."

The new job became a discordant symphony of new faces, new lives, and new characters. Presents began to arrive by mail, all of which were returned. Harry Markson, in charge of boxing for Madison Square Garden, brought in the Garden's counsel one morning, Truman Gibson, whom Joe Louis had introduced to the Garden and who later got into big trouble. Sugar Ray Robinson sent in George Gainford to look me over. I had to learn the hard way—not only about the boxing game itself, but about my own commission to find out who were friends and who were foes, and who, if any, were available for a consideration. Each morning brought a new string of job-seekers, hopeful prospective licensees, boxers looking for a last chance, and innumerable calls from the press, each reporter looking for an edge over his pals. It was all in a day's work.

We were a black sport, with more rock and roll than soul, although occasionally a white meteor crossed the horizon. Such had been the ethnic history of the game, not 100 per cent of one group all the time, but enough to show who were the underdogs in the American melting pot. First came the Irish, suffering from the American Protective Association—Morrissey, Heenan, Paddy Ryan, John L. Sullivan ("I can lick any man in the house"). Then the Jews, discriminated against in labor, housing, public accommodations, and community life, and influenced by the history of the British prize ring, where Sephardic Jews from Spain and Portugal had become heavyweight champions. Then the Italians had their day—and many a son of Italy fought under a good fighting Irish name, until finally Rocky Marciano, alias Marchegiano, became heavyweight champion of the world and retired undefeated.

After that came the black flood, and with it a distinguished roll of champions. And now with the black group we were in the middle of a long line of Latin-American licensees, mostly from Puerto Rico in the lesser weights, but with some South American hopefuls in the heavier classes.

It was all fine and dandy, or so it appeared, this noble art of self-defense. I liked the game, but we hadn't had a heavyweight championship in the Garden or anywhere else in New York City for years, not since the Hurricane Jackson fight in 1957. The heavyweight title bouts had migrated to Seattle, Los Angeles, and Indianapolis. There was trouble in boxing in New York—big trouble—and as one underworld character put it, "Mel the Gom" fell into it with both feet. Jim Norris, head of the Garden, was in close contact and on a first name basis with Frankie Carbo, an underworld character exerting an important and malevolent influence on boxing.

Cus D'Amato, the champion's manager, whom Truman Gibson called "our arch enemy," wasn't so saintly himself, and was certainly not above playing both ends against the middle, as in the case of the Roy Harris championship bout in Los Angeles, which Floyd Patterson won. D'Amato took out some insurance on Floyd's future by making his office assistant, Charley Black, the manager of Roy Harris just in case Floyd lost. Cus then had it going and coming, since his own office hanger-on would not only have control of Harris if he beat the champion, but would also get 10 per cent of Harris's purse in the event of a return match. But that was past history, and when Bill Rosensohn came in waving a contract with Ingemar Johansson for a championship match with Floyd, it looked like heavyweight boxing was coming back to New York. Even Governor Rockefeller remarked with a broad smile at a luncheon in Albany, "You've started off running." But the honeymoon was short.

The Athletic Commission was grossly over-staffed, with more than 100 inspectors, most of whom we never saw. The two commissioners were Julie Helfand, now Justice Helfand of the Supreme Court, a former Brooklyn assistant district attorney and young Jim Farley, son of Jim Farley the great boxing commissioner who was known as Mr. Democrat, and who broke with F.D.R.

over his third and fourth terms. Dan Parker of the *New York Mirror* said that as the lone Republican on the Commission, sitting with two Democrats, I took office "with two strikes on me," and that "Julius and his Democratic colleague, Jim Farley, Jr., will hold the balance of power."

I decided to give Rosensohn Enterprises a license to promote the Patterson-Johansson world heavyweight championship fight in New York, and announced my intention from the bench. Farley shouted for an adjournment. We went into executive session in my office for a 10-minute tirade by the opposition. Though the Garden was violently against the licensee, the real reason for their outburst was that they knew that if they opposed the license in public, the press, eager for the bout, would tear them apart. Helfand was the more knowledgeable of the two, and he was smart. It wasn't long before the newspapers were reporting that Helfand was running the Commission, since he had the know-how and most of his appointees were still in office, but this state of affairs did not last long. We disagreed on many things, mostly politics, but on the whole I found him an able and honest public servant.

But if Farley and Helfand were difficult at times, the cross of Sam Duberstein was the heaviest. Duberstein was an auctioneer who continued to ply his trade while holding the top staff job on the Commission. A Brooklyn district leader, he was appointed executive secretary of the Commission on the recommendation of the Kings County Republican organization, of which Johnny Crews was the chairman. When a sale by Duberstein Auctioneers was advertised in the daily press, which was often, we knew he would not be with us that day. That would have been bad enough, but one day a call came through to my desk at 9:30 A.M. and an angry voice took me to task, saying, "You sunner bitch, where wuz you this mawning?"

Startled, I asked, "Who are you?"

Back came the violent reply, "You know me you bastid! Where's my money from the auction?"

I hung up and rang for Duberstein, who wasn't in. You could never reason with Dubie. When you called him to account for some failure to do his job or some infraction of the rules, he would look at you reproachfully, as though you were the guilty one.

One of the best deputies we had on the job was a Democrat, Pat Callahan. I liked Pat for his ability and his honesty, and when several Republican leaders, prompted by Duberstein, asked why I kept him, I closed the subject by answering, "Pat Callahan is a better man than anyone you ever sent over." The Chief Deputy, Frank Morris, was also able and honest, and when I put little Petey Scalzo in as Chief Inspector, I had the nucleus of a good working group. Petey tried to kiss me when I told him I'd appoint him, and said "I'm going home to burn a candle." His son married a nice little Jewish girl who, like a good wife, took possession of all the gift checks at the wedding.

It was an interesting period in which to take office. Into the peaceful, somnolent atmosphere of the Commission had come the order of the United States Supreme Court affirming Judge Sylvester J. Ryan's decree of June 24, 1957, dissolving the unlawful combination of the Chicago International Boxing Club and the New York International Boxing Club. These were owned, respectively, by Chicago Stadium and Madison Square Garden, which were in turn controlled by the two central figures in national boxing, Jim Norris and Arthur Wirtz. On February 18, 1959, Judge Ryan approved the sale of the Norris-Wirtz stock interests in the Garden to the Irving Mitchel Felt group, doing business under the name of Graham-Paige Corporation. This didn't bother us too much at the Commission, since Judge Ryan's decree was two years old, and Felt, having been the President of the Federation of Jewish Philanthropies, with its 130 agencies, was a well-known do-gooder.

But I had a visitor that week. An appointment had been made by my secretary, without my knowledge or consent, with Billy Brown, one-time matchmaker at the Garden, a short, stocky, Italian type whose alias was Dominick Mordini and who sought a license of any kind—second, manager, or matchmaker. He was rather short with me when I presented him with proof of his connection with Frankie Carbo, the underworld boxing king, who at that time was a fugitive from justice. The district attorney had set forth in the report of his lengthy investigation of boxing the evidence of Billy Brown's association with Carbo and other

shady characters, but to my surprise, Mordini attempted to deny
it. He left in a huff, saying I'd hear from him. I never did and
Mordini's bout was over. But this was just a preliminary to the
main event—Frankie Carbo and his stooge, Gabe Genovese,
now·appeared on the scene.

Also known as Paul Carbo, Paul John Carbo, Frank Tucker,
and Frank Russo Carbo, Frankie was still a fugitive from justice.
But he was no fugitive from the Garden's Jim Norris, Gabe
Genovese, Blinky Palermo, or Carmen Basilio, all of whom knew
about his hideaway in Miami and discussed boxing business with
him there. Upstate promoter Norman Rothschild, for instance,
had to pay some $10,000 to Genovese to get Basilio's managers,
DeJohn and Nitro, to agree to the Carmen Basilio-Johnny Saxton
welterweight championship match held in Syracuse in 1956. Since
Blinky Palermo, a long-time friend and associate of Carbo, was
also the manager of Saxton, Carbo had it all down the line—
both managers in his pocket and even a cut from promoter
Rothschild.

But the end of the road was now in sight for Carbo. He was
picked up in New Jersey, and after a fight against extradition,
brought to New York, where he pleaded guilty to acting as an
undercover manager and matchmaker. In December, 1959, he
was sentenced to two years' imprisonment in the Rikers Island
Penitentiary. At Carbo's sentencing the prosecutor stated:

> The evil influence of this man has, for many years, perme-
> ated virtually the entire professional sport of boxing. I be-
> lieve it is fair to say that the name of Frank Carbo today
> symbolized the degeneration of professional boxing into a
> racket.

But the big heat did not come until 1961, the year after his
release from Rikers Island. Boxing was still under his control,
although he was no longer the all-powerful eminence. Illness had
begun to work its inroads, and so had the Kefauver hearings.
Truman Gibson, Jim Norris' associate in both the New York and
Chicago ends of the empire, named 14 outstanding managers and
promoters as being so close to Carbo as to be controlled by him.

Carbo's connection with organized crime dated from his early youth. Homicide and robbery figured in the long list of his offenses, and the fear inspired by his murderous reputation was the basis of his power. But he was also able to deliver. His stable of managers and fighters always made a living when Carbo was in the picture, not as good as it might have been, but better than the complete screwing they might well have received without him. When he could get champions like Davey Moore, Johnny Saxton, and Carmen Basilio in his clutches, either directly or through managers or go-betweens, he naturally attracted the smaller fry, the preliminary-bout boxers. Here his close relationship with Jim Norris and the Garden paid off. Again and again, in the many investigations by state and federal law enforcement agencies, *omerta,* the seal of silence, was harshly and inexorably enforced, and it was only when Jackie Leonard, a manager and promoter, refused to kick in and was threatened with death, that Carbo's hold was finally broken. Leonard collaborated with the police and nailed Carbo, Palermo, and their associates. Carbo was sentenced to 25 years in prison and a fine of $10,000; Palermo received 15 years and a fine of $10,000, and Truman Gibson, a suspended 5-year term and a $10,000 fine. The ball was over.

The prospects now looked bright in New York. We had a heavyweight championship coming up, something not seen for years, with a new and attractive Great White Hope who had a professional boxing record of 21 wins and no losses. Bill Rosensohn had signed up Ingemar Johansson and paid $10,000 for a 40-day option on a Patterson fight.

We didn't know Rosensohn, but had been advised by the California Athletic Commission that he had been given a temporary license to co-promote the Patterson-Roy Harris fight in Los Angeles after the California Commission had disqualified Al Weill as a promoter. Bill went into boxing, he said, "with the highest of hopes, and this was to me the realization of a dream." The big fight was slated for June 25, 1959, and preparations went on at a furious rate. All the local politicians put in bids for free tickets, and friends of yesteryear of whom we hadn't seen hair nor hide for decades, appeared on the scene with ear-to-ear smiles of intimate friendship. This I later learned was Standard Operating Behavior (S.O.B.) for all championship fights, and Pat Callahan advised me to reserve and pay for a couple of hundred ringside seats, and then to pray for reimbursement. For weeks before the fight, the Commission was lobbied by Republican Party officials and district and county political leaders in behalf of various nominees for referee of the main event, and this too was a curse that had to be borne.

Then clouds began to gather on the horizon. There was something that smelled, and smelled bad, and the boxing writers started playing it up in their columns. Who was this manager of Ingemar? What made him manager? What did he know about the game? We ordered a hearing, and to our consternation found that Cus D'Amato had done it again. When Johansson returned to Sweden, he published a story stating that he had been compelled to sign a slave contract for a manager selected by Cus D'Amato, his opponent's manager. The press promptly characterized the Commission as The Three Blind Mice: Winken, Blinken, and Nod; and more pointedly, The Three Dumb Dukes. As the investigation progressed, we found that D'Amato had dug up a stooge, one Harry Davidow, an ancient friend who ran a small store in Brooklyn, and then forced Johansson, under threat of losing the championship fight with Patterson, to sign a contract making Davidow his manager for five years. Davidow piously affirmed that he had been satisfied to take only 10 percent as manager since "I didn't feel that I was entitled to any more because I didn't have anything to do with the development of Mr. Johansson." Prior to the day they signed the contract, Davidow hadn't even met the fighter. We unanimously disapproved the contract, and fiery Judge Helfand went on record with the opinion that "the whole thing stinks to high Heaven."

The boxing press fell upon this episode with a ravenous appetite. Rosensohn reported that Cus D'Amato had threatened to pull the fight out of New York, and this was confirmed by his attorney. D'Amato, fearing that this might hurt the gate, then denied it in a few thousand well-chosen words, although Rosensohn had made a trip to California to look for an alternate site. In fact, up until the day before the fight, Rosensohn feared that D'Amato would cancel it. Next to this, our subsequent discovery—that a deal had been made (so Rosensohn testified), between D'Amato, Rosensohn, and three others to divvy up the sale of 200 working press tickets, the closest tickets to the ring and worth a minimum of $20,000—seemed almost minor. Rosensohn later testified that he had received his one-fifth share of the money. The other four denied everything.

The fight was postponed from June 25th because of rain. It rained again on the 26th. I walked around all day with a sinking sensation in the pit of my stomach, remembering that the law had required the promoter to file with the state a bond of only $2500 to protect the ticket holders against failure to stage the fight, and that some $400,000 worth of tickets had already been sold. After visiting Yankee Stadium for a last-minute inspection, I had cut off all telephones to the office, and was seeing only important officials of the promotion, when our chief inspector, Petey Scalzo, a former world's featherweight champion, came in with a word of comfort. "Don't let nuthin' bother you," he said, "Jest roll with the punch!"

The rain continued, but at about 8 P.M. it slackened off, and the ensuing knockout of champion Floyd Patterson by Ingemar Johansson is boxing history. It was a good clean end to three months' bickering over the details of the promotion—the rights to closed-circuit television, radio rights, and movie rights, and the foreign rights to all three. (Irving Berlin Kahn, a friend of D'Amato and the president of Teleprompter, a corporation specializing in closed-circuit television, had made a pitch for the business, and there had been headlines about the sale of these rights for $400,000 and even $600,000. When Cus D'Amato's lawyers failed to file their ancillary agreements with us, I called in the police and threatened to have all the closed-circuit equipment pulled out of the Stadium. Then and only then were the contracts filed with us, under protest.)

But the worst was yet to come. Early in August, Frank Hogan, the distinguished district attorney of New York County, asked me to drop by the Criminal Courts Building, where he had his office. He then told me that the entire promotion had been tainted by outside influences. Fearing for his life, Rosensohn had gone to the district attorney about the 'fierce jungle' of professional box-

ing. Through a professional gambler, he had been played for a
sucker.

Our investigation turned up a ripe crew of characters. First was
Gil Beckley, a professional gambler and bookmaker whom Bill
had used in the past to place an occasional bet on a football game
or some other sports event. Beckley was no altar boy. He had a
police record way back to 1933. Beckley had introduced Bill to
Anthony Salerno, who had an even more staggering background.
Known to the New York City Police Department as "Fat Tony,"
he had also used the name of Tony Russo. The records of the
Commission had indicated that William P. Rosensohn was the sole
stockholder of Rosensohn Enterprises. We then learned the shocking news that Salerno and Charlie Antonucci, also known as
Charley Black, Cus D'Amato's closest friend, each was reported
to have had a one-third interest in the profits of the promotion.
Charley Black was the man D'Amato had used as a dummy
manager of Roy Harris, Patterson's opponent in the Patterson-
Harris championship fight.

The fourth principal in this drama was Vincent J. Velella, a
lawyer and Republican political leader of an East Harlem assembly
district. Rosensohn testified that Salerno had introduced Velella
to him and throughout all their investigations, contended that
while he, Rosensohn, had a one-third interest, Charley Black a
third, and Velella the remaining share, Salerno was at all times
the party in interest in that corporation. Rosensohn under oath
testified:

> *Q.* "What was Salerno's relationship to All Star Sports, Inc.
> (the corporation in question)?"
> *A.* "He was a man who originally brought this company into
> being. He was the man who introduced me to Vincent Vel-
> ella, who formed the company. He was the man who Vincent
> Velella represented and who, I believe, Vincent Velella was
> the nominee for in the company."

Throughout the entire inquiry, despite the established fact that
at every important conference between Velella and Rosensohn,
Salerno was present—whether at Ronnie's Steak House, Velella's
office, Rosensohn's apartment, McCarthy's Steakhouse, the Sherry

Netherland, or the Hampshire House—Velella claimed the presence of Salerno was just social or mere coincidence. Velella also denied that any money passed between Salerno and Rosensohn, but on the evidence, particularly the evidence of a tape recording that was taken at Rosensohn's request of a conversation between himself and Velella, the Commission held by unanimous opinion:

> This Commission cannot accept the fact that Salerno was an innocent by-stander at these meetings and it believes that the $10,000 loan was made by Salerno to Rosensohn in Velella's office and that Salerno was a part of the promotion. The tape recording of the conversations at the meeting of July 31, 1959, in Rosensohn's office strongly supports this conclusion.

The hearings before the Commission provided a field day for the press. Each new disclosure brought a new flurry of publicity and fresh recriminations of the "I'm-as-honest-as-you-you-dirty-liar" type. I casually mentioned to Martin Kane of Sports Illustrated that Iwo Jima was never like this, and the press had another headline.

The licenses of Cus D'Amato as manager and second were revoked by the Commission, and Rosensohn's licenses were suspended for three years. Bill could never understand why we took this action against him. In the U.S. Senate hearings he testified:

> The dream actually ended before the New York State Athletic Commission. You see, this was a strange, sad ending, because while all this was happening, still, I felt that while I may have made mistakes of judgment, I had done nothing that was dishonest. I had done nothing—and I had been, as far as I know, one of the few people in boxing who had taken it upon himself to go to a law-enforcement agency and jeopardize his future to try to help what was right, what was good.
>
> And, frankly, I must say the district attorney's office was very helpful. The State Attorney General's office was very helpful. The U.S. Attorney's office was very helpful.
>
> Then I came before an outfit called the New York State Athletic Commission. . . . I must say I spent many hours before the Commission and tried in every way to help them when it came to their rendering a final judgment, which

I had hoped would find—well, at least would exonerate me for what I had tried to do.

Instead, the State Athletic Commission, for reasons which are not entirely clear to me, suspended my matchmaker's license for three years. This is the end of the story.

The Commission's opinion gave the reasons:

Rosensohn was the promoter of the Patterson-Johansson fight. It was he who was introduced to Tony Salerno by Beckley, a bookmaker, and it was through Salerno that Rosensohn made his contact with Velella.

While credit inures to Rosensohn for his candor subsequent to the promotion, we cannot condone his violation of the rules of this Commission and the fact that through his instrumentality there was brought into this picture a shady character, whom neither the district attorney of New York County, the Attorney General of the State of New York, nor the New York State Athletic Commission was able to subpoena for questioning.

Rosensohn has sworn to his own hurt and has completely cooperated and offered his assistance and cooperation, *on his own initiative,* in the several investigations in this community. His cooperation was of material assistance in uncovering the background of the promotion and the part played by those individuals who acted "undercover" and behind the scenes. Credit must be given him for this assistance. These facts constitute a vital factor in our thinking, consonant with the primary interest of the public and the welfare of the boxing industry.

The New York County district attorney has stressed Rosensohn's complete cooperation and assistance rendered in his investigation and has indicated his position to this Commission, not by way of trespassing on our jurisdiction but to indicate the material assistance rendered to him by Rosensohn.

Rosensohn violated the rules of this Commission in failing to advise us of the changes in the stock ownership of his corporation, a licensee of this Commission. Not only must the Commission be advised immediately of any new stockholders or directors (Rules, Subdivision 10, Page 22) but such changes must be upon notice to and with the consent of the Commission (Rule 23, Page 49).

There was likewise, although uncorroborated, a violation of the Commission's rules by Rosensohn in connection with

the sale of working press tickets (Subdivision 9, Page 31).
Moreover, the public interest requires that from any promotion as well as any licensed activity in professional boxing,
there be excluded individuals whose character is such as to
bring into bad repute both the boxing industry and the
licensed individuals connected with it, and in this regard
there was violation by Rosensohn.

Rosensohn feared for his life, and he let it be known that he
had dictated a tape recording of the most secret details of the
Patterson-Johansson promotion, and had left it with his attorney
in a safe deposit box for release in the event that anything happened to him. During those hectic days, he was also accompanied by a detective assigned for his protection, and his fears
were not entirely unjustified. A year later we were informed "that
sombody had been coming from the West Coast to take care of
Rosensohn." That somebody never materialized—nor did Bill
Rosensohn's dream of a boxing empire.

★

24. A Child of Misfortune

CHARLES "SONNY" LISTON was born May 8, 1932, in St. Francis County near the small town of Forest City, 20 miles from Little Rock, Arkansas. A field hand at 12, he preferred to give the city as his residence and afterwards referred to it as his first home. When Liston was 13, his mother moved her brood of 12 children to St. Louis, leaving his father and his children from a previous marriage in Little Rock. For the first time, Sonny went to school, but his big size in a class of small children set him apart from the others, and he could not endure their laughter and ridicule.

> My mother put me in school [he was to tell Senator Kefauver's committee] and then after I started going to school, other kids, you know, seen me coming out of . . . I was such a large boy. Other kids would see me coming out such small kids' room. So they made fun of me and start laughing and I started fighting. . . . I started fighting—that isn't when I really started fighting; and when I started playing hookey; and from hookey I led to another thing, so I wound up in the wrong school.
> What school did you wind up in? [asked Kefauver]
> Well, the house of detention.
> Where was that?
> That was in St. Louis.
> How old were you then?
> I was about 14.

After his mother had gotten him out of the house of detention, it was Father Stevenson, a Catholic priest in Jefferson City, who led him into professional boxing. ("He was the one who got me

217

started.") The good father brought manager Frank Mitchell to him, and when Sonny beat Mitchell's boy, Mitchell took him on. After winning the Golden Gloves Championship, sponsored by the *St. Louis Globe-Democrat,* in 1953, Sonny turned pro with Frank Mitchell as his manager.

Mitchell, with 18 arrests, was only the first. Before long, Sonny was working for John Vitale, whose record included some 20 arrests or pick-ups, and the late Raymond Sarkis, who was described as the president of a labor union. Sonny was arrested while driving Sarkis' Cadillac. Sonny also met Frank (Blinky) Palermo, a close friend of his manager of record, and Pep Barone, with whom he signed a five-year contract on March 11, 1958. Up to that day Sonny had never even seen Barone.

Sonny became a highly merchantable asset as the years passed. Up to December, 1962, he had won 33 of his 34 bouts, losing a single decision to Marty Marshall, whom he knocked out seven months later. But by then he was locked in with a group of associates he could never cast off. He lost no other fight until 1964, when his seconds threw in the towel after the end of the sixth round of the championship fight with Cassius Clay in Miami Beach on February 25th, 1964. We watched that fight in Walter Cronkite's private office at CBS with Gene Tunney and Hank Greenberg. When Liston failed to come out for the seventh round, Gene threw up his hands and shouted, "This is the end of professional boxing."

It didn't turn out that way.

Liston did not fight again for 15 months, until his return bout with Cassius Clay, which ended with what many of the boxing world called a dive in the first round. No one saw the so-called phantom punch, and Cassius Clay stood in the center of the ring and called on Liston to get up.

I rather liked Liston. He had some—perhaps too few—good qualities. As a prize fighter he was self-reliant and self-sufficient and loyal to his own hurt, to his gang of "advisors" or so-called managers, a bunch of hangers-on and blood-sucking self-seekers. Coarse, brutal, ignorant, and friendless, Liston fought against the world every moment of his working day, but for all his history of violence, there was a moving sincerity in his answer to Senator

Kefauver when he was asked about John Vitale, Frank (Blinky) Palermo, Frank Mitchell, and others:

"Do you believe that people like this ought to remain in the sport of boxing, Mr. Liston?" Kefauver asked.

"Well, I couldn't pass judgment on no one," Sonny replied. "I haven't been perfect myself."

I had been introduced to Liston on several occasions but had never gotten to see him closely. I was surprised, therefore, in March, 1962, to receive a buoyant telephone call from Pete Rademacher, who said he'd like to come up with Liston and see me. They had an idea, he said, that looked good for boxing and would I see them? Pete was a handsome young American boy whose professional boxing career had ended almost before it began. Having won the Olympic Heavyweight Championship at Melbourne in 1956, he had been misled into a bout for the world's heavyweight championship. Floyd Patterson flattened him in six rounds at Seattle on August 22, 1957.

Liston wore a dark suit and open collar shirt. His muscles bulged through the tight fit of his jacket. He was solid and poised, without fear or anxiety, dead-pan but not sullen. He smiled when I mentioned that he had a great record as a boxer, but Pete did most of the talking. He unfolded a weird tale that the FBI was going to give Sonny a clean bill of health and that he, Pete, was to be Liston's manager. I said I'd look into it, and asked about Pep Barone, Mitchell, and Blinky. Liston turned to Pete and said, "Didn't I tell you they would ask that?" Then he asked me, "Do you know George Katz?" Unversed in boxing history I had to say no, but later we found that Katz had become a manager of Sonny Liston for a 10 per cent share. Who was to receive the rest of the customary managerial share, was never disclosed.

I told Liston we would make no decision based on his record alone; if he was otherwise qualified, we would consider his application on its merits. We had frequently licensed boxers with records in the hope that the sport would help them come back. We shook hands and the meeting broke up. Within the hour, the FBI informed me that there was nothing to Rademacher's story about a clean bill of health for Sonny. Partly for this reason, when Teddy Brenner, Markson's matchmaker and buffer, asked me to permit Sonny Liston to be introduced before a main event at the Garden, I turned him down. To permit Sonny to appear there in the midst of our investigation might have indicated some form of endorsement. Dick Young, widely-read columnist of the *Daily News,* ran a story about this under a sub-head, "Garden was off-limits to Sonny:"

> What really galled Sonny Liston, was that he could not even get an introduction from the Madison Square Garden ring when others were fighting. There are nights when a guy with two decisions over his wife gets introduced to the crowd by Johnny Addie, but the taboo on Sonny Liston, undesirable, stuck.

I had lunch at the City Athletic Club on 54th Street with Tom Bolan, Roy Cohn's partner in the promotion, during the week before our decision was due, and cautioned him as one lawyer to another not to take anything for granted. I told him that a title fight in New York would turn on whether or not we licensed Liston. Others who inquired, including the press, were advised that the matter was before the Commission, and was *sub judice.* Clamoring for a decision, some sports writers jumped the gun. The *Journal-American* of February 14th reported the Liston-Patterson fight in New York. Hugh Bradley had the story:

> **FLOYD, SONNY MAY MEET IN P. G. IN JUNE.**
> **Unless there is a sudden hitch or switch, heavyweight champion Floyd Patterson will announce on Friday the he will defend his title against Sonny Liston, the No. 1 contender, in June. The place is expected to be the Polo Grounds.**

Rumors flew thick and fast on the fight and its location. Al Buck, by-lined sports writer for the *New York Post,* had the story of a trip by Julius November, Patterson's attorney, to the West Coast, to look into an offer to hold the fight in Los Angeles. Then Al announced in his columns that the fight was to be held at the Yankee Stadium in New York. In answer to requests for information, I merely stated, to quote Al Buck, that "Liston is not licensed in New York State." Then came a blast in the *Post,* March 12th, announcing the fight in New York without qualification or reservation:

THE BIG FIGHT'S SET FOR OUR TOWN IN JUNE.
Confirming what Floyd Patterson had told The Post exclusively 10 days ago, Julius November, his attorney and spokesman, today announced the heavyweight champion will fight Sonny Liston No. 1 contender. The site of the title fight will be in New York. The time will be June.

Jim McCulley of the *Daily News* was not lost in the shuffle. Although Jim was cautious enough to use an interrogation point in his story, the growing expectations for a championship fight in New York were reinforced:

PAT VS. LISTON HERE IN JUNE?
Heavyweight champ Floyd Patterson is expected to announce within 48 hours the date, site and opponent for his next title defense. A night late in June, Yankee Stadium and Sonny Liston—that's how the announcement is expected to read.

On March 16, 1962, Floyd Patterson, the champion, and Sonny Liston, the contender, signed for a "June Multi-Million Dollar Heavyweight Title Fight, The Richest in History," in the words of the *Daily Mirror*. Liston applied for a license on April 17, 1962, and as the *World-Telegram* reported, I promised to act promptly on the request. Some of the press and many in the boxing world believed that I had already discussed the matter with Governor Rockefeller or Attorney General Louis Lefkowitz, whom several writers described as my brother-in-law, a relationship we both denied with an exchange of compliments. In fact, I never discussed the matter with Louis or Rocky. Contrary to all that has been written, they knew no more than those in the sport about what our decision was to be.

The late Dan Parker, the most accomplished of all the sardonic Doubting Thomases among the boxing writers, could not refrain from a last, well-barbed shaft. Writing of the pressures to bring the fight to New York, he said:

It is assumed that, if the fight would help business by drawing a large crowd here, they'd be willing to let the Boxing Commission decide whether approval of the contest would be a victory for sin over virtue. In this crisis, Gen. Krulewitch, Chairman of the Commission, can be expected to react in such a manner that the public will exclaim in unison: 'Don't be cruel to Krulewitch! He seen his duty and he done it!'

On April 26, 1962, the night before the announcement was due, I wrote the opinion. The following morning the press gathered in our conference room for the story, which I had had secretly mimeographed, and there was Marvin Kohn, press secretary, handing out the report. It was the *coup de grace* for Sonny. We dissected his vitals, and laid them out for all to see:

On April 17, 1962, Charles Liston, ring name Sonny Liston, made application for a license as a boxer to this Commission. Liston will be 29 years old on May 8th of this year. He has been a professional boxer since 1953, with a ring history of 34 professional contests. He has been licensed over the years in the states of Pennsylvania, Texas, Colorado, Missouri, Illinois, Washington, and in parts of Florida. On occasion his license has been suspended because of arrests in Missouri and (this past year) for five months in the state of Pennsylvania after two arrests, to which we shall hereinafter refer.

Liston's offense record has been widely publicized and we refer to it only to indicate that his first offense, which included robbery and larceny from the person, occurred when he was 17 years of age. Some six years later, he was sentenced to nine months in the workhouse on a charge of assault to kill, and was released after serving approximately four to five months. These are the only convictions in Liston's record. There are listed a number of arrests, but comparatively few in number, as indicated by our Department of Correction report. Two of the arrests took place in 1961, the charges being the impersonation of an officer, and disorderly conduct, both of which charges were dismissed.

We express our appreciation to Commissioner Paul D. Mc-Ginnis of the State of New York, Department of Correction, and Director Paul D. McCann of the Division of Identification for their courtesy in promptly processing the fingerprint application in this matter so that the results could be available at the earliest possible moment.

Liston's background is of importance in this proceeding. He is one of a household of 25 children, his own mother having had 13. He has had very little schooling, if any. As early as the age of 14, he was in the House of Detention in St. Louis, and at the age of 17 began serving his prison term of some four years. In prison he learned to box and his ability in the ring has brought him to the position of the Number One Contender for the World's Heavyweight Title.

The investigation conducted by the United States Senate's Subcommittee on Antitrust and Monopoly of the Committee of the Judiciary included testimony by Liston, John Vitale of St. Louis, Frank Palermo of Philadelphia, and Frank Mitchell of St. Louis, all of whom were well-known to Sonny Liston.

A contract had been entered into between Joseph "Pep" Barone, manager, and Sonny Liston, boxer, dated March 11, 1958, for a period of five years, but during those hearings which explored the background of Sonny Liston, Barone was not able to testify because of ill health. Frank Palermo, John Vitale, and Frank Mitchell, all of whom have extensive arrest records, took the Fifth Amendment when questioned on all subjects including their relationship with Sonny Liston.

Frank Mitchell was one of Liston's early managers; Vitale was his employer in St. Louis; and Palermo, recently sentenced to 15 years after trial in the United States District Court in California (from which an appeal is pending), was a friend.

Sonny Liston was represented at the Kefauver hearings by Jacob Kossman, an eminent attorney in Pennsylvania, who was recommended to Liston by Palermo, and his present attorney in this proceeding, Morton Witkin, Esq., represented Palermo before the Senate Subcommittee. These attorneys are gentlemen of standing and we refer to them without derogation as to their good reputation and standing in their community.

It was through Pep Barone, Liston's manager, that he met Blinky Palermo in 1958, and in that year the Pep Barone-Liston contract was executed.

The history of the Barone-Liston contract is of interest. In 1961, it was dissolved for a consideration of $75,000, to be paid by Sonny Liston within two years to Pep Barone. A portion of these monies was paid to Barone out of the December, 1961, Liston-Westphal bout, leaving a balance still due to Barone of some $57,000.

George Katz subsequently entered into an agreement with Liston as manager under which the division between manager and boxer was 10 percent–90 percent, a most unusual distribution. Out of the Westphal fight, Katz received some $7,500.

In the present proceeding before this Commission, George Katz, the manager under the contract dated April 24, 1961, between Katz and Liston, does not appear either as manager or in any other capacity, although his name is mentioned. Liston states: "In connection with this bout with Floyd Patterson, Mr. Katz has not and will not act in my behalf. I am represented by my counsel, Morton Witkin, 911 Finance Building, Philadelphia, Pennsylvania."

We address ourselves to the issue before this Commission. Liston, the Number One Contender for the World's Heavyweight Title, has proved himself an outstanding performer in the ring. Outside of the square circle, he has not been so fortunate. A child of circumstances, without schooling and without direction or leadership, he has been the victim of those with whom he has surrounded himself. As Senator Kefauver said to Liston, 'You have undoubtedly been taken in by many improper people who made connections with you, whether you knew it or not.'

We do not take the position that Liston's police record alone bars him from a license in this State. We do on occasion in the processing of rehabilitation, license applicants with records. Important figures in the boxing world have achieved distinction, despite an original unsavory background including a police record. Since the Kefauver hearings, Liston has been twice arrested.

The history of Liston's past associations provides a pattern of suspicion. His association with Vitale, Palermo, Mitchell, and others is a factor which can be detrimental to the best interests of professional boxing and to the public interest as well. We cannot ignore the possibility that these long-time associations continue to this day. The wrong people do not disengage easily.

There would be more than a calculated risk in the issuance of a license on this application.

The Commission unanimously disapproves the application and denies the license to Charles Sonny Liston.

Five months later, Sonny Liston won the World Heavyweight Championship in Chicago, flattening Floyd Patterson in exactly 126 seconds.

New York State recognized him as the World's Title Holder.

★

25. *Orchids for a Change*

IT WAS OPEN SEASON on state athletic commissions and boxing commissioners. Nobody had a kind word for us. Whatever we did was wrong, and that went for the industry too. We all needed something new and different. So, when the word was passed that the golden boy of the National AAU Light Heavyweight Championship, the National Golden Gloves Heavyweight Championship and the Olympic Games Light Heavyweight Championship, had gone pro and was coming to New York for a license, we were offered, to say the least, a refreshing prospect of change. Floyd Patterson had lost the championship, won it back, and was to lose it again to Sonny Liston. We still had a list of rated boxers longing (as were their managers, seconds, trainers, bottle holders, cut men, and families), for the pot of gold at the end of the rainbow—but the sport was dead as Kelsey's.

The new boy came to New York in 1962 and brought us a new look in boxing. Born in 1942, he came to New York sponsored by the most socially prestigious group ever to follow in the train of a boxing hopeful. Cassius Marcellus Clay, Jr., had been named for his father, who in turn had been given the name of the most sensational figure in 19th-century Kentucky history, an abolitionist who voted for Lincoln. The Dictionary of American Biography records:

> When very young, he fought his mother, his schoolmaster, and a slave companion; the day before his wedding he canned a rival in the streets of Louisville; and when 93 years old, suffering under the hallucination that people were plotting against his life, he converted his ancestral mansion into a fortified castle, protected by a cannon. His

career was turbulent in politics, in the Army, within the circle of his family, and in all his social and diplomatic relations. In 1841, he fought a duel in Louisville with Robert Wickliffe, Jr.; four years later he so mutilated with a bowie knife Sam M. Brown as to be indicted for mayhem; in 1850 he stabbed to death Cyrus Turner; and in his old age he shot and killed a Negro. In all his early political campaigns he carried a bowie knife and two pistols.

Our own Cassius Clay approached the New York State Athletic Commission for a license with the Louisville Sponsorship Group in attendance. This financial, political, and social galaxy was a sight to behold. It comprised:

W. L. Lyons Brown, Sr.	Chairman of the Board, Brown–Forman Distillers Corporation.
William S. Cutchins	President, Brown–Williamson Tobacco Co.
Patrick Calhoun, Jr.	Retired Chairman of the Board, American Commercial Barge Line.
Robert Worth Bingham	Station WHAS radio and TV, *Courier-Journal & Times*.
J.D.S. Coleman	Oil magnate.
Archibald McG. Foster	Vice-President, Ted Bates Advertising Co.
William Faversham, Jr.	Vice-President, Brown–Forman Dist. Corp., member of the New York Stock Exchange.
George W. Norton, IV	Executive, Station WAVE (and nephew of Thurston Norton, Chairman of Republican National Committee).

Vertner D. Smith, Sr.	Chairman of the Board, Vertner Smith Distributing Co. Member of Kentucky Racing Commission.
Elbert Gary Sutcliffe	Millionaire farmer.
James Ross Todd	Executive, W. L. Lyons & Co., Louisville, Kentucky.

We licensed Cassius Clay and his managerial group, and then Angelo Dundee, who had been training Cassius, applied for a license as his second. There had been some question at one time involving Angelo's associations, but since he had no criminal record and was being sponsored by the Louisville group, we gave him his license too.

Cassius Clay, now known, of course, as Muhammad Ali, is the most colorful, preposterous, conceited, and shrewd figure in professional boxing since John L. Sullivan. He talked and fought his way to the championship and then, discarding the sponsors who had guided him to the crown, changed his name to Mohammed Ali and joined a religious group called the Black Muslims, an organization of American blacks who follow the religious practices of Islam and propose segregation of the races with a view toward the establishment of a separate black national group.

"And so what?" said we, anticipating Senator Russell, who later said in Congress, "I note that Clay has now changed his name to Muhammad Ali. This may seem strange, but the right to change one's name for boxing purposes has been exercised by hundreds of boxers without anyone questioning the right."

The change of name and the change of religion brought headlines on every sports page in the country, and the furor reached its peak in the deliberations of the National Boxing Association. The NBA was a monumental creation of futility, starting nowhere and ending similarly. In its fumbling efforts to clean up the sport, it brought to mind Abe Lincoln's judgment of a neighbor's incompetent efforts at farming: "That's as useless as trying to fertilize a quarter section with a fart."

In Cassius Clay's change of name the World Boxing Association, the thinly disguised successor of the NBA, saw a providential opportunity to snatch victory from the poverty of its achievements, and proclaimed to all the world its impending annulment of Cassius's world heavyweight title. As the *Washington Post* reported:

> **WBA Commissioner Abe J. Greene said in Paterson, N. J. that Clay should be given a chance to decide whether he wants to be a religious crusader or the heavyweight champion. "As a champion he is neither a Muslim nor any other religionist, because sports are completely nonsectarian," Greene said. "I think Clay should be given the choice of being the fighter who won the title or the fanatic leader of an extraneous force which has no place in the sports arena. The decision will be his."**

The WBA president agreed:

> **WBA president Ed Lassman, who hopes to have Clay's title vacated within the week "for conduct detrimental to boxing" said at Miami, Fla., "Of course, Clay might be reinstated as champion within five or six months" if his conduct improves. Meanwhile, at New Orleans, chairman Emile Bruneau of the WBA's world championship committee began a telephone poll of his seven fellow committeeman to see whether they will vote to dethrone Clay.**

The New York State Athletic Commission, its head bloodied but unbowed, took the opposite tack, and to its surprise, came up smelling like a rose. We announced that we would continue to recognize "Gaseous Cassius" as champion, regardless of any action that the World Boxing Association might take. This stand brought together from the ends of the political spectrum Senator Jacob K. Javits, liberal Republican of New York, and Senator Richard B. Russell, Democrat of Georgia, who agreed, perhaps for the only time, on a civil rights issue. Senator Russell:

> Cassius Clay, in common with 180 million other American citizens has a right to join the religious sect of his choice without being blackmailed, harassed, and threatened with the severe punishment of being deprived of the heavyweight boxing championship. Incidentally, this is a very valuable

property right, but these arrogant men, who apparently are directing the World Boxing Association, propose to take it away from Clay without the slightest pretext of a court hearing.

No one denies that professional boxing has now fallen to a low estate. I must say that if those who direct this World Boxing Association are so intolerant, narrow-minded and bigoted as to threaten to strip a champion of his title because of his religious belief, it is no wonder that professional boxing is at a low ebb. Any American citizen who becomes the head of the World Boxing Association should maintain that great principle of the American Constitution that every citizen is entitled to worship according to the dictates of his conscience.

Senator Javits:

First, I was much pleased to hear a good word said for New York by the distinguished Senator from Georgia in regard to the matter of Cassius Clay. I agree with the Senator on this matter. I am proud of the statement made by Gen. Melvin L. Krulewitch, Chairman of the New York State Boxing Commission. I know him very well. He is an ex-Marine general who has an outstanding war record. It is typical of him and typical of my state that we are not panicked by the ukase of the World Boxing Association, that one should be deprived of his title because of some affiliation of which the association disapproves and of which I disapprove. As General Krulewitch so properly says, "That is no reason for taking a man's title away from him." That is not the American way.

So I register my pride in New York for standing up in this way, as it always will, in my judgment, for the dictates of the basic constitutional functions of our country. Perhaps it is a good thing to demonstrate to the country that whatever may be the differences between the Senator from Georgia and me—and probably they are as pronounced as any in this Chamber on the issue of civil rights—we can also see eye to eye on a question such as this without inhibition.

I do not believe that Muhammad Ali has gone Kosher, as required by strict Islamic observance, and turned his back forever on spare ribs, richly larded crackling bread, and good Virginia ham. But I do believe in the statement I issued in behalf of the Commission and which appeared verbatim in most of the country's newspapers. This is how it appeared in the Hearst syndicated press:

SETTING IT RIGHT

The New York State Athletic Commission has moved to project reason and fairness into efforts to deprive Cassius Clay of the world's heavyweight championship.

Officials of the World Boxing Association advanced the specious argument that the fighter's conduct, particularly his membership in the Black Muslims, justified denying him recognition as heavyweight champion.

Former Marine Corps General Melvin L. Krulewitch, chairman of the New York Commission, has voiced the rest of this editorial for us. He said:

Within the limits of the Constitution, the right to freedom of speech and to religious beliefs are inviolate. No title of a world champion has ever been vacated because of religion, race, or personal beliefs. The State Athletic Commission will continue to recognize Cassius Clay as Heavyweight Champion.

★

26. Death of a Fighter

THE EVENING OF Saturday, March 24, 1962, was an evening long to remember. In white tie and tails, I went from the wedding of Percy Uris's daughter in the Jade Room at the Waldorf to the world championship fight at Madison Square Garden between Benny (Kid) Paret, the welterweight champion of the world, and Emile Griffith, the former champion, who had lost his title to Paret the previous September 30 by a split decision.

As I took my seat at ringside during the concluding rounds of the bout preceding the main event, I saw that the staff were all in position. Deputy Commissioner Frank Morris, a retired New York Police Department sergeant and its heavyweight champion, was in Griffith's corner, seated by Deputies Dan Dowd and Pat Callahan. Petey Scalzo, chief inspector and a former featherweight champion, was in Paret's corner, and I noted with pleasure the presence at ringside of the chairman of the Medical Advisory Board, Dr. Marv Stevens, former Yale football player and coach, together with our staff physicians Dr. Ira McCown, Dr. Alexander Schiff, and Dr. A. H. Kleiman, a professor at Polyclinic Hospital.

The press were jammed in the first six rows of ringside seats, with the photographers leaning on the aprons around the ring. Johnny Adee, the announcer, waved to me from the judges' seats, and the eyes of George Bannon, the 80-year-old timekeeper, were glued to his watch, one hand on the gong-beater ready to sound the end of the round. The ring officials whom I had asked Mary O'Keefe, our chief clerk, to notify were all present. The job of selecting the judges and referee is the sole prerogative of the chairman of the Commission, who also has the responsibility of keeping the names secret, to guard against the possibility of gamblers and fixers tampering with them or even sending an honest referee temporarily on the sick list by staging an "accident." Time and again politicians would try to get a friend assigned to a particular fight, but all such requests had to be turned down. The only requests we considered were for appointments as wrestling judges. Professional wrestling exhibitions are not contests. The judge's duty is to sit in a ringside seat and keep awake during the program.

For that night's championship fight, I had picked the cream of our officials. Ruby Goldstein was the referee. With over 30 years of experience in boxing including 20 years as a professional referee, his reputation, ability, and integrity were above reproach. As judges, I put in Frank Forbes, who had been one of our officials for 27 years including seven years as a timekeeper, and Tony Rossi, a former professional boxer and an official judge for 17 years. These men were the best. Ruby Goldstein, for instance, was quoted in Frank Graham's book, *Third Man in the Ring,* as saying:

> One of the most important things to know is when to stop a fight and when to let it go on. In this you must be neither too hasty nor too slow. If you act too quickly, you may prevent a fighter who hasn't been really hurt, though his face may be bloodied, from going on to win. You must strike at just the right moment—to give a boy another chance or to intercede to save him from a crippling beating, or worse.

It looked as if it were going to be a hard fight. At the weigh-in at the commission offices at noon that day, where the usual crowd of managers, trainers, seconds, and friends had been in attendance, there had been some disorder between the boxers. Ed Brennan of the *Journal-American* described the incident:

> **This was the third fight between Griffith and Paret. There was bad blood between them. This stemmed from the fact that Paret, who speaks only Spanish, taunted and teased Emile about his manhood. Benny did this at the Saturday noon-time weigh-in. He used a word which in Spanish means a man is effeminate. This boiled Emile's blood and they almost came to blows.**

Now, at the Garden, the fighters were in their corners and Johnny had begun the introduction of the champs of yesteryear and present title holders. The national anthem was then sung, and Ruby called the fighters to the center of the ring for the same last-minute instructions that they'd heard for years. He waved them to their corners, the gong sounded, and they came out boxing.

Griffith had the edge during the first five rounds, but in the manner that had characterized Paret in previous fights and earned him the reputation as a "come-on" fighter, Paret came from behind in the sixth and cleanly knocked Emile down, hurting him so much that Emile had to hang on in a clinch for the remainder of the round. Paret continued to do well in the next five rounds, winning three of them, and in the tenth round, although Griffith was ahead in the first two minutes, Paret came on again and finished strongly.

The eleventh round went to Griffith however, and then, in the twelfth, Griffith cut loose with a whirlwind of blows. Forcing Paret into a corner and blocking him in, he rained down a storm of punches, right and left, which Paret tried to duck, even sticking his head outside the ring at one point, to avoid this savage barrage. Paret was never off his feet. His left arm clung instinctively to the topmost rope as the attack, centered on the jaw, continued during a five-second outrage of brute force. Then Ruby Goldstein jumped in between them, screaming, "Hold it," and enfolded Griffith in his arms to prevent any further action. Paret was still upright. From the ringside, shocked into a deepening sickness at heart, we watched him sink to the floor. All four doctors climbed into the ring and began to minister to the unconscious Paret.

Moments later a stretcher was brought and Paret was carried out and rushed to Roosevelt Hospital, where I remained at his side until 3 A.M., having appointed a committee to investigate the incident and feeling more than ever a growing burden of futility and hopelessness. The telephone was ringing when I got home, but after the first call, I took it off the hook. The call was from a life-long boxing fan and a classmate of mine at Columbia.

"Mel, did you see the television coverage of the fight?"

"No," I said. "I was there at ringside."

"The playback of the last five seconds was the most nauseating, revolting picture of brutal savagery I've ever seen."

I hung up and got into bed but not to sleep. After an hour or two of pitching and tossing, I shaved, bathed, fixed a bite for myself, and returned to the hospital. Dr. Schiff was still there. I stayed until lunchtime and in the afternoon a telegram arrived from Governor Rockefeller:

> I AM DEEPLY CONCERNED AND DISTURBED, AS I AM SURE ARE ALL SPORTS FANS AND THE PEOPLE OF THE STATE GENERALLY, OVER THE SERIOUS INJURIES RECEIVED BY BENNY PARET IN LAST NIGHT'S WORLD WELTERWEIGHT BOXING MATCH. WILL YOU PLEASE FURNISH ME WITHIN 24 HOURS A FULL AND SPECIFIC REPORT ON THE FIGHT, PARTICULARLY THE INCIDENTS OF THE 12TH ROUND PRECEDING THE STOPPAGE OF THE FIGHT BY THE REFEREE, TOGETHER WITH A DETAILED REPORT OF THE MEDICAL AND OTHER MEASURES WHICH THE STATE ATHLETIC COMMISSION TOOK IN THIS CASE AND TAKES GENERALLY TO PREVENT OR AVOID SERIOUS INJURIES TO CONTESTANTS.
>
> NELSON A. ROCKEFELLER

By now, Paret, who had never regained consciousness, had undergone three hours of brain surgery to relieve the subdural hemorrhage suffered during the last seconds of the fight.

The press had learned about the Governor's telegram, and writers and columnists swarmed down upon the commission, each and every one snooping, probing, and trying to nose out some new angle for a story. But we had only 24 hours to make our report, and I clamped down the lid. Gabe Pressman threatened to complain to the Governor that we were keeping out the press, which we were, but we had to get out that report.

Late Monday afternoon we finished it, complete with statements from all interested parties, including the ring officials, the ringside doctors, and the Medical Advisory Board, which Governor Dewey had appointed to protect the boxer. The Board had recommended important safeguards in professional boxing, all of which we had observed. What had provoked the blistering flood of telephone calls to the Governor's office had been the agonizing television playback of those last fatal seconds, accentuating in slow motion each crashing, repeated punch against Paret's jaw and head. The finished report, absolving all parties from blame, was signed, sealed, and delivered by courier within the 24 hours ordered by the Governor. The disgruntled sports writers left in disgust when they heard that any further information must come from the Governor since the report was now in his hands. But I had counted without. the usual leak. Despite every precaution, someone close to me had passed the word about our conclusions. Don McClennan, the assistant night editor of the *Daily News* and my press officer during the 1957 campaign for borough president called up in righteous wrath to notify me that the *Mirror* had the story and to demand that I come clean. I told him there was no story and that the Governor had the report. He hung up, unhappy, cold, and resentful. He was also quite right. The *Mirror did* have the story. Our conclusion, based on our investigation, was short and to the point: "It is our opinion that all possible medical pre-caution had been taken prior to the contest and Referee Goldstein acted in good judgment in stopping this contest when he did."

The Associated Press closed out the story on April 3, 1962: "Benny (Kid) Paret died today—10 days after his head was bashed 20 times or more as he hung helpless in the ropes in losing his world welterweight title. He never came out of a coma after being pounded senseless by Emile Griffith in the 12th round of their nationally televised title fight. . . ."

★

27. *Laugh, Clown, Laugh*

THE COMMISSION had investigated itself and found it was in the clear, although not smelling like a rose. Dr. Ira McCown, the Commission's medical director, and Dr. Marvin A. Stevens, chairman of the New York State Medical Advisory Board, reported that all of the medical standards for boxers as recommended by the Advisory Board and approved by the Boxing Commission had been fully complied with in the case of Benny Paret, including complete physical examinations on March 1, March 15, and March 24, plus a last examination two hours before the fight in Paret's dressing room.

But Paret was dead.

Had Griffith been goaded into the brutal savagery of the last few seconds of the fight by the insult offered by Paret at the weigh-in? Had the 200 rounds of hard fighting during the past three years, including 10 with Gene Fullmer in Las Vegas, when Paret was knocked out, and 27 with Griffith, all within a period of six months, finally caught up with Benny?

There was no way of knowing.

By our whitewash, legitimate and legal though it was, we had cleared the commission, the state of New York, the ring officials, the doctors and the Garden of all blame, and there was no litigation. But four days later, the state legislature created an investigating committee on boxing, gave it an ample appropriation, and turned it loose. Elections were slated for the fall!

I recall with quiet enjoyment a gathering of this committee at Al Schacht's steak emporium—at least to the point where the tab was presented. I took with me some members of the commission staff, three only out of the 14 members of the committee attended. We dined in a private room decorated with boxing prints—John Groth's "Stillman's Gym," so true to life that you could almost smell the sweat, and portraits of Tom Sayers, champion of England at only 150 pounds, and John Morrissey, the American heavyweight champion and future congressman.

After dinner—mostly roast prime ribs and steaks (the most expensive items on the menu, since the state was picking up the tab)—we came to the business of the evening. After the second round of drinks, there was a general lessening of tension. The acting chairman, a research assistant visibly impressed by the responsibility of his office, turned to Fargo, his assistant, who was fumbling with a folder of papers which appeared to include a well-thumbed copy of the day's racing form, and whispered, "What do we do now?" "We read the resolution, sir." "As I was about to say," said the acting chairman, "when I was interrupted by my assistant, we will read the resolution."

After the reading, the chairman called to Globber, the second assistant, who was speaking at the far end of the table. "Globber," he shouted, "you're drunk."

"I haven't had a drink today," Globber replied, pointing to a glass of ginger ale.

"How dare you contradict me. I can smell the whiskey all the way up here. Isn't he drunk, Fargo?"

"Yes, sir," Fargo answered. There was indeed a smell of hard liquor in the air.

"That's what I thought," the chairman said. "What shall I do with him?"

"Let him sleep it off," Fargo suggested.

"As I was about to say when I was again interrupted by my assistant—Globber, leave the room at once!"

Fargo leaned over and whispered to the chairman, "He has the pay vouchers for the meeting. And he was employed by the Speaker of the Assembly."

"Since you've asked for clemency," the chairman went on, although Globber hadn't said a word, "we will allow you to sit in for the rest of the evening." Turning to the stenographer taking the minutes of the evening, "Did you get the clemency part?"

A soft snore was the only response. After the last round of vodka ginger ales, the stenographer had gone out like a light.

"Well," announced the chairman, "We have concluded the business of the meeting." Turning to the representatives of the New York State Athletic Commission, he added, "We thank you for your contribution and we are happy to have had you as our guests tonight."

Since I, as chairman of the commission, had invited my colleagues to the dinner meeting, I naturally picked up the tab: $109.50. Months later, on looking over the committee's final accounting to the legislature of the State of New York, I found an item that brought back memories of that evening: "For entertainment of the staff and the chairman of the Athletic Commission at a dinner conference and meeting at Al Schacht's Restaurant. . . . $109.50."

That was an unusual day. Usual days began with me walking through Central Park, down to the 59th Street and Sixth Avenue exit, across to Seventh and then down to the 47th Street offices of the New York State Athletic Commission. My usual time was 9 A.M. and of course I couldn't hope for any of the staff to be in, although the civil service rules specified 8:55. As I had long since discovered, they made their own rules, and it was too much to continue to argue, wheedle, threaten, or bribe them to get in on time.

The commission had three floors of a narrow-fronted building, my office being on the tenth floor along with the conference room and the hearing room, which had ample space for the press and a small room for per diem counsel and secretary. The outer office, separated from the dingy foyer by a three-foot wooden unvarnished rail with a swinging, squeaking gate, had just enough space for the files and a secretary. It had been rumored both before and during my time that there was a pipeline from the commission to the press, and I was never more conscious of this fifth column than during the time we were putting together our report on the Paret fatality. More and more I had come to realize that the regulation of boxing was a one-man job.

I picked up the mail lying on the floor, unlocked the door to my office, and sat down in the chair previously occupied by the Honorable Julius Helfand, Brooklyn racket buster (he acknowledged that he had sent 23 men to the chair), Bob Christenberry, unsuccessful candidate for mayor and later postmaster of New York City, and the late Eddie Eagan, Rhodes scholar and amateur boxing champ. I opened the first letter. It was addressed in long-hand—no signature, no address. "You bastid you, you sell out to big bizness. You work for Madison Square Garden and you fix all the fights. I fix you soon."

Next was a typed communication from one Poltava, seeking a license. He advised me that he was a giant, very strong, weight 400 pounds, careful of his diet, ate yogurt.

The next letter was from a high state official asking why his brother had not been receiving assignments as a boxing inspector. Inspectors are paid only when assigned to a show, but their biggest asset is a large silver-plated badge which can be flashed at ticket-takers, uncertain broads, and traffic police. (I later wrote the high-ranking politician that I liked his brother very much, but that we had scheduled no shows in the vicinity of the small village where he lived. However, we planned to set one up in Palmyra, 200 miles away, and I would gladly pay for a pair of tickets for him. I was sorry, but I could not pay his railroad fare. I closed the letter pleasantly, wishing him success in the forthcoming elections.)

At 10 o'clock my secretary tiptoed in, and attempting appease-ment for her tardiness, asked if I would like some black coffee. I gave her a dollar for the java and turned to the next letter, which was from the Governor. It was the usual formal reference to the commission of a letter he had received and for which he wanted us to draft a reply. The letter was a 15-page, single-spaced docu-ment describing a cover-all invented by the writer to prevent injury to any boxer in any circumstances. From the schematic drawings enclosed, it was not dissimilar to an astronaut's space suit. It was air-filled and covered the entire body. In my draft for the Gov-ernor's signature, I ventured to remark that he must have spent a lot of time on his project, that we would look into the matter, and that we appreciated his devotion to the manly art of self-defense. My fear, sustained by past experience, was that in due course I would receive a further communication, this time perhaps of 30 pages.

The morning wore on. My first visitor was an applicant for a boxing license, accompanied by a friend and advisor. The boy had no experience, no training, and no job, and I told his advisor I'd think it over. "Why not now?" he replied, pulling out his trump card—a letter from the boy's mother stating that her son had no police record.

"So what?" I replied. "We occasionally get boxers with no police records."

"But," he persisted, "where he lives, no police record is like a college education." I politely ushered them out.

The next callers were a pair who had applied the previous week for a license. In the interim I had gotten an FBI report on the applicant, who had stated that he had never been arrested. They came into the office and I did not ask them to sit down. This would be a short one.

"You have a record of eight arrests for robbery and assault and battery, including on your wife," I said. "Why did you tell me you hadn't been arrested?" The advisor answered, "They were all thrown out. He had a jealous wife."

Eight arrests and all thrown out. This boy must have had some friends at court. I didn't like the smell of it. "Listen to me," I said, "You go back, keep your nose clean, keep training, and come back to me next year and I'll look you over again."

Their pride hurt, they hustled out of the room but not without a parting shot. "We'll go to a good state for a license, like New Jersey or maybe Illinois. Liston got a license in Chicago."

My next two visitors were Fargo and Globber of the investigating committee. I joined them at the conference table, and Globber began. He was swarthy and middle-sized with shiny black ringlets plastered to his skull. A droplet hung from the end of his enormous hooked nose, and my surprised look caused him to pull out a large handkerchief and scrub it away vigorously. "We'd like to ask you a few questions," he said.

Fargo, his superior, immediately interrupted him. Fargo was tall, blond, and pale. "We'd like to ask you a few questions," he said. "Shoot," I replied. "That's what we're here for."

"We'd like to know what you think of boxing," said Globber.

"I think it's a good sport if properly regulated."

"Did you get that, Globber?" asked Fargo. Globber, writing furiously on a grubby white pad, nodded.

"Now we come to the important part," said Fargo, pulling out a long white printed form from his inside coat pocket. "Globber, do you have a copy?"

"Yes, sir."

"Make copies of everything the witness says."

He turned in my direction a look of fatherly Christian charity. "Since you are the chairman of the New York State Athletic Commission, we will not take your testimony under oath." Globber looked steadfastly at his pencil and a blank sheet of paper.

"How old are you?" Fargo began. I told him.

"Married?"

"Yes."

"Previous arrests, convictions, sentences, time served in confinement?" he read from the form.

"What's all this about?" I queried, with some impatience. "I'm not applying for a boxer's license."

"Did you make a note of this, Globber? The man is not applying for a boxer's license."

Looking at the length of the questionnaire, to save time I pulled out a copy of my biography, kept ready for publicity purposes and handed it to him.

Fargo took a look and turned to Globber, "Mark this 'Exhibit A.' " The paper was duly marked and returned to the inside coat pocket.

"This completes the examination," said Fargo. "Many thanks for your cooperation. You don't by any chance have an inspector's badge with you?"

"Exhibit B," Globber said helpfully.

"As I was about to say, Exhibit B," said Fargo with a withering look.

"This is a matter of serious importance," I answered, with a straight face. "I shall take it up in executive session at the next meeting of the commission."

I rose, they followed suit, and I escorted them through the door to the elevator.

The committee worked for a year, overspent its allowance and made a report exonerating the commission and all its officials and recommending that professional boxing be continued in New York. But the pressure of the investigation, as well as the Paret death, had the effect of making referees ultra cautious. They would stop a fight whenever there was the slightest risk of injury to a boxer. In a bout between Dick Wipperman, a Buffalo policeman, and a giant by the name of Jim Beattie, the referee stopped the fight in Beattie's favor early on. Wipperman recovered quickly, ran to the center of the ring, seized the announcer's microphone, and shouted to a gleeful audience that the fight had been fixed, that we were all fixers, and that he was ready to go ahead—all this, of course, after taking a nice little rest. He was hustled out of the ring, suspended, and ordered to appear before the commission on charges.

On the day of the hearing, my Marine Corps buddy, Supreme Court Justice Carlton A. Fisher, of Buffalo, called me up and told me that he would like to appear as a character witness for a young Jewish friend, Dick Wipperman, who was up before me on charges. I suspected the telephone call was a word to the wise, but it was *garnicht helfen*—it didn't help. Wipperman received a peremptory warning—one more and he'd be out of boxing—and was fined $100.

We had another one like that, but a little more serious. Oscar Bonavena, a great Argentinian heavyweight, fought Tom McNeeley in the Garden. McNeeley was a tough fighter who fought all his matches in a frenzy. He had been taking a beating in the earlier rounds, and was staggered again and again by Bonavena in the fifth round. The referee stepped in and stopped the fight. At once there was a great tumult in the ring and among Tom's friends at ringside. Ned Irish, president of Madison Square Garden, came across to my seat and stood towering over me. In a loud and insulting voice, he exclaimed, "This is what *you* did," pointing a finger at me and then at the confusion in the ring. All the seat-holders in earshot turned around to listen as Irish continued. "We pay your salary," he thundered, "and you do *this* to us." He was still ranting when several of the Garden officials intervened.

Since this was an affront to the state as well as to the Commission and to me personally, I didn't take it sitting down. I issued an order to the Garden to show cause why disciplinary action should not be taken against it for conduct detrimental to the best interest of the sport. Several of the Garden's coterie of boxing writers covered the incident the next day, exonerating Irish and characterizing me as ultrasensitive. I got a laugh out of that—former regular Marine Corps sergeants are not known for their ultra sensitivity. The chairman of the board of the Garden, Irving Mitchel Felt, a millionaire sportsman and public benefactor, came to see me at the Commission's offices, to apologize personally for the incident. Then I received a letter from Irish himself:

August 26, 1964

Dear General Krulewitch,

Since I have been unable to reach you by telephone this week in order to apologize personally for the incident in Madison Square Garden last Friday evening, I would like to set forth my feelings in the matter.

There is no question that my remarks to you were not proper. I sincerely regret the impetuousness which caused me to act in this fashion and I apologize for any embarrassment which they have caused you.

Please be assured that my conduct was no more than a regrettable reaction to an unusual sporting incident occurring at a time when we are all deeply involved in the struggle to maintain boxing as a major sport.

I have always had, and continue to have, the greatest personal respect for you. Your efforts toward insuring the present and future welfare of boxing and the progress which the Commission under your direction has made are most laudable.

Again my apologies.

Sincerely yours,
s/Ned Irish

The state had had more than its pound of flesh—I called it quits. The Paret death was the last boxing fatality in New York to date, and in support of boxing it must be said that the deaths from contact sports in our state in hockey, football, polo, skiing, auto racing, and numerous others are far more frequent. Boxing ranks only tenth in fatalities. But even a single fighter's death is one too many, and what with the political acrobatics, the brain fag, the continuous sniping from every quarter, and the heartache of the fatality itself, it was almost too much to bear.

It was at a Gold Medal dinner of the United Service Organization, with which I was connected, that I first mentioned to Rocky that I was turning in my uniform as boxing commissioner. He replied as he had when I had mentioned it before, that he didn't have a replacement. I answered that the woods were full of politicians who'd jump at the salary, the car, and the $3000 expense allowance. The Governor smiled and said that he knew all about that, but if I was going to resign, would I do it while the legislature was in session, so that he would not have to make an interim appointment? This I agreed to do, and the Governor in his press release accepted my resignation, and spoke very flatteringly of my service to the state.

Eventually, a politician was found who happily agreed to accept the car, the $3000 expense account, and the $25,000 salary (it had been increased from the $16,000 I had received) and the commission and the loyal party workers breathed easy. But not before other possibilities had been canvassed. The late Jackie Robinson was once reported as a possible successor. I thought it a good appointment, and invited him down to the commission for a look-see. At that time, boxing was very much a black sport and since Jackie had broken the color line in major league baseball, I thought he would have done well as boxing commissioner. But the howls in the sports columns that he was a resident of Connecticut (which would not in itself have been enough to preclude him from the job) led to an investigation of his affairs, and it was found that there might be a conflict of interest in view of the fact that he had, or was about to have, a business association with Floyd Patterson, former heavyweight boxing champion of the world, who was still a licensee of the commission. Some years later, Jackie was appointed a member of the commission, an office he still held at the time of his death.

My term as chairman not only helped me get over the death of my first Helen, but also led me to my second. On an official visit to Los Angeles, I called up a number highly recommended by the wife of a boyhood chum, and left my name with the answering service. The call was returned and we made a date for dinner the night before I left for New York. And that was how I met Hellen, the former Hellen Floss Sulzbacher. Two years later we were married, and I presented her with an army of relatives, including children and grandchildren.

Upon my resignation an appointment to the Public Service Commission was touted in the press, but never materialized. Inevitably, I turned again to the law. Happily, I became associated with one of the greatest lawyers whom I have ever encountered, either as a colleague, or adversary, student or teacher, in court, in politics, or in public life. Murray I. Gurfein ranks as one of the great lawyers of our time, not solely because of his brilliance—many lawyers were *magna cum laude* and members of the *Harvard Law Review* in their youth—but because his eminence was leavened by a warming, earth-roots compassion for people. He was a genius in his profession and was so regarded by his confrêres. In 1967 I joined Murray Gurfein's law firm, and enjoyed and profited by the association. In 1971 Murray was appointed to the United States District Court for the Southern District of New York, and the first case he tried was the prosecution of *The New York Times* by the Federal Government for its disclosure of the Pentagon papers. A lifelong Republican, Judge Gurfein's opinion in that celebrated case won him national and international acclaim.

My passion for the law was so great that even in my early years at Columbia Law School I began to collect antiquarian law books. I was particularly attracted to Littleton, an early writer on the law of real estate, *inter alia,* who flourished in the 15th century. There have been literally hundreds of editions of his book, which was originally printed in Legal French and was acclaimed throughout the world. *Les Tenures de Monsieur Littleton* was even quoted in the French courts.

One of the greatest of English jurists, Littleton coined the adage, *Lex plus laudatur quando ratione probatur* ("Law is more to be praised when it is proved by reason"). In my small way, I joined the legions of dedicated worshippers of the proven word. I picked up copies of his work all over the world, and gloated when I could send Rosenthal, the bookseller at Oxford, to Paris to pick up a rare edition with no price limit on the acquisition. I bought the magnificent, parchment-bound Wight edition of 1604, with both books in the copy, the Legal French and the English, and with the magnificent Hoar family coat of arms on the bookplate. And when I purchased in London a copy of a Companie of Stationers Edition printed in 1640, I bought it only for the doodle on the colophon page. There on the last page of the book was a contemporary caricature of a cavalier, high crowned hat, goatee, mustache, and all—a symbol of the cavalier opposition during the period of the Puritan Revolution and the continuing ideological war between the Cavaliers and Roundheads. Almost three and a half centuries later, I can't determine whether it was a Roundhead or a Cavalier who made the drawing.

I gave the collection to Columbia Law School in 1970, and this is what the Columbia Law Bulletin wrote about it:

PRESENTATION OF KRULEWITCH RARE BOOK COLLECTION

"Whether you have a taste for antiquities, enjoy seeing how our predecessors in the profession prepared, or simply love books, I know you will share the thrill of pleasure I feel at having this magnificent collection in our Library," said Dean Michael I. Sovern in accepting a collection of rare law books, the gift of Major General and Mrs. Melvin L. Krulewitch. At a reception held November 24, 1970, in the George Bowen Case Lounge, the Dean and Faculty of Law gathered to honor Major General and Mrs. Krulewitch and to accept the presentation. The gift volumes, which will be designated the *Krulewitch Collection,* will be housed in the Law Library's Treasure Room.

The collection focuses on Littleton's Tenures, an early work on the Common Law of England. Many of the books, dating from 1534, are extensively annotated in minute script by the lawyers who used them. One volume, still in excellent condition after four hundred years, contains annotations written by two lawyers who practiced law more than one hundred years apart.

In accepting the collection on behalf of the University, Dean Sovern noted that the gift of rare books was but one of many generous contributions which General and Mrs. Krulewitch had made. For many years, the General has been the donor of the Krulewitch Fellowship, awarded annually to a graduate student in law who is committed to a career in legal education or government service.

Of the General, who is a Class of 1918 alumnus of the Law School, Dean Sovern said: "His career has been an extraordinary mixture of bravery, erudition, loyalty, high intelligence, and generosity."

★

Postscript

I WAS ORDERED BACK to temporary active duty by the Marine Corps in February, 1972, to participate in the Memorial Day Services at Belleau Wood—on full pay and allowances! Since I can speak French after a fashion, I delivered the memorial address in that language. I give a little of it here—in English— because I know of no better way to express the feelings that have stayed with me all my life:

> We return after 54 years to these woods, where in the flower of our youth, we withstood the murderous attacks of the enemy's best regiments. We beat him at his own game and then we counter-attacked and resolutely and unflinchingly imposed our will on him.
> Closely adjoining these woods, we endured our poisonous, suffocating gas attack on June 12, 1918, when our company, the 78th, was reduced from a strength of 200 officers and men to a remnant of 11 men, of whom I happened to be the senior in command. We were all wounded, bloodied, gassed, burned, and weary to the bone, but every one of us refused to be evacuated.
> Here we made our stand, and in that moment of decision we did not fail our fallen comrades. We held these woods and its surrounding area against every violent counter-attack during the succeeding days and as we moved forward we left behind us the bodies of our beloved comrades.
> I have come back to Belleau Wood.
> We loved France in springtime and the flowers were as beautiful then as now. There is a true nostalgia among all of us who knew France in our youth, and whose friendship and affection for this country have never changed.
> The muguet whose fragrance we enjoyed on that May day

Ceremonies in Trinity Churchyard, New York City, 1972, honoring Major Franklin Wharton—Commandant of the U.S. Marines Corps in 1804.

in 1918 brought luck to some of us—it's just chance and fate that we are here today—but to our comrades who lie so peacefully in this eternal city, it brought the fulfillment of their destiny.

Say not that these young men who rest around us were cut off in their youth. Life is not measured by years, but rather by accomplishments. To them was granted the opportunity to give their all for freedom, and in that moment of supreme dedication they reached the highest summits of devotion. Let us never forget them, because in their reflected radiance, shines the eternal light of freedom.

★

Index